Lecture Notes in Computer Science

Edited by G. Goos and J. Hartmanis

369

Dirk Taubner

Finite Representations of CCS and TCSP Programs by Automata and Petri Nets

Springer-Verlag

Berlin Heidelberg New York London Paris Tokyo Hong Kong

Author

Dirk A. Taubner
Institut für Informatik, Technische Universität München
Arcisstraße 21, D–8000 München 2, Federal Republic of Germany

CR Subject Classification (1987): D.1.3, D.3.1, F.1.1–2, F.3.2–3, F.4.3

ISBN 3-540-51525-9 Springer-Verlag Berlin Heidelberg New York
ISBN 0-387-51525-9 Springer-Verlag New York Berlin Heidelberg

Printing and binding: Druckhaus Beltz, Hemsbach/Bergstr.
2145/3140-543210 – Printed on acid-free paper

To my parents

Foreword

There are two main approaches to a theory of concurrent distributed computations: the theory of Petri nets and the Milner/Hoare theory of CCS/CSP. They are based on different philosophies and emerged from two different classical notions of computability. The Petri net approach developed (in the early 60s) from the ideas around Turing machines and automata; it has concurrency and causality as its basic concepts. CCS/CSP grew (in the middle of the 70s) out of ideas around the λ-calculus and concepts in programming; it has communication and composition as its basic notions.

Petri nets are equipped with a natural notion of partial order semantics (the processes introduced by Petri in 1976, which model concurrency explicitly), while originally CCS/CSP has an interleaving semantics (which models concurrency by nondeterminism).

In recent years both approaches began to influence each other and to converge. In particular Petri nets are being developed such that they can be used for a variety of purposes: for system description, as a specification and programming language, and as a formal semantics for languages like CCS and CSP. We are now in the phase where constructions allowing compositionality and modularity are built into Petri nets, where we look for hierarchical net constructions and refinement techniques, and for methods of formal reasoning (about or by using nets) — see for example the ESPRIT Basic Research Action 3148 "Design Methods Based on Nets" (DEMON). The deep and broad theory developed around CCS/CSP and related concepts has a great impact on this development.

On the other hand, ideas and techniques from the field of Petri nets influence more and more the CCS/CSP domain. And, at least in my opinion, the power and the problems inherent in the application of the CCS/CSP operators as well as in the implementation of CCS/CSP-based languages, can be particularly well understood and studied by translating these operators into constructors for nets and for automata. This thesis is an especially good proof for this opinion.

Munich, June 1989 Wilfried Brauer

Foreword

Preface

This work relates different approaches for the modelling of parallel processes.

On the one hand there are the so-called 'process algebras' or 'abstract programming languages' with Milner's Calculus of Communicating Systems (CCS) and the theoretical version of Hoare's Communicating Sequential Processes (CSP) as main representatives.

On the other hand there are machine models, viz. the classical finite state automata (transition systems), for which however more discriminating notions of equivalence than equality of languages are used; and secondly there are differently powerful types of Petri nets, namely safe, respectively general (place/transition) nets, and predicate/transition nets.

Within a uniform framework the syntax and the operational semantics of CCS and TCSP are explained. We consider both, Milner's well-known interleaving semantics which is based on infinite transition systems, as well as the new distributed semantics introduced by Degano, De Nicola, Montanari, and Olderog which is based on infinite safe nets.

The main part of this work contains three syntax-driven constructions of transition systems, safe nets, and predicate/transition nets respectively. Each of them is accompanied with a proof of consistency.

Due to intrinsic limits, which are also investigated here, neither for transition systems and safe nets, nor for general place/transition nets does a finite consistent representation of all CCS and TCSP programs exist. However sublanguages which allow finite representations are discerned. On the other hand the construction of finite predicate/transition nets is possible for all CCS programs in which every choice and every recursive body starts sequentially.

The work is a revised version of my PhD thesis. I am particularly grateful to my supervisor Prof. W. Brauer for his kind guidance, for many helpful discussions, and for his continuous very efficient support. Additionally I thank Prof. Mogens Nielsen for his advice and for having acted as the second referee.

My special thanks go to Walter Vogler. In numerous discussions and with many suggestions for improvements he has been a great help. I have also benefitted from valuable comments of Volker Diekert and Ursula Goltz.

I thank the Siemens AG and in particular Prof. H. Gumin for supporting my work by an Ernst von Siemens Scholarship. Especially I appreciate the additional time which made it possible for me to do this revision.

Munich, June 1989 Dirk Taubner

Contents

Introduction 1

1 Abstract programming languages 7
1.1 Syntax 8
1.2 A general language 12
1.3 Interleaving operational semantics 21
1.4 Equivalence notions 25
1.5 Reachable subsystems and quotients 30
1.6 Correspondence with CCS 33
1.7 An alternative rule for recursion 39
1.8 Correspondence with TCSP 43

2 Connections with formal language theory 46
2.1 Terminating traces 46
2.2 Turing power 48
2.3 Counters 52
2.4 Decidability questions 57

3 Representation by finite automata 61
3.1 Extended transition systems 62
3.2 Syntax-driven construction 64
3.3 The extended transition system for a term 76
3.4 Consistency 86
3.5 Finitely representable subsets 91

4 Representation by finite and safe Petri nets 95
4.1 Definitions and terminology of net theory 97
4.2 Syntax-driven construction 101
4.3 Consistency, definedness, and finiteness 107
4.4 Further properties of the constructed nets 113

5 A remark on the representation by finite Petri nets 118

6 Representation by finite and strict predicate/transition nets . . 123
6.1 Predicate/transition nets 126
6.2 Syntax-driven construction 133
6.3 Distributed operational semantics following Degano, De Nicola, Montanari, and Olderog 140
6.4 Distributed consistency 145

Conclusion 156

Bibliography 159

Mathematical notations, abbreviations 165

Index 166

Introduction

Parallel processes have been a topic of intensive research on both a practical and a theoretical level for quite a long time. Starting out from well-known theoretical models for parallel processes this work aims at giving finite graphical representations of processes.

In the literature there are a number of formalisms for parallel processes which concentrate on the aspect of control and data flow, they abstract from the data values and the decisions depending on values. We call such a formalism an abstract programming language. Well-known examples are Milner's CCS, the theoretical version of Hoare's CSP, ACP by Bergstra and Klop, COSY by Lauer et al., and MEIJE by Austry and Boudol. Abstract programming languages (sometimes also called 'process algebras' or 'calculi of processes') are used for modelling, specifying, and analyzing parallel processes.

For this work we choose a language which encloses pure finitary CCS and the main part of TCSP. This enclosure is proven formally. Furthermore our language also captures most aspects of the other abstract programming languages.

The immediate goal of this work is to find for programs of this language finite representations by automata and by Petri nets (of different types) respectively to study the intrinsic limits of the finite representability.

Additionally this investigation serves the following broader goals. Firstly it supplies finite graphical representations which support comprehension by humans. Secondly a complementary but formally related mathematical representation is given. This helps understanding the interrelationship, provides a way to transfer analyzing methods, gives insight into the complexity of the constructs of abstract programming languages, and facilitates further investigation. Furthermore the net representations explicitly model parallelism and can also be understood as a distributed semantics. Finally the representation by well-known machine models (automata, Petri nets) supplies an aid for the implementation of parallel processes.

Of course any representation should be semantically consistent. For the semantics of an abstract programming language there are two mainstreams of research: The *interleaving* semantics, where parallelism is modelled by arbitrary interleaving and the *distributed* semantics, where parallelism is modelled explicitly. While the theory for the former is rather settled, this appears not to be true for the latter.

In this work, as usual, the interleaving operational semantics of an abstract programming language is in a first step given as an arc-labelled transition system, which can be derived by a set of rules. This technique is due to Plotkin and Milner. In a second step some equivalence notion on transition systems is chosen and programs with equivalent transition systems are considered to be equal.

For our research we choose as equivalence the strong bisimulation equivalence of Milner and Park. All other well-known interleaving equivalences are implied by strong bisimularity, hence if we find some representation which is consistent with respect to strong bisimularity, it is also consistent with respect to the other equivalence notions.

In general the transition system of an abstract program is infinite, even if the attention is restricted to the reachable subsystem. Consider for example $P :\equiv rec\, p.\big((ac\, nil \mid b\bar{c}p) - C\big)$ where two parallel subprocesses are forced to synchronize by the restriction $C := \{c, \bar{c}\}$ before the second subprocess continues recursively. The reachable part of the transition system for P according to the standard interleaving semantics is

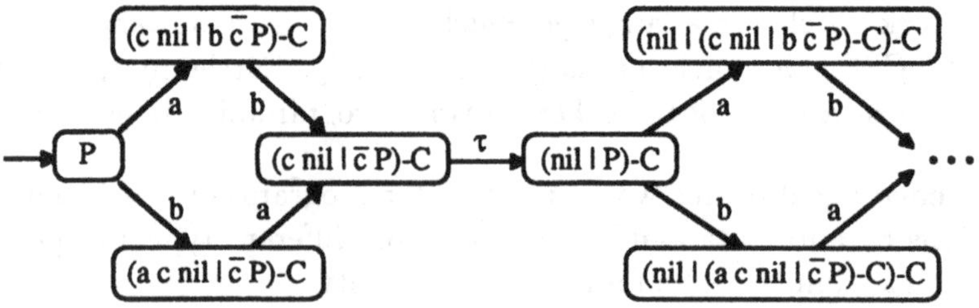

although the finite transition system

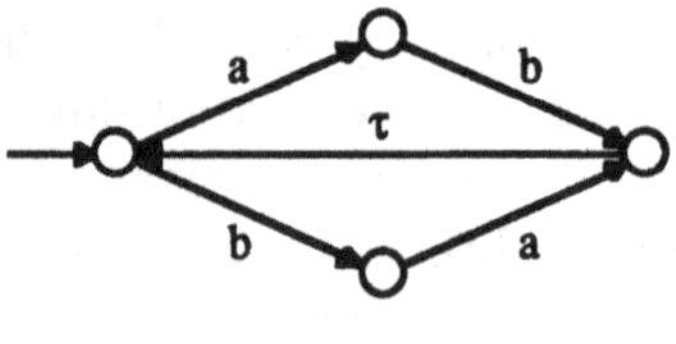

is strongly bisimular to it.

A similar example is $Q :\equiv rec\, q.a(qf)$ for the renaming function f with $f(a) = b$ and $f(b) = b$. For Q the reachable part of the transition system according to the standard semantics can be sketched as

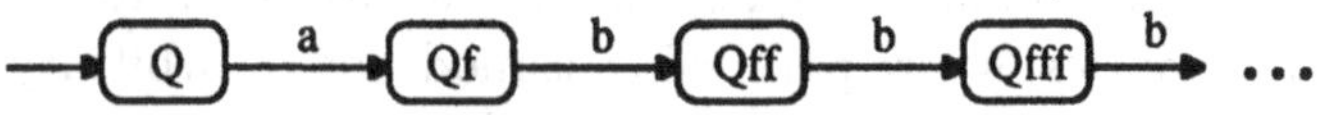

and the finite transition system strongly bisimular to it is as follows.

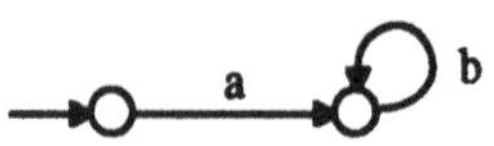

The aim of this work is to systematically construct for as many abstract programs as possible a consistent representation as a

1. finite automaton (= finite transition system),

2. finite and safe place/transition net,

3. finite place/transition net,

4. finite predicate/transition net.

In this context consistency means the following (let $\mathcal{T}[\![P]\!]$ be the transition system for the abstract program P):

For 1 consistency means that $\mathcal{T}[\![P]\!]$ is strongly bisimular to the automaton. For 2 and 3 that $\mathcal{T}[\![P]\!]$ is strongly bisimular to the interleaving reachability graph of the net. And for 4 that $\mathcal{T}[\![P]\!]$ is strongly bisimular to the interleaving reachability graph of the safe-net-semantics of the predicate/transition net.

We show that there exists no effective procedure which for an arbitrary abstract program outputs some strongly bisimular finite transition system if it exists, and otherwise states its non-existence.

But for the class of abstract programs, where every renaming function changes a finite set of actions only and where certain intertwinings of recursion and parallelism are disallowed, it is possible to present a systematic construction of strongly bisimular finite transition systems. This considerably extends a construction of finite transition systems ('charts') by Milner for programs with prefixing, choice and recursion only.

Similarly we give a consistent construction of safe nets. These nets also model explicitly the parallelism of the abstract programs. Nevertheless the interrelation of both constructions is very tight as the interleaving reachability graph of the net constructed for some program is isomorphic to the finite transition system constructed for that program.

With respect to 3 Goltz presents a construction of finite place/transition nets for a subset of CCS where restriction and renaming of actions is not allowed, but where arbitrary intertwinings of recursion and parallelism are allowed. We show that this construction cannot be extended for restriction or renaming by exhibiting CCS programs for which no bisimular finite place/transition net exists.

Finally with respect to 4 we give a systematic construction of finite and strict predicate/transition nets for a class of programs, which encloses almost all of CCS. The only exceptions are that we require every sum to offer alternatives which start with a single action (either visible or not) and every body of a recursion to start with the invisible action τ. The latter assumption is sensible to model divergence correctly and to enforce guardedness. The former assumption is motivated by the choice constructs of concrete programming languages such as Ada, Occam or Chill; and secondly by the wish to avoid fruitless technical complications encountered by other authors.

For this construction we do not only prove the consistency as stated above. But we even have consistency to a distributed semantics, namely we have that the reachable part of the safe-net-semantics of the predicate/transition net for some program P *equals* the reachable part of the safe net for P given by the distributed operational semantics of Degano, De Nicola, Montanari and Olderog.

The latter point is quite interesting insofar as we did not aim at getting this equality, but we looked for a finite representation which intuitively adequately models the inherent parallelism. Ending up with a closely related structure shows that the structure discovered by Degano, De Nicola and Montanari indeed is very fundamental.

In summary this work gives systematic constructions of automata and Petri nets of several types for rather large classes of abstract programs. Although we investigate aspects of parallel processes theoretically we think that this also may help with respect to practical aspects. In chapter 3 we indicate that the set of abstract programs which can be represented by finite automata and by finite and safe nets suffices to model the control flow of semi-static concrete parallel programming languages, such as for example Occam.

Furthermore in particular the net representations can support the development of a distributed implementation of parallel processes as they reflect the parallelism explicitly. Finally our considerations may help to transfer techniques for proving correctness and methods for the modular construction from automata and net theory to concrete parallel programming languages.

The rest of this introduction gives a chapterwise summary of the contents emphasizing the contributions which are new. A more detailed discussion, also of the related literature, is given at the end of each chapter.

CHAPTER 1 introduces the syntax and interleaving semantics of the abstract programming language we will be working with throughout (the distributed semantics is given in chapter 6). The basic definitions and properties of transition systems and equivalence notions are collected. Most of this chapter is known from the literature. Nevertheless the particular choice of the operators is very convenient, as it allows to work with few operators while being able to model the parallel composition operators of the other abstract programming languages. Moreover we show how an alternative rule for recursion can be investigated by using the standard rule but considering a certain subset of programs only.

CHAPTER 2 proves that the subsets of our language which correspond to CCS, TCSP respectively, are Turing powerful. This fact is known by folklore. We carried out the proof in order to see how these subsets could be restricted to allow finite representations. In particular we show that counters can be programmed without using any renaming.

Additionally we show that there exists no effective procedure which for a given program outputs some finite transition system which is strongly bisimular to the transition system of the program if it exists and states its non-existence otherwise.

CHAPTER 3 gives the first of three syntax-driven constructions for abstract programs. This one leads to transition systems. It starts out from Milner's construction of charts [Milner 84], but additionally takes into account the parallel composition operator and most importantly the action manipulation operator (renaming, restriction, hiding). The latter may occur in any combination with recursion. We therefore had to refine the so-called extensions of Milner's charts with information about the action manipulation functions which are to be applied recursively. We call these generalized charts extended transition systems.

In order to prove the consistency of our construction we develop a set of rules to derive the extensions of the transition system of a program, similar to the set of rules which allows to derive the transitions. Then we can carry out an induction on the structure of the programs, even though the subprograms may contain free identifiers.

The essential contribution of this chapter is the refinement of Milner's extensions and the set of rules to derive them.

We give sufficient conditions for the definedness and finiteness of our construction. These conditions are fulfilled for a set of programs which disallows the intertwining of recursion and parallel composition but which allows recursion with respect to the second component of sequential composition (tail-recursion) and arbitrary recursion with respect to the other operators. This subset in turn allows to model the control flow of Occam programs.

CHAPTER 4 transfers the construction from chapter 3 to safe Petri nets while modelling the concurrency explicitly. In general this leads to graphically smaller objects. The transitions of a Petri net are natural generalizations of the transitions of a transition system. The construction for the transitions of the Petri nets which we present in this chapter is well-known from the literature. On the other hand the information for the recursive binding is rarely treated in Petri net constructions. Only Goltz has generalized Milner's construction of charts for Petri nets [Goltz 87]. She labels certain places of the nets with the binding information. We take a different approach here and generalize the extensions of a transition system presented in chapter 3 to special transitions of a Petri net. This also implies that our construction for the recursion is different.

We are able to prove a very tight relation to the construction from chapter 3, namely if the net construction is defined then the reachability graph of the net constructed for some program is isomorphic to the transition system constructed in chapter 3. With this result we can easily transfer the results on consistency, definedness, and finiteness from chapter 3 to this chapter. Additionally we show the state machine decomposability and the coverability by place invariants of the constructed nets.

CHAPTER 5 is a comment to Goltz's representation of CCS programs (without renaming and restriction) as finite but not necessarily safe Petri nets [Goltz 87]. For that construction we prove that in general it can be extended neither for restriction nor for renaming. For the first case the counter without renaming from chapter 2 is used, and a similar term which is almost a counter is used for the second case.

CHAPTER 6 gives the third syntax-driven construction. It leads to a powerful high-level form of Petri nets, called predicate/transition nets. Such a predicate/transition construction for an abstract programming language has not appeared in the literature so far.

The idea for this construction is based on the observation that in the transition system of a term the set of reachable states (= terms) mainly differs with respect to action manipulation functions and with respect to the parallel context. Although there may be infinitely many reachable terms, each of them is built from a finite set of 'cores'. These cores form the places of the predicate/transition net construction while the action manipulation functions together with some information on the parallel contexts are represented by the individual tokens. See the introduction to chapter 6 for a more detailed informal explanation.

The distributed operational semantics for our language following Degano, De Nicola, Montanari, and Olderog is given. Due to a minor syntactic limitation its definition becomes very simple and moreover a clearer intuitive interpretation is possible.

In contrast to the previous constructions, for the one of this chapter we prove consistency with respect to the distributed semantics. Furthermore this construction is defined and leads to finite predicate/transition nets for all CCS programs where every choice and every body of a recursion starts sequentially, no limitations are imposed concerning the intertwining of recursion with parallel composition and action manipulation.

Apart from the first chapter all chapters can be read independently, the needed cross-references are indicated in the text as well as in the index.

Chapter 1

Abstract programming languages

For the modelling of parallel processes and programs one line of research takes an approach similar to automata and formal language theory. This approach considers uninterpreted actions as the basic execution unit, and by doing so it concentrates on the control flow and data flow aspects of parallel processes, i.e. it concentrates on aspects of causal and temporal dependencies and on aspects of synchronization.

On the other hand this approach abstracts from data values (as the actions are uninterpreted) and from decisions (branchings) which depend on data values. In contrast to automata and formal language theory this approach uses more discriminating semantics with respect to non-determinism and recently also with respect to concurrency.

Usually this approach starts with a little grammar (syntax) producing the language of all processes under consideration, and this syntax offers operators which correspond to the most important program constructs of concrete parallel programming languages such as Ada, Occam, and Chill.

For these two reasons (abstraction from data values, resemblance to parallel programming languages) we call such an approach an *abstract programming language*, and the parallel processes under consideration are called *abstract programs*.

The two main representatives of this line of research are Milner's Calculus of Communicating Systems (CCS) [Milner 80], and Hoare's Theory of Communicating Sequential Processes (TCSP) [Brookes et al. 84]. They have initiated a lot of research and the development of more languages. To name but a few there are ACP [Bergstra, Klop 85], SCCS, ACCS [Milner 83], MEIJE [Austry, Boudol 84], [de Simone 85], and CIRCAL [Milne 85].

Related research has been carried out by [Arnold 82], and [Nivat 82]. Furthermore COSY [Lauer, Campbell 75] and extended regular expressions may be seen as precursors of abstract programming languages. But the recursion mechanism used in the latter approaches is not as general as in abstract programming languages.

What we call an 'abstract programming language' is sometimes also called a 'process algebra' or a 'calculus of processes'.

In this chapter we present the basic aspects of abstract programming languages. We start in section 1.1 with the syntax, carefully taking into account the notion of syntactic substitution. We adopt the technique of Barendregt to identify α-congruent terms syntactically. In section 1.2 we present the syntax of our language **A**, which encloses most features of the other abstract programming languages with very few operators. The syntactic relation to CCS and TCSP, and the modelling of termination and sequential composition by means of the basic operators are discussed.

The following two sections state the interleaving operational semantics by giving a labelled transition system (section 1.3) and equivalences on transition systems (section 1.4). The distributed operational semantics is deferred to chapter 6. For non-operational semantics the reader is referred to [Hennessy 88] who provides an excellent general and systematic introduction.

In section 1.5 we discuss how attention can be concentrated on the relevant portion of a transition system. Finally in the last three sections we formally show that our semantics is the same as that of CCS and TCSP with respect to the corresponding subsets of **A**. Furthermore we discuss an alternative rule for recursion and exhibit a subset of **A** fulfilling the proper termination property. On first reading we recommend to skip the rest after Proposition 1.33 of this chapter and to directly continue with chapter 2 or 3.

1.1 Syntax

Definition 1.1 The syntax of an abstract programming language is specified by a one-sorted *signature* $Sig = \langle Op, \rho \rangle$ where Op is a set of function (= operator) symbols and $\rho : Op \to \mathbb{N}$ gives the arities. The *syntax* is given as

$$P ::= \quad op(\underbrace{P, \ldots, P}_{\rho(op)\ \text{times}}) \quad \text{for } op \in Op$$

$$\mid \ p \ \mid \ rec\, p.(P) \quad \text{for } p \in Idf$$

where Idf is a countably infinite set of identifiers.

Elements produced by this syntax (grammar) are called *plain terms*. □

Terms of an abstract programming language are built from function symbols of the signature and a notation for recursion. Unary operators are sometimes written in postfix notation, binary operators are usually written infix. Parentheses are omitted if no confusion arises. To save parentheses we let unary operators precede over binary operators.

Intuitively the meaning of $rec\, p.(P)$ is the definition and an immediate call of a parameterless function. The meaning of p is just a recursive call of a function.

In the literature this notation for recursion is called μ-notation [de Bakker 80, p. 259], [Olderog, Hoare 86, p. 13], since instead of $rec\, p.(P)$ they write $\mu p.(P)$. Others (e.g. [Milner 83]) write $fix\, p.(P)$. The letter μ appears to be chosen due to the strong resemblance to λ-calculus, and indeed a number of notions, such as the notion of free and bound occurrences of identifiers and the notion of substitution are transferred from λ-calculus [Barendregt 85, pp. 22ff.] to the terms of an abstract programming language. They are defined next.

Definition 1.2 Let P be produced by the syntax in Definition 1.1. The set of free identifiers $FI(P)$ of P is defined inductively as follows.

$$\begin{aligned} FI(p) &= \{p\} \\ FI(rec\, p.Q) &= FI(Q) - \{p\} \\ FI(op(P_1, ..., P_{\rho(op)})) &= \bigcup_{i \in \{1,...,\rho(op)\}} FI(P_i) \end{aligned}$$ □

An identifier p occurs *free* in P if p is not in the scope of a $rec\, p.-$, otherwise p occurs *bound*. For example in $op_2(p, rec\, p.op_1(p))$ the leftmost p occurs free while the other two occurrences of p are bound.

Syntactic substitution, α-congruence

Next we define the syntactic substitution of a term Q for every free occurrence of an identifier p in another term P, denoted by $P[Q/p]$. It is well-known that some care has to be taken to avoid name clashes, i.e. confusion of free and bound identifiers.

For example in $rec\, p.op_2(p, q)[op_1(p)/q]$ for some operators op_1 and op_2 and identifiers $p \neq q$ the incautious (naïve) substitution, i.e. the textual replacement of q by $op_1(p)$, would lead to $rec\, p.op_2(p, op_1(p))$, thus binding the right-most occurrence of p recursively, which is not wanted. Instead some renaming of bound identifiers is needed. In our example the bound occurrences of p should be renamed to $r \notin \{p, q\}$ leading to $rec\, r.op_2(r, op_1(p))$ as the result of the substitution. In the λ-calculus such a renaming of bound identifiers is called α-conversion [Church 41] or α-congruence [Barendregt 85, p. 26].

In order to be able to work with terms in the naïve way we adopt the technique of [Barendregt 85, p. 26] and identify α-congruent terms on the syntactic level. E.g. we will have $rec\, p.p \equiv rec\, q.q$, where $\equiv$ denotes syntactic equality. But in order to do so we need the following definitions and propositions. Let $\doteq$ denote absolute syntactic identity (without identification of α-congruent terms).

Definition 1.3 (syntactic substitution)
Let U, V be produced by the syntax in Definition 1.1, $p \in Idf$, then

$$U[V/p] :\doteq \begin{cases} V & \text{if } U \doteq p \\ q & \text{if } U \doteq q \wedge q \neq p \\ op(U_1[V/p], ..., U_n[V/p]) & \text{if } U \doteq op(U_1, ..., U_n) \\ U & \text{if } U \doteq rec\, p.R \\ rec\, r.(R[r/q][V/p]) & \text{if } U \doteq rec\, q.R \text{ and } q \neq p, \text{ and} \\ \quad \text{where } r = q \text{ if } p \notin FI(R) \vee q \notin FI(V), \\ \quad \text{else } r \text{ is the first identifier in } Idf, \text{ which does occur neither} \\ \quad \text{in } R \text{ nor in } V \text{ (to this end we assume an order on } Idf). \end{cases}$$

□

Definition 1.4 1. A *change of bound identifiers* in U is the replacement of a part $rec\, p.V$ of U by $rec\, q.(V[q/p])$, where q does not occur (at all) in V.

2. U is *α-congruent* with V, notation $U \equiv_\alpha V$, if V results from U by a series of zero or more changes of bound identifiers. □

Proposition 1.5 ($\equiv_\alpha$ is a congruence w.r.t. substitution)
For any U, U', V, V' produced by the syntax in 1.1 and $p \in Idf$.

$$U \equiv_\alpha U' \wedge V \equiv_\alpha V' \Rightarrow U[V/p] \equiv_\alpha U'[V'/p].$$

Proof [Barendregt 85, Prop. C2, p. 577], he in turn refers to [Curry et al. 58, pp. 94-104]. Note that the syntactic case 'application of an operator $op(P_1, ..., P_{\rho(op)})$' of abstract programming languages corresponds to the syntactic case 'application PQ' in λ-calculus (cf. the definitions for free identifiers and substitution), this is why the proof of Barendregt/Curry can be carried out here analogously.
Similar proofs have been carried out in [Dosch 87, pp. 37ff.]. □

Fact 1.6 For U, U' as above $\quad U \equiv_\alpha U' \Rightarrow FI(U) = FI(U')$. □

From now on let us identify α-congruent terms: Let a *term* be an α-congruence class of plain terms. Recall that a plain term is an element produced by the syntax in 1.1. Throughout we understand plain terms P, Q, R to represent their α-congruence class. We write $P \equiv Q$ if P's and Q's α-congruence classes are equal, i.e. if $P \equiv_\alpha Q$. If plain terms are not to be understood as representing their α-congruence class (this is the case in section 1.6 only) we will explicitly say so, in this case we will use the letters U, V, W.

Due to the above propositions free identifiers and substitution are uniquely defined for terms using any representatives. And even better: If we obey the Barendregt convention (1.8), which can always be obeyed (1.9), then substitution may be carried out in the naïve way (1.10).

Definition 1.7 (term, closed term, subterm)

1. $Rec(Sig) := \{[U]_{\equiv_\alpha} \mid U$ is produced by the syntax in Def. 1.1 $\}$ (the set of recursive terms of an abstract programming language given via a signature Sig).
2. Let $P \in Rec(Sig)$, then P is *closed* if $FI(P) = \emptyset$.
3. Let $X \subseteq Rec(Sig)$, then $cl(X) := \{P \in X \mid P$ is closed$\}$.
   Notation: We omit parentheses when applying cl, e.g. $cl(Rec(Sig))$ is written $clRec(Sig)$.
4. For $P \in Rec(Sig)$ the notion of *subterm* is defined inductively: P is a subterm of P, if $P \equiv op(P_1, \ldots, P_n)$ then for all $i \in \{1, \ldots, n\}$ every subterm of P_i is a subterm of P, and if $P \equiv rec\, q.Q$ then every subterm of Q is a subterm of P. □

Definition 1.8 (Barendregt convention)
A collection of plain terms $P, Q, R, \ldots$ satisfies the *Barendregt convention*, if no identifier, which occurs bound in any of the plain terms $P, Q, R, \ldots$, also occurs free in any of the plain terms. □

Fact 1.9 For any finite collection of terms there exist representatives fulfilling the Barendregt convention.

Proof Choose any representatives and then change the bound occurrences of identifiers to new identifiers. □

This fact enables us always to assume that the plain terms representing some terms are satisfying the Barendregt convention.

Proposition 1.10 Let $P, Q \in Rec(Sig)$, $p \in Idf$, then

$$P[Q/p] \equiv \begin{cases} Q & \text{if } P \equiv p \\ q & \text{if } P \equiv q \wedge q \not\equiv p \\ op(P_1[Q/p], ..., P_{\rho(op)}[Q/p]) & \text{if } P \equiv op(P_1, ..., P_{\rho(op)}) \\ rec\, q.(R[Q/p]) & \text{if } P \equiv rec\, q.R \end{cases}$$

Proof We may choose the representatives such that P, Q, p as plain terms satisfy the Barendregt convention. Then for the last clause $P \equiv rec\, q.R$ implies $q \not\equiv p$ and $q \notin FI(Q)$. The claim follows from Definition 1.3. □

The following facts will be used in proofs.

Proposition 1.11 Let $P, Q, R \in Rec(Sig)$, $p, q, r, \in Idf$, then

1. $P[p/p] \equiv P$
2. $p \notin FI(P) \Rightarrow P[Q/p] \equiv P$
3. ('substitution lemma')
   $q \neq r \wedge q \notin FI(R) \Rightarrow P[Q/q][R/r] \equiv P[R/r][\, Q[R/r] \,/q]$
4. $q \notin FI(P) \Rightarrow P[q/p][Q/q] \equiv P[Q/p]$

Proof 1. and 2. Analogous to [Curry et al. 58, p. 95, Theorem 1 a) b)].
3. Analogous to [Barendregt 85, p. 27, Substitution Lemma] using Prop. 1.10.
4. Induction on the structure of P.

$\underline{P \equiv r}$ for $r \in Idf$. If $r \neq p$, then $P[q/p] \equiv r \equiv P[Q/p]$, and as $q \notin FI(P)$ we know $r \neq q$, hence $r[Q/q] \equiv r$. Else if $r = p$, $P[q/p] \equiv q$, and then $q[Q/q] \equiv Q \equiv p[Q/p]$.

$\underline{P \equiv op(P_1, \ldots, P_n)}$ Then as $q \notin FI(P)$ we know $\forall i : q \notin FI(P_i)$. Hence
$P[q/p][Q/q] \equiv op\big(P_1[q/p][Q/q], \ldots, P_n[q/p][Q/q]\big)$
$\overset{\text{i.h.}}{\equiv} op(P_1[Q/p], \ldots, P_n[Q/p]) \equiv P[Q/p]$.

$\underline{P \equiv rec\, r.R}$ By Fact 1.9 we may assume that P, q, p, and Q satisfy the Barendregt convention. Hence $r \notin \{q\} \cup FI(Q)$, and $q \notin FI(P) = FI(R) - \{r\}$ implies $q \notin FI(R)$.
And then $P[q/p][Q/q] \equiv rec\, r.(R[q/p][Q/q]) \overset{\text{i.h.}}{\equiv} rec\, r.(R[Q/p]) \equiv P[Q/p]$. □

In many papers [Olderog, Hoare 86], [Olderog 87], [Degano et al. 87] the problem of name clashes is neglected, other papers [Milner 85], [Goltz 87] mention it, but do not give a precise definition for the substitution. Using the Barendregt convention allows us to carry out proofs precisely but nevertheless avoids many fruitless technicalities.

1.2 A general language

In this section we define the syntax of the language **A**, the abstract programming language we will be working with throughout. The letter A stands for 'anonymous'.

It is rather general, it contains the whole finitary pure CCS [Milner 80], [Milner 85] and almost the whole TCSP [Brookes et al. 84], [Brookes, Roscoe 85] as special cases. Additionally the more general parallel operators used in ACP [Bergstra, Klop 85] and by Winskel [Winskel 87] can be expressed in **A**. We also distinguish a number of useful subsets of **A**, in particular those corresponding to CCS and TCSP.

The operators

For the language **A** we start out from a countably infinite alphabet

$$Alph$$

of names for the basic visible actions. Next we postulate a disjoint copy of *Alph*

$$\overline{Alph}$$

of conames together with a bijection $\bar{\cdot} : Alph \rightarrow \overline{Alph}$. For simplicity also the inverse of $\bar{\cdot}$ is denoted by $\bar{\cdot}$, and hence for $a \in Vis$, where

$$Vis := Alph \cup \overline{Alph}$$

we have $\bar{\bar{a}} = a$. We will also use the extended set of actions consisting of the unordered pairs over *Vis*.

$$EVis := \Big\{ [a, b] \mid a, b \in Vis \Big\}$$

Note that the unordered pair $[a, a]$ of two a's is in *EVis*. Finally there is the special action τ not in $EVis \cup Vis$ which is Milner's *invisible action*. To some extent it plays the rôle of ε (the empty word) in formal language theory, but in other respects it is treated differently; that is why Milner chose a different symbol. Let

$$Act := \{\tau\} \cup Vis \cup EVis$$

be the set of *actions*. Furthermore the special symbol $\perp$, which is not an action ($\perp \notin Act$), is used to indicate 'undefined' in functions. Define $Act_\perp := Act \cup \{\perp\}$.

We are now ready to define the signature $Sig_{\mathbf{A}}$ of **A**. In passing we also state the intuitive meanings of the operators.

$Sig_{\mathbf{A}}$ contains one nullary operator

$$nil$$

denoting a process which has stopped, i.e. which is inable to perform any action.

For every $a \in \{\tau\} \cup Vis$ there is a unary operator (called *prefixing*).

$$a(\cdot)$$

Intuitively aP can perform a and then behaves as P.

Let *Fun* be the set of functions $f : Act_\perp \rightarrow Act_\perp$ with $f(\perp) = \perp$ and $f(\tau) = \tau$. Functions in *Fun* will be written in postfix notation, and usually we omit parentheses. E.g. $f(\perp)$ is written $\perp f$, and for $f, g \in Fun$ the application of g on the application of f on a is written $(a)f \cdot g$ or just afg.

For every $f \in Fun$ there is a unary operator written in postfix notation.

$$(\cdot)f$$

We call this operator *action manipulation.* It is a combination of renaming, restriction, and hiding (= abstraction): In Pf an action a is renamed to an element of $Vis \cup EVis$ if $af \in Vis \cup EVis$; an action a (and the behaviour dependent on it) is restricted (= disallowed) if $af = \perp$; and it is hidden (= made invisible) if $af = \tau$. Note that τ is never affected, and that $\perp$ is not considered as an action but as indicating 'undefined', hence $\perp f = \perp$ states that f is strict.

There are two binary operators written in infix notation.

$$\cdot + \cdot \quad \text{and} \quad \cdot \nmid \cdot$$

The *sum* $P + Q$ behaves either like P or like Q, depending on whether the first executed action belongs to P or to Q.

The *parallel composition* $P \nmid Q$ allows P and Q to proceed independently and additionally, if P can perform $a \in Vis$ and Q can perform $b \in Vis$ then $P \nmid Q$ can perform the joint action $[a, b] \in EVis$. Note that $P \nmid Q$ is different from Milner's $P \mid Q$, where $a, b \in Vis$ can only synchronize if $a = \bar{b}$ resulting in the action τ. Below we show that our parallel composition in conjunction with action manipulation can be used to express all other known parallel operators for abstract programming languages even the very general $\textcircled{L}$-operator of [Winskel 87]. However it is technically as simple as Milner's $\mid$ and it clearly distinguishes between parallelism and manipulation of actions.

This completes the signature $Sig_{\mathbf{A}}$.

Let $terms := Rec(Sig_{\mathbf{A}})$. In summary these recursive terms (which are also called *abstract programs*) are produced by the following grammar.

$$P ::= nil \;\Big|\; p \;\Big|\; aP \;\Big|\; Pf \;\Big|\; P + P \;\Big|\; P \nmid P \;\Big|\; rec\, p.P$$

where $p \in Idf$, $a \in \{\tau\} \cup Vis$, $f \in Fun$.

Note that we do not specify a syntax for identifiers, actions, and action manipulation functions. For identifiers and actions we will provide enough constants, and for functions in *Fun* we will use standard mathematical notation. Often only the non-trivial part of the function will be given, i.e. that part of a function f with $af \neq a$. In particular a function is often denoted by its set of pairs which differs from identity. E.g. the meaning of $\{b \mapsto c, c \mapsto \perp\}$ is the function $f : Act_\perp \rightarrow Act_\perp$, where

$$af = \begin{cases} c & \text{if } a = b, \\ \perp & \text{if } a = c, \\ a & \text{otherwise.} \end{cases}$$

Abbreviations

An advantage of $Sig_{\mathbf{A}}$ is that due to the very small number of operators we save a large amount of cases in the case analyses which are necessary in many proofs. We now define a number of operators inspired by other abstract programming languages, which are interpreted as syntactic abbreviations of terms of **A**. This way we avoid the necessity of additional cases.

Definition 1.12 (abbreviating notations) Let $P, Q \in terms, A \subseteq Vis$.

1. $P \textbf{ or } Q \quad :\equiv \quad \tau P + \tau Q$ (internal non-determinism)
2. $P \setminus A \quad :\equiv \quad P\{a \mapsto \tau \mid a \in A\}$ (hiding)
3. $P\text{–}A \quad :\equiv \quad P\{a \mapsto \bot \mid a \in A\}$ (restriction)
4. $P \mid Q \quad :\equiv \quad (P \mathbin{\mid\!\!\ast} Q)g$ (CCS parallel composition)

   where $(a)g := \begin{cases} a & \text{if } a \in Vis \cup \{\tau\} \\ \tau & \text{if } a = [b,c] \in EVis \wedge b = \bar{c} \\ \bot & \text{otherwise.} \end{cases}$
5. $P \parallel_A Q \quad :\equiv \quad (P \mathbin{\mid\!\!\ast} Q)g_A$ (TCSP parallel composition)

   where $(a)g_A := \begin{cases} a & \text{if } a \in \{\tau\} \cup Vis - A \\ b & \text{if } a = [b,b] \in EVis \text{ for } b \in A \\ \bot & \text{otherwise.} \end{cases}$
6. Let $L : (Vis \cup \{\bot\})^2 \rightarrow Vis \cup \{\tau, \bot\}$ be a function with $L(a,b) = L(b,a)$ for all $a, b \in Vis \cup \{\bot\}$ and $L(\bot,\bot) = \bot$.

   $P \textcircled{\scriptsize L} Q \quad :\equiv \quad (P \mathbin{\mid\!\!\ast} Q)g_L$ (Winskel's parallel composition)

   where $(a)g_L := \begin{cases} L(a,\bot) & \text{if } a \in Vis \cup \{\bot\} \\ L(b,c) & \text{if } a = [b,c] \in EVis \\ \tau & \text{if } a = \tau. \end{cases}$

If $A = \{a\}$ we drop the braces, i.e. then $P \parallel_A Q$ ($P \setminus A$, $P\text{–}A$) is written $P \parallel_a Q$ ($P \setminus a$, $P\text{–}a$). □

1. - 5. stem from CCS and TCSP and are discussed later. We will prove that their semantics in **A** agrees with the usual one. For 6. let us just remark that it corresponds to Winskel's parallel composition [Winskel 87, p. 352], which is based on a synchronization algebra $(L_{\mathrm{Win}}, \bullet, *, 0)$. L_{Win} corresponds to $Vis \cup \{\tau, \bot\}$ and $\bullet$ corresponds to L. If $*$ is used as an argument of $\bullet$, it corresponds to $\bot$, and if 0 is the result of $a \bullet b$, this also corresponds to $\bot$. The other usages of $*$ and 0 are not needed. There is one difference to [Winskel 87]: He even allows the manipulation (renaming or restriction) of the invisible action τ, this is not allowed above.

We will frequently use certain subsets of *terms*.

Definition 1.13 For $p \in Idf$, $a \in \{\tau\} \cup Vis$, $f \in Fun$ define the following subsets of recursive terms.

1. $terms_\tau$ is generated by the grammar

$$T ::= nil \;\Big|\; p \;\Big|\; aT \;\Big|\; Tf \;\Big|\; T+T \;\Big|\; T \nmid T \;\Big|\; rec\, p.\tau T$$

2. *singterms* is generated by the following grammar, choosing S as start symbol; *qterms* is generated by the same grammar, but choosing Q as start symbol

$$S ::= nil \;\Big|\; p \;\Big|\; aQ \;\Big|\; S+S \;\Big|\; rec\, p.\tau Q$$
$$Q ::= S \;\Big|\; Qf \;\Big|\; Q \nmid Q$$

□

The only difference between elements of *terms* and elements of $terms_\tau$ is that in the latter every body of a recursion is prefixed with τ.

An element of *singterms* (called a *singular term*) always starts with a choice between none or more single actions, which are not in the scope of an action manipulation operator.

An element of *qterms* (called a *qterm*) is constructed from some singular term(s) with action manipulation and/or parallel composition. The 'q' has been chosen for this subset of terms, as every choice and every recursive body starts sequentially. We have the following fact, see also p. 165.

Fact 1.14 $Rec(Sig_{\mathbf{A}}) = terms \supset terms_\tau \supset qterms \supset singterms$ □

CCS terms

Milner's pure CCS is the best known abstract programming language, its syntax is contained in the language **A**.

Definition 1.15 (CCS terms)
Define $terms_{CCS}$ to be the set of terms produced by the following syntax

$$P ::= nil \mid p \mid aP \mid Pf \mid P{-}A \mid P+P \mid P|P \mid rec\, p.P$$

where (1) $p \in Idf$,
(2) $a \in \{\tau\} \cup Vis$,
(3) $f \in Fun$, such that $f\lceil_{EVis} = id \wedge \forall a \in Vis : af \in Vis \wedge \overline{af} = \bar{a}f$
(4) $A \subseteq Vis$, such that $a \in A \Rightarrow \bar{a} \in A$.

($f\lceil_X$ is used to denote the restriction of f to X, cf. p. 165) □

Fact 1.16 $terms_{CCS} \subset terms$ □

Let us now comment on the correspondence to the syntax chosen in [Milner 85, pp. 199f.]. In the above syntax we do not allow infinite summation or infinite families of equations for recursion, i.e. we consider *finitary* CCS. We only allow an empty or two elementary index set for summation, i.e. Milner's $\sum < P_i >_{i\in\emptyset}$ is denoted *nil*, and Milner's $\sum < P_i >_{i\in\{1,2\}}$ is denoted $P_1 + P_2$.

Furthermore only a singleton index set is allowed for recursion, i.e. Milner's $fix_1 < p_i >_{i\in\{1\}} < P_i >_{i\in\{1\}}$ is denoted $rec\, p_1.P_1$. These three constructions suffice for the modelling of any finite sum and any finite family of equations. Contrary to [Milner 85] we denote restriction by the minus sign in order to distinguish restriction from hiding. Hiding is not included in the syntax of [Milner 85] but it can be simulated, see e.g. Lemma 2.12 below.

The other syntactic differences are so small that they are not worth to be mentioned, but note that [Milner 85] syntactically distinguishes α-congruent terms.

Milner's set $\Lambda = \Delta \cup \overline{\Delta}$ corresponds to $Vis = Alph \cup \overline{Alph}$. It is not hard to see that the elements of $terms_{CCS}$ naturally correspond in a one-to-one manner to the α-congruence classes of agent expressions of [Milner 85, p. 199], where every summation has an empty or two elementary index set and every recursion has a singleton index set.

It will be shown in section 1.6 that this correspondence is also true semantically.

Sequential Composition

As Milner has shown [Milner 80, p. 128] [Milner 85, p. 217] termination and sequential composition may be added to CCS as derived operators. We adopt his technique for **A**. To this end let

$$Alph = Alph' \cup \{\surd, \surd_1, \surd_2\},$$

such that $Alph' \cap \{\surd, \surd_1, \surd_2\} = \emptyset$. $\surd$ (pronounced 'tick') is used to indicate successful termination, the other new actions are used for auxiliary purposes. In particular they are used to define an operator for sequential composition as shown in the definition below.

The idea to use a special action to indicate termination suggests itself. The particular symbol $\surd$ has been used e.g. by [Brookes et al. 84] and [Brookes, Roscoe 85]. Nevertheless there an additional operator is introduced for sequential composition while below sequential composition is considered as an abbreviation of previously defined operators.

Definition 1.17 (further abbreviations) Let $P, Q \in terms$.

1. $skip :\equiv \surd nil$

Let $g_i := \{\surd \mapsto \surd_i, \bar{\surd} \mapsto \bar{\surd}_i\}$ for $i \in \{1,2\}$.

2. $P \,;\, Q :\equiv \big(Pg_1 \mid \bar{\surd}_1 Q\big) - \{\surd_1, \bar{\surd}_1\}$
3. $P \mid_{\surd} Q :\equiv \big((Pg_1 \mid Qg_2) \mid (\bar{\surd}_1\bar{\surd}_2\surd nil + \bar{\surd}_2\bar{\surd}_1\surd nil)\big) - \{\surd_1, \bar{\surd}_1, \surd_2, \bar{\surd}_2\}$
4. Define $Ticks := \{\surd, \surd_1, \surd_2, \bar{\surd}, \bar{\surd}_1, \bar{\surd}_2\} \cup \Big\{ [a,b] \mid a, b \in \{\surd, \surd_1, \surd_2, \bar{\surd}, \bar{\surd}_1, \bar{\surd}_2\}\Big\}$.
   Let $terms_{\surd} \subseteq terms$ be defined by the following syntax.

$$P ::= nil \;\Big|\; skip \;\Big|\; p \;\Big|\; aP \;\Big|\; Pf \;\Big|\; P+P \;\Big|\; P\,;P \;\Big|\; P \mid_{\surd} P \;\Big|\; P \parallel_A P \;\Big|\; rec\, p.P$$

where (a) $a \notin Ticks$
(b) $f\lceil_{Ticks} = id \;\wedge\; (Act - Ticks)f \subseteq Act - Ticks$
(c) $\surd \in A \subseteq (Vis - Ticks) \cup \{\surd\}$. □

Fact 1.18 For $P, Q \in terms_{CCS}$: $skip$, $P\,;Q$, and $P|_{\surd}Q \in terms_{CCS}$. □

When termination is indicated by $\surd$, it should be ensured that no term can execute any action after executing $\surd$, since such a behaviour would have no interpretation. In general $\nmid$ and also the abbreviations $|$ and $\parallel_A$ can introduce such a behaviour. Milner [Milner 85, p. 217] therefore defined a stronger version of his parallel composition which demands a synchronization on the termination actions of its components before it can terminate itself (see the above definition 3.).

If we do not allow the general $\nmid$, but only $;$, $|_{\surd}$, and $\parallel_A$, where $\surd \in A$ (cf. def. 4. above), then all terms have the wanted property (cf. Theorem 1.47).

TCSP terms

There are many versions of TCSP in the literature [Brookes et al. 84], [Brookes 83], [Brookes, Roscoe 85], [Olderog, Hoare 86]. The language **A** contains almost all operators found in these references. The main exception is that the external choice operator ($P \mathbin{[]} Q$) is contained in **A** for certain P and Q only. We decided to live with this exception in order to keep the number of basic operators as small as possible. Moreover the exception is not very severe. For many considerations of this work we foresee no fundamental problems with the general $[]$-operator, for others we demand a similar limitation anyway.

Definition 1.19 (TCSP terms) Define $terms_{\mathrm{TCSP}}$ to be the set of terms produced by the following syntax, where P is used as the start symbol.

$$P ::= V \;\Big|\; p \;\Big|\; Pf \;\Big|\; P{-}A \;\Big|\; P \setminus A \;\Big|\; P \,\mathbf{or}\, P \;\Big|\; P\,;P \;\Big|\; P \parallel_A P \;\Big|\; rec\, p.P$$
$$V ::= nil \;\Big|\; aP \;\Big|\; V + V$$

where (1) $p \in Idf$
(2) $a \in Alph$
(3) $f \in Fun \;\wedge\; f\lceil_{(Act-Alph)} = id \;\wedge\; (Alph)f \subseteq Alph$
$\wedge\; \forall a \in Alph:\; |(a)f^{-1}| \in I\!N$
(4) $A \subseteq Alph$. □

Let us comment on the TCSP syntax. The second syntactic clause (using the non-terminal V) causes every alternative of a sum produced by this clause to start with a visible action. For this case $+$ and $[]$ coincide semantically as will be formalized in section 1.6. Hence we may interpret a sum produced by this clause as external choice.

In the literature on TCSP *nil* is usually written *stop*, and **or** is sometimes denoted by $\sqcap$. Furthermore some authors (e.g. [Brookes, Roscoe 85]) do not offer the general $\parallel_A$-operator, but only the special cases for $A = Alph$ (which is denoted $\parallel$) and $A = \emptyset$ (denoted $|||$). Note that some authors (e.g. [Olderog, Hoare 86]) demand *Alph* to be finite.

In section 1.6 we formally show that the interleaving semantics of **A** coincides with that of [Olderog, Hoare 86] for the subset of $terms_{\mathrm{TCSP}}$ which is treated there.

Finally let us remark that the sequential composition ($P\;;\;Q$) is based on CCS parallel composition and CCS action manipulation (cf. 1.17). One could alternatively base sequential composition solely on TCSP parallel composition and action manipulation, e.g. by defining

$$P \;;_{\mathrm{TCSP}}\; Q :\equiv \big(P\{\surd \mapsto \surd_1\} \parallel_{\{\surd_1\}} \surd_1 Q\big) \setminus \{\surd_1\}.$$

It is then possible to prove that $;_{\mathrm{TCSP}}$ and $;$ coincide semantically for TCSP terms, this is why we do not elaborate this point.

ACP

Bergstra's and Klop's Algebra of Communicating Processes (ACP) has been developed from CCS. For an overview see [Bergstra, Klop 86].

The parallel composition of ACP is similar to Winskel's Ⓛ. It starts out from a binary *communication function* $|_{\mathsf{ACP}}$: $Vis^2 \rightarrow Vis \cup \{\bot\}$ which is written infix and for which $a \,|_{\mathsf{ACP}}\, b = b \,|_{\mathsf{ACP}}\, a$ holds for all $a, b \in Vis$. This function may be either extended to the special synchronization algebra

$$L(a,b) := \begin{cases} a \,|_{\mathsf{ACP}}\, b & \text{if } a \in Vis \wedge b \in Vis \\ a & \text{if } b = \bot \\ b & \text{if } a = \bot \end{cases}$$

and then Ⓛ corresponds to the parallel composition of ACP, or the latter can be defined directly as

$$P \,\|_{\mathsf{ACP}}\, Q := (P \nparallel Q)g_{\mathsf{ACP}}, \quad \text{where } (a)g_{\mathsf{ACP}} := \begin{cases} b \,|_{\mathsf{ACP}}\, c & \text{if } a = [b,c] \in EVis \\ a & \text{if } a \in Vis \cup \{\tau, \bot\}. \end{cases}$$

In ACP the sequential composition is not treated as a derived operator but as a basic one. Instead of introducing a special action $\surd$ for termination, in order to distinguish terminated from deadlocked processes, Bergstra and Klop introduce a special action δ for deadlocking. For a corresponding treatment it would also in **A** be necessary to introduce sequential composition as a basic operator.

Further differences are the auxiliary left merge operator $\lfloor\!\lfloor$ and the approach to specify the semantics of ACP by a set of axioms instead of providing an operational semantics as done in the next section. Because of these differences we do not consider ACP formally here.

1.3 Interleaving operational semantics

In this section we describe the technique for the definition of the operational semantics of an abstract programming language.

For simplicity we concentrate for the moment on the *interleaving* semantics. That means that every computation is modelled as a linear (= totally ordered) sequence of actions. If the abstract programming language contains a parallel operator it has to be modelled as arbitrary *interleaving*.

Interleaving semantics have several advantages. They are well-studied, they are usually not too complicated, and they capture non-determinism and several aspects of parallelism, such as correctness and deadlock-freedom. On the other hand some aspects of parallelism are not modelled satisfactorily by interleaving semantics, in particular the speed up, which is reachable if more than one processor is available; the number of processors needed to reach the maximal speed up; and the causal dependence between actions are not modelled satisfactorily.

This is the reason why many non-interleaving semantics which aim at modelling more aspects of parallelism are being investigated. They usually are indicated by the catchword "true concurrency". We prefer to call them *distributed* semantics in order to avoid emotional discussions about truth. Interleaving semantics are just more abstract than distributed semantics and it depends on the application, whether they are too abstract.

When we use Petri nets for the representation of **A** we will aim at consistency with a distributed semantics. In chapter 6 we will define the distributed operational semantics of **A**.

The operational semantics of an abstract programming language has two stages. The first is a labelled transition system, whose states are the terms of the language and whose transitions are given in the structured-operational-semantics technique (SOS-technique) developed by Plotkin [Plotkin 81]. Then for a particular term P this term (= state) is chosen as starting state in the transition system, resulting in the transition system of P.

The second stage is an equivalence relation on transition systems.

Via these two stages two terms P and Q are defined to have the same meaning if their transition systems lie in the same equivalence class.

Definition 1.20 (transition system)

1. A *transition system* T over Act is a triple $\langle S, D, z\rangle$, where

S	is the set of states,
$D \subseteq S \times Act \times S$	is the set of transitions,
$z \in S$	is the starting state.

2. T is *finite* if S and D are finite.

3. T is *finitely branching* if $\forall s \in S : \{\langle a, s' \rangle \mid \langle s, a, s' \rangle \in D\}$ is finite.

We write $r \,{-a\rightarrow_D}\, s$ for $\langle r, a, s \rangle \in D$, and $r \,{-a\rightarrow_i}\, s$ for $\langle r, a, s \rangle \in D_i$ etc. □

A transition system may be seen as an edge labelled multi-graph with one special node (the starting state) and hence it can be represented graphically in the standard way indicating the starting state with an extra incoming arrow ($\rightarrow\!\!\bigcirc$). The name 'transition system' is due to [Keller 76]. The Rabin-Scott-automaton (finite automaton) is a finite transition system over a finite alphabet, where a subset of states is indicated as being final.

Definition 1.21 Let $T = \langle S, D, z \rangle$ be a transition system.

1. ($-\rightarrow_D$ is extended for sequences $w \in Act^*$)
   For all $s \in S$ $\quad s \,{-\varepsilon\rightarrow_D}\, s$ is true.
   $s \,{-w\rightarrow_D}\, s'$ iff
   $\exists v \in Act^*,\ a \in Act,\ r \in S :\ w = va \ \wedge\ s \,{-v\rightarrow_D}\, r \ \wedge\ r \,{-a\rightarrow_D}\, s'$.
2. ($=\Rightarrow_D$ is as $-\rightarrow_D$ but τ's are cancelled)

$$\text{For } v \in Act^* \text{ define} \quad v \setminus \tau := \begin{cases} \varepsilon & \text{if } v = \varepsilon, \\ v' \setminus \tau & \text{if } v = v'\tau, \\ (v' \setminus \tau)a & \text{if } v = v'a \wedge a \neq \tau. \end{cases}$$

   $s \,{=w\Rightarrow_D}\, s'$ iff $\exists v \in Act^* :\ v \setminus \tau = w \ \wedge\ s \,{-v\rightarrow_D}\, s'$.
3. (shorthands)

$$\begin{array}{llll} s \,{-w\rightarrow_D} & :\Leftrightarrow\ \exists s' : s \,{-w\rightarrow_D}\, s' & s \,{-w\not\rightarrow_D} & :\Leftrightarrow\ \neg(s \,{-w\rightarrow_D}) \\ s \,{=w\Rightarrow_D} & :\Leftrightarrow\ \exists s' : s \,{=w\Rightarrow_D}\, s' & s \,{=w\not\Rightarrow_D} & :\Leftrightarrow\ \neg(s \,{=w\Rightarrow_D}) \\ s \rightarrow_D & :\Leftrightarrow\ \exists a \in Act : s \,{-a\rightarrow_D} & s \not\rightarrow_D & :\Leftrightarrow\ \neg(s \rightarrow_D) \end{array}$$

4. (a state s from where an infinite τ-path starts is indicated by $s \uparrow_D$)
   $s \uparrow_D$ iff there exists a function $f : \mathbb{N} \rightarrow S$ such that
   $f(0) = s \ \wedge\ \forall i \in \mathbb{N} :\ f(i) \,{-\tau\rightarrow_D}\, f(i+1)$. □

Usually we will not distinguish isomorphic transition systems, i.e. systems where the only difference is that the states are named differently.

Definition 1.22 Two transition systems $\langle S_1, D_1, z_1 \rangle$ and $\langle S_2, D_2, z_2 \rangle$ are called *isomorphic* if there exists a bijection $\varphi : S_1 \rightarrow S_2$, such that $z_2 = \varphi(z_1)$, $\langle r, a, s \rangle \in D_1$ iff $\langle \varphi(r), a, \varphi(s) \rangle \in D_2$. We write $T_1 \cong T_2$ if T_1 and T_2 are isomorphic. □

The transition system of a recursive term P of an abstract programming language has as states all recursive terms and as starting state P. For our language **A** we have the following definition.

Definition 1.23 (the transition system of a term)
Let $P \in terms$, then $\mathcal{T}[\![P]\!]$ is the transition system $\langle terms, \mathbf{D}, P\rangle$ over Act, where $\mathbf{D}$ is as defined below. □

The transitions of the transition system are given in Plotkin's SOS-technique. The first step is to define a set of inference rules for transitions based on the syntactic structure of the terms. And secondly the transitions are defined to be those which are finitely provable using the inference rules, i.e. the set of transitions is the least relation satisfying the inference rules.

For our language **A** we have:

Definition 1.24 (**D** and the inference rules for **A**)
$\mathbf{D} \subseteq terms \times Act \times terms$ is defined to be the least relation satisfying the rules below. Only for this transition relation we completely drop the index on arrows, e.g. $\langle P, a, Q\rangle \in \mathbf{D}$ is written $P \overset{a}{\longrightarrow} Q$.

For every $P, P', Q, Q', R \in terms$, $a, b \in Act$, $c \in Vis \cup \{\tau\}$, $f \in Fun$, $r \in Idf$ there exist rules:

act) $$cP \overset{c}{\longrightarrow} P$$

fun) $$\frac{P \overset{a}{\longrightarrow} P' \ \wedge\ af \neq \bot}{Pf \overset{af}{\longrightarrow} P'f}$$

sum) $$\frac{P \overset{a}{\longrightarrow} P'}{P + Q \overset{a}{\longrightarrow} P' \ \wedge\ Q + P \overset{a}{\longrightarrow} P'}$$

asyn) $$\frac{P \overset{a}{\longrightarrow} P'}{P \nparallel Q \overset{a}{\longrightarrow} P' \nparallel Q \ \wedge\ Q \nparallel P \overset{a}{\longrightarrow} Q \nparallel P'}$$

syn) $$\frac{a, b \in Vis \ \wedge\ P \overset{a}{\longrightarrow} P' \ \wedge\ Q \overset{b}{\longrightarrow} Q'}{P \nparallel Q \overset{[a,b]}{\longrightarrow} P' \nparallel Q'}$$

rec) $$\frac{P \equiv rec\, r.R \ \wedge\ R[P/r] \overset{a}{\longrightarrow} P'}{P \overset{a}{\longrightarrow} P'}$$

Some derived rules

The general parallel composition ($\nparallel$) allows us to model in conjunction with action manipulation functions all other known parallel composition operators for abstract programming languages. The latter are incorporated into **A** by considering them as abbreviations. Our set of operators is chosen in order to minimize the number of defining inference rules and then to minimize the number of cases in the proofs, since very many proofs proceed by an induction on the length of the proof for some transition.

Yet to calculate examples and to see the relationship to operational semantics of other abstract programming languages it is convenient to derive some inference rules for the abbreviations.

Proposition 1.25 Let $P_1, P_2, Q \in terms,\ a \in Act, A \subseteq Vis$. Then

1. $(P_1 \textbf{ or } P_2) -a\rightarrow Q$ iff $a = \tau \wedge (P_1 \equiv Q \vee P_2 \equiv Q)$
2. $P_1 \mid P_2 -a\rightarrow Q$ iff $\exists Q_1, Q_2 \in terms,\ b \in Act,\ c \in Vis:$

$$\begin{aligned} &(Q \equiv Q_1 \mid P_2 \wedge P_1 -b\rightarrow Q_1 \vee Q \equiv P_1 \mid Q_2 \wedge P_2 -b\rightarrow Q_2) \\ &\wedge (a = b \in Vis \cup \{\tau\} \vee a = \tau \wedge b = [c, \bar{c}]) \\ \text{or}\ \ &Q \equiv Q_1 \mid Q_2 \wedge P_1 -c\rightarrow Q_1 \wedge P_2 -\bar{c}\rightarrow Q_2 \wedge a = \tau. \end{aligned}$$

3. $P_1 \|_A P_2 -a\rightarrow Q$ iff $\exists Q_1, Q_2 \in terms,\ b \in Act:$

$$\begin{aligned} &(Q \equiv Q_1 \|_A P_2 \wedge P_1 -b\rightarrow Q_1 \vee Q \equiv P_1 \|_A Q_2 \wedge P_2 -b\rightarrow Q_2) \\ &\wedge (a = b \in \{\tau\} \cup Vis - A \vee b = [a, a] \wedge a \in A) \\ \text{or}\ \ &Q \equiv Q_1 \|_A Q_2 \wedge P_1 -a\rightarrow Q_1 \wedge P_2 -a\rightarrow Q_2 \wedge a \in A. \end{aligned}$$

If additionally for $i \in \{1,2\} : P_i -a\rightarrow\ \Rightarrow a \in \{\tau\} \cup Vis$ we even have

4. $P_1 \mid P_2 -a\rightarrow Q$ iff $\exists Q_1, Q_2 \in terms, c \in Vis:$

$$\begin{aligned} &(Q \equiv Q_1 \mid P_2 \wedge P_1 -a\rightarrow Q_1 \vee Q \equiv P_1 \mid Q_2 \wedge P_2 -a\rightarrow Q_2) \\ \text{or}\ \ &Q \equiv Q_1 \mid Q_2 \wedge P_1 -c\rightarrow Q_1 \wedge P_2 -\bar{c}\rightarrow Q_2 \wedge a = \tau. \end{aligned}$$

5. $P_1 \|_A P_2 -a\rightarrow Q$ iff $\exists Q_1, Q_2 \in terms:$

$$\begin{aligned} &a \notin A \wedge (Q \equiv Q_1 \|_A P_2 \wedge P_1 -a\rightarrow Q_1 \vee Q \equiv P_1 \|_A Q_2 \wedge P_2 -a\rightarrow Q_2) \\ \text{or}\ \ &a \in A \wedge Q \equiv Q_1 \|_A Q_2 \wedge P_1 -a\rightarrow Q_1 \wedge P_2 -a\rightarrow Q_2. \end{aligned}$$

Now let $P, \tilde{Q} \in terms,\ a \in Act,\ A \subseteq Vis$. Then

6. $(P{-}A) -a\rightarrow \tilde{Q}$ iff $\exists Q \in terms : \tilde{Q} \equiv Q{-}A \wedge P -a\rightarrow Q \wedge a \notin A$.
7. $(P \setminus A) -a\rightarrow \tilde{Q}$ iff $\exists Q \in terms:$

$$\tilde{Q} \equiv Q \setminus A \wedge (a \notin A \wedge P -a\rightarrow Q \vee a = \tau \wedge \exists b \in A : P -b\rightarrow Q).$$

Proof Straightforward from the rules. For 4. and 5. use 2. and 3. □

1.4 Equivalence notions

The second stage of the operational semantics is an equivalence relation on transition systems. In the literature there exists a large variety of notions of equivalence. Up to now there is no general agreement which notion is the right one. It even may be the case that such an agreement is impossible and that different equivalence notions will be used depending on the aspects which one wants to capture.

In this section we define the best known equivalence notions and show their interrelation.

Definition 1.26 (strong bisimulation)
For $i \in \{1,2\}$ let $T_i = \langle S_i, D_i, z_i \rangle$ be transition systems.

1. Let $s_1 \in S_1$ and $s_2 \in S_2$, then $B \subseteq S_1 \times S_2$ is *a strong bisimulation for* s_1 *and* s_2 if $\langle s_1, s_2 \rangle \in B$ and $\forall \langle r, s \rangle \in B, a \in Act$:

$$\begin{array}{lll} \text{i)} & r \xrightarrow{a}_1 r' \;\Rightarrow\; \exists s' : s \xrightarrow{a}_2 s' \wedge \langle r', s' \rangle \in B & \text{and} \\ \text{ii)} & s \xrightarrow{a}_2 s' \;\Rightarrow\; \exists r' : r \xrightarrow{a}_1 r' \wedge \langle r', s' \rangle \in B. & \end{array}$$

   s_1 and s_2 are *strongly bisimular* if there exists a strong bisimulation for s_1 and s_2. If $T_1 = T_2$ we call B a *strong autobisimulation on* T_1.

2. $T_1 \sim T_2$ if z_1 and z_2 are strongly bisimular i.e. if there exists a strong bisimulation $B \subseteq S_1 \times S_2$ for z_1 and z_2. In this case we also say that B is a *strong bisimulation for* T_1 *and* T_2.
   $\sim$ is called *strong bisimulation equivalence* or *strong bisimularity.*

3. For $T = \langle S, D, z \rangle$ define $\overset{S,D}{\sim} := \{\langle r, s \rangle \in S^2 \mid \langle S, D, r \rangle \sim \langle S, D, s \rangle\}$.
   Note that $\overset{S,D}{\sim}$ is independent of the starting state. For $P \in$ *terms* and $\mathcal{T}[\![P]\!] = \langle terms, \mathbf{D}, P \rangle$ we abbreviate $\overset{terms,\mathbf{D}}{\sim}$ as $\sim_{\$}$. □

Park introduced the notion of bisimulation for finite automata [Park 81, p. 179], but much of the idea behind it is already contained in [Milner 80, Theorem 5.6]. The attribute *strong* refers to the fact that no abstraction from the invisible action τ is made.

Proposition 1.27 (analogous to [Milner 85, Prop. 2.1])
Let $T, T_1, \ldots$ be transition systems.

1. id_S is a strong bisimulation for T and T.
2. If B is a strong bisimulation for T_1 and T_2 and B' is a strong bisimulation for T_2 and T_3 then $B \circ B'$ (the composition of relations) is a strong bisimulation for T_1 and T_3.

3. If B is as above, then B^{-1} (the converse relation) is a strong bisimulation for T_2 and T_1.
4. $\sim$ is an equivalence relation on the set of transition systems. □

For 4. we have to ensure that the class of transition systems actually is a set. This is no problem if an appropriate fixed universe for states is chosen. We are assuming the latter.

Proposition 1.28 Let $T = \langle S, D, z \rangle$ be a transition system. Then

1. $\overset{S,D}{\sim}$ is an equivalence relation on S.
2. $\overset{S,D}{\sim} = \bigcup\{B \subseteq S^2 \mid B \text{ is a strong autobisimulation on } T\}$.
3. $\overset{S,D}{\sim}$ is a strong autobisimulation for T.

(2. and 3. imply that $\overset{S,D}{\sim}$ is the largest strong autobisimulation on T.)

Proof 1. Follows from 1.27 4.
2. If $r \overset{S,D}{\sim} s$, then $\langle S, D, r\rangle \sim \langle S, D, s\rangle$, and then there exists a strong autobisimulation B (on T) for r and s, hence $\langle r, s\rangle \in B$.
If $\langle r, s\rangle \in B$ for a strong autobisimulation on T, then $\langle S, D, r\rangle \sim \langle S, D, s\rangle$ and hence $r \overset{S,D}{\sim} s$.
3. Clearly $\langle z, z\rangle \in \overset{S,D}{\sim}$. Let $\langle r, s\rangle \in \overset{S,D}{\sim}$, $a \in Act$. Then there exists a strong autobisimulation B for r and s.
i) If $r \xrightarrow{a}_D r'$, then $\exists s' : s \xrightarrow{a}_D s' \wedge \langle r', s'\rangle \in B \subseteq \overset{S,D}{\sim}$.
ii) Symmetrically. □

Theorem 1.29 $\sim_\$$ is a congruence for the operators

$$a\cdot\,,\ \ \cdot f\,,\ \ \cdot + \cdot\,,\ \text{and}\ \ \cdot \nmid \cdot\,.$$

I.e. for all $P, P', Q, Q' \in terms$: $P \sim_\$ P'$ and $Q \sim_\$ Q'$ implies

1. $aP \sim_\$ aP'$ for all $a \in \{\tau\} \cup Vis$
2. $Pf \sim_\$ P'f$ for all $f \in Fun$
3. $P + Q \sim_\$ P' + Q'$
4. $P \nmid Q \sim_\$ P' \nmid Q'$.

Proof These facts are easily checked using the following strong bisimulations: 1. $\{\langle aP, aP'\rangle\} \cup \sim_\$$, 2. $\{\langle Rf, R'f\rangle \mid R \sim_\$ R'\}$, 3. $\{\langle P + Q, P' + Q'\rangle\} \cup \sim_\$$, and 4. $\{\langle R_1 \nmid R_2, R_1' \nmid R_2'\rangle \mid R_1 \sim_\$ R_1' \wedge R_2 \sim_\$ R_2'\}$. □

Note that $\sim_\$$ is not a congruence for $rec\, p.\cdot$, as $a\, nil \sim_\$ ap$ but $rec\, p.a\, nil \not\sim_\$ rec\, p.ap$.

Definition 1.30 (weak bisimulation, bisimulation congruence)
Let T_1, T_2 be transition systems.

1. $B \subseteq S_1 \times S_2$ is a *weak bisimulation for T_1 and T_2* if

   i) $\langle z_1, z_2 \rangle \in B$
   ii) $\forall \langle r, s \rangle \in B,\ w \in (Act - \{\tau\})^* :$
   $$r =w\Rightarrow_1 r' \;\Rightarrow\; \exists s' : s =w\Rightarrow_2 s' \wedge \langle r', s' \rangle \in B$$
   $$\text{and } s =w\Rightarrow_2 s' \;\Rightarrow\; \exists r' : r =w\Rightarrow_1 r' \wedge \langle r', s' \rangle \in B$$

2. $T_1 \approx T_2$ if $\exists B \subseteq S_1 \times S_2 :\ B$ is a weak bisimulation for T_1 and T_2.
   $\approx$ is called *weak bisimulation equivalence* or *weak bisimularity.*

3. $T_1 \approx_+ T_2$ if $\forall a \in Act$:
   $$z_1 -a\rightarrow_1 r \;\Rightarrow\; \exists s \in S_2, n \in I\!N : z_2 -a\tau^n\rightarrow_2 s \wedge \langle S_1, D_1, r \rangle \approx \langle S_2, D_2, s \rangle$$
   $$\text{and } z_2 -a\rightarrow_2 s \;\Rightarrow\; \exists r \in S_1, n \in I\!N : z_1 -a\tau^n\rightarrow_1 r \wedge \langle S_1, D_1, r \rangle \approx \langle S_2, D_2, s \rangle.$$
   $\approx_+$ is called *bisimulation congruence.* □

For the weak bisimulation we have adopted the definition for bisimulation in [Milner 85, 2.1.]. For the bisimulation congruence we have adopted the characterization in [Milner 85, Prop. 2.6]. As presented here the name congruence is only justified by its resemblance to that characterization of Milner's congruence.

Definition 1.31 Let $T = \langle S, D, z \rangle$ be a transition system.

$$\begin{array}{lcl}
\mathit{initials}(s) & := & \{a \in Act \mid s =a\Rightarrow_D \} \quad \text{for } s \in S \\
\mathit{traces}(T) & := & \{w \mid z =w\Rightarrow_D \} \\
\mathit{divs}(T) & := & \{vw \mid z =v\Rightarrow_D s \wedge s \uparrow_D \wedge w \in (Act - \{\tau\})^*\} \\
\mathit{divergences}(T) & := & \big\langle \mathit{traces}(T) \cup \mathit{divs}(T),\ \mathit{divs}(T) \big\rangle \\
\mathit{failures}(T) & := & \Big\langle\ \big\{\langle w, X \rangle \mid z =w\Rightarrow_D s \wedge X \subseteq Act - (\{\tau\} \cup \mathit{initials}(s))\big\} \\
 & & \quad \cup \big\{\langle w, X \rangle \mid w \in \mathit{divs}(T) \wedge X \subseteq Act - \{\tau\}\big\}, \\
 & & \quad \mathit{divs}(T)\ \Big\rangle
\end{array}$$

T is called *divergence free* if $\mathit{divs}(T) = \emptyset$. □

The next equivalence notions are well-known from the literature. For $=_{\text{tr}}$, $=_{\text{div}}$, and $=_{\text{fail}}$ see e.g. [Olderog, Hoare 86]. The testing equivalence has been introduced by [De Nicola, Hennessy 84]. We have transferred these notions to the transition systems used here. For a transference to Petri nets see [Pomello 86].

Definition 1.32 (trace, divergence, failure, and testing equivalence)
For transition systems T_1 and T_2 we define

$$\begin{array}{llll}
T_1 =_{\text{tr}} T_2 & :\Leftrightarrow & \mathit{traces}(T_1) = \mathit{traces}(T_2) \\
T_1 =_{\text{div}} T_2 & :\Leftrightarrow & \mathit{divergences}(T_1) = \mathit{divergences}(T_2) \\
T_1 =_{\text{fail}} T_2 & :\Leftrightarrow & \mathit{failures}(T_1) = \mathit{failures}(T_2) \\
T_1 =_{\text{test}} T_2 & :\Leftrightarrow & T_1 =_{\text{tr}} T_2 \wedge T_1 =_{\text{fail}} T_2
\end{array}$$
□

The next proposition states the relationship of all equivalences on transition systems. It shows that (apart from isomorphism) strong bisimularity is the finest equivalence. Hence if we find a finite transition system, which is strongly bisimular with that of a term, we have a finite representation of that term, which is not only consistent with respect to strong bisimularity, but also with respect to *all* other equivalences presented above. This is the reason why we will search for strongly bisimular finite representations.

Proposition 1.33

a)

$$\begin{array}{ccccccc}
 & & & \approx_+ \longrightarrow \approx & & & \\
 & & \nearrow & & \searrow & & \\
\cong \longrightarrow \sim & & & & & =_{\mathbf{tr}} & \\
 & & \searrow & & \nearrow & & \\
 & & & =_{\mathbf{test}} & & & \\
 & & & & \searrow & & \\
 & & & & & =_{\mathbf{fail}} \longrightarrow =_{\mathbf{div}} &
\end{array}$$

where $R \rightarrow R'$ stands for $\forall T_1, T_2 : \; T_1 \, R \, T_2 \;\Rightarrow\; T_1 \, R' \, T_2$.

b) For divergence free transition systems

$$\cong \longrightarrow \sim \longrightarrow \approx_+ \longrightarrow \approx \longrightarrow =_{\mathbf{test}} \rightleftarrows =_{\mathbf{fail}} \longrightarrow =_{\mathbf{div}} \rightleftarrows =_{\mathbf{tr}}$$

where $R \rightarrow R'$ stands for
$\forall \, T_1, T_2$ with $divs(T_1) = divs(T_2) = \emptyset : \; T_1 \, R \, T_2 \;\Rightarrow\; T_1 \, R' \, T_2$.

Proof Let T_1, T_2 be transition systems.

a) "$T_1 \cong T_2 \;\Rightarrow\; T_1 \sim T_2$" For the isomorphism $\varphi : S_1 \rightarrow S_2$, clearly $\{\langle s, \varphi(s)\rangle \mid s \in S_1\}$ is a strong bisimulation for T_1 and T_2.
"$T_1 \sim T_2 \;\Rightarrow\; T_1 \approx T_2$" Let B be the strong bisimulation for T_1 and T_2. An induction on the length of v proves for all $\langle r, s\rangle \in B$, $v \in Act^*$ that $r -v\rightarrow_1 r'$ implies $\exists s' : s -v\rightarrow_2 s' \;\wedge\; \langle r', s'\rangle \in B$ and the symmetrical implication, which in turn proves that B is also a weak bisimulation for T_1 and T_2.
"$T_1 \sim T_2 \;\Rightarrow\; T_1 \approx_+ T_2$" Let B be as above. Let $z_1 -a\rightarrow_1 r$, then since B is a strong bisimulation for T_1 and T_2 we have $\langle z_1, z_2\rangle \in B$ and $\exists s : z_2 -a\rightarrow_2 s \;\wedge\; \langle r, s\rangle \in B$ (i.e. $z_2 -a\tau^n\rightarrow_2 s$ for $n = 0$) and clearly $\langle S_1, D_1, r\rangle \sim \langle S_2, D_2, s\rangle$. Then the first condition for $T_1 \approx_+ T_2$ follows by the previously proved implication, the second condition is proved symmetrically.
"$T_1 \approx_+ T_2 \;\Rightarrow\; T_1 \approx T_2$" Define $B :=$
$$\begin{array}{l}\{\langle z_1, z_2\rangle\} \cup \bigcup\{B' \mid \exists a \in Act, n \in \mathbb{N}, r, s : \\ \qquad (z_1 -a\rightarrow_1 r \;\wedge\; z_2 -a\tau^n\rightarrow_2 s \;\vee\; z_1 -a\tau^n\rightarrow_1 r \;\wedge\; z_2 -a\rightarrow_2 s) \\ \qquad \wedge\; B' \text{ is a weak bisimulation for } \langle S_1, D_1, r\rangle \text{ and } \langle S_2, D_2, s\rangle\}.\end{array}$$
To see that B is a weak bisimulation for T_1 and T_2 it suffices to check for $\langle r, s\rangle \in B$, $w \in (Act - \{\tau\})^*$, and $r =w\Rightarrow_1 r'$ that $\exists s' : \; s =w\Rightarrow_2 s' \wedge \langle r', s'\rangle \in B$.

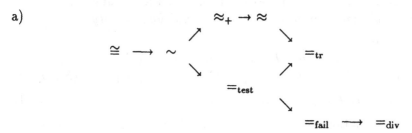

As $r \overset{w}{\Longrightarrow}_1 r'$ there exists $v \in Act^*$ such that $v \setminus \tau = w \wedge r \overset{v}{\longrightarrow}_1 r'$.
In case of $r = z_1$, if $v = \varepsilon$ then $r' = r$ and $s \overset{\varepsilon}{\Longrightarrow}_2 s$, else if $v = av'$ for $a \in Act$, $v' \in Act^*$ then $z_1 \overset{a}{\longrightarrow}_1 \bar{r} \wedge \bar{r} \overset{v'}{\longrightarrow}_1 r'$. Since $T_1 \approx_+ T_2$ there exist $n, \bar{s}$ such that $z_2 \overset{a\tau^n}{\longrightarrow}_2 \bar{s} \wedge \langle S_1, D_1, \bar{r}\rangle \approx \langle S_2, D_2, \bar{s}\rangle$. Now for any weak bisimulation B' for $\langle S_1, D_1, \bar{r}\rangle$ and $\langle S_2, D_2, \bar{s}\rangle$ by definition $B' \subseteq B$. Hence $\exists s' : \bar{s} \overset{(v' \setminus \tau)}{\Longrightarrow}_2 s' \wedge \langle r', s'\rangle \in B$. And since $w = (av') \setminus \tau$ we conclude that $s \overset{w}{\Longrightarrow}_2 s'$.
In case of $r \neq z_1$ we have that $\langle r, s\rangle \in B' \subseteq B$ for some weak bisimulation for $\langle S_1, D_1, r\rangle$ and $\langle S_2, D_2, s\rangle$. This clearly implies $\exists s' : s \overset{w}{\Longrightarrow}_2 s' \wedge \langle r', s'\rangle \in B' \subseteq B$.

Before proving the remaining inclusions let us first show the following facts. Let B be a weak bisimulation for T_1 and T_2.
(*a) $\forall \langle r, s\rangle \in B : \ initials(r) = initials(s)$.
If B additionally is a strong bisimulation for T_1 and T_2 then
(*b) $\forall \langle r, s\rangle \in B : \ r \uparrow_1 \Leftrightarrow s \uparrow_2$
(*c) $divs(T_1) = divs(T_2)$.

(*a) is immediate. To check (*b) let $\langle r, s\rangle \in B$. We prove $r \uparrow_1 \Rightarrow s \uparrow_2$, the other direction is symmetrical. As $r \uparrow_1$ there exists a function $f : \mathbb{N} \to S_1$ such that $f(0) = r \wedge \forall i \in \mathbb{N} : f(i) \overset{\tau}{\longrightarrow}_1 f(i+1)$.
Now let $g : \mathbb{N} \to S_2$, where $g(0) := s$ and for $j \in \mathbb{N}_1 : g(j) := s'$ where $s' \in S_2$ is one of the states such that $g(j-1) \overset{\tau}{\longrightarrow}_2 s'$ and $\langle f(j), s'\rangle \in B$.
The fact that g is not defined uniquely is no problem as any such g proves $s \uparrow_2$; but we have to show that it is defined for all $j \in \mathbb{N}$. To this end we inductively prove $\forall j \in \mathbb{N} : \ \exists s' : \ g(j) \overset{\tau}{\longrightarrow}_2 s' \wedge \langle f(j+1), s'\rangle \in B$.

<u>$j = 0$</u> $\quad \langle f(0), g(0)\rangle = \langle r, s\rangle \in B$ and $f(0) \overset{\tau}{\longrightarrow}_1 f(1)$, hence since B is a strong bisimulation $\exists s' : g(0) \overset{\tau}{\longrightarrow}_2 s' \wedge \langle f(1), s'\rangle \in B$.

<u>$j \mapsto j+1$</u> $\quad$ By ind. hyp. $g(j+1)$ exists and $\langle f(j+1), g(j+1)\rangle \in B$. Hence $f(j+1) \overset{\tau}{\longrightarrow}_1 f(j+2)$ implies $\exists s' : \ g(j+1) \overset{\tau}{\longrightarrow}_2 s' \wedge \langle f(j+2), s'\rangle \in B$.

(*c) Follows from (*b) and the fact that every strong bisimulation for T_1 and T_2 is also a weak bisimulation for T_1 and T_2.

Proof of Proposition 1.33 a) continued.

"$T_1 \approx T_2 \Rightarrow T_1 =_{tr} T_2$" is trivial, "$T_1 \sim T_2 \Rightarrow T_1 =_{fail} T_2$" follows from (*a) and (*c), and then also "$T_1 \sim T_2 \Rightarrow T_1 =_{test} T_2$" follows.
To check "$T_1 =_{fail} T_2 \Rightarrow T_1 =_{div} T_2$" let $T_1 =_{fail} T_2$. Clearly $divs(T_1) = divs(T_2)$. It remains to show $w \in traces(T_1) \Rightarrow w \in traces(T_2) \cup divs(T_2)$ (the other implication is symmetrical). If $w \in traces(T_1)$ then $z_1 \overset{w}{\Longrightarrow}_1$, hence $\langle w, \emptyset\rangle \in pr_1(failures(T_1)) = pr_1(failures(T_2))$, thus either $w \in traces(T_2)$ or $w \in divs(T_2)$.

b) Let $divs(T_1) = divs(T_2) = \emptyset$. "$T_1 =_{div} T_2 \Rightarrow T_1 =_{tr} T_2$" and "$T_1 =_{fail} T_2 \Rightarrow T_1 =_{test} T_2$" are trivial. By (*a) $T_1 \approx T_2$ implies $T_1 =_{fail} T_2$, and hence also "$T_1 \approx T_2 \Rightarrow T_1 =_{test} T_2$" follows. Proposition 1.33 □

1.5 Reachable subsystems and quotients

Above we have shown that strong bisimularity is the finest (interleaving) equivalence we want to consider. We do not wish to distinguish strongly bisimular transition systems. Next we show that the reachable part of a transition system T contains all information needed, i.e. it is strongly bisimular with T.

Definition 1.34 (reachable subsystem)
Let $T = \langle S, D, z\rangle$ be a transition system, and S' a set with $z \in S' \subseteq S$. We define

1. $\mathit{Reach}(T, S') := \left\langle \hat{S}, D \cap (\hat{S} \times \mathit{Act} \times \hat{S}), z \right\rangle$
   where $\hat{S}$ is the smallest set such that $S' \subseteq \hat{S}$ and
   $\langle r, a, s\rangle \in D$ for $r \in \hat{S}$ implies $s \in \hat{S}$.
2. $\mathit{Reach}(T) := \mathit{Reach}(T, \{z\})$. □

Property 1.35 Let $T = \langle S, D, z\rangle$ be a transition system, and $z \in S' \subseteq S$.

1. $T \sim \mathit{Reach}(T, S')$.
2. $T \sim \mathit{Reach}(T)$.
3. $\mathit{Reach}(T, S') = \left\langle \hat{S}, D \cap (\hat{S} \times \mathit{Act} \times \hat{S}), z \right\rangle$,
   where $\hat{S} = \{s \in S \mid \exists s' \in S', w \in \mathit{Act}^* : s' -w\rightarrow_D s\}$.

Proof 1. Let $\mathit{Reach}(T, S') = \langle \hat{S}, \hat{D}, z\rangle$ then the identity on $\hat{S}$ is a strong bisimulation for T and $\mathit{Reach}(T, S')$. 2. Follows from 1. 3. Trivial. □

Definition 1.36 (quotient of a transition system)
Let $T = \langle S, D, z\rangle$ be a transition system. Let R be an equivalence relation on S. Then define the *quotient of T with respect to R*

$$T/R := \left\langle S/R,\ \{\langle [r]_R, a, [s]_R\rangle \mid \langle r, a, s\rangle \in D\},\ [z]_R \right\rangle.$$

Here S/R denotes the quotient of S with respect to R, and $[s]_R$ denotes the equivalence class of R which contains the representative s. □

Proposition 1.37 Let $T = \langle S, D, z\rangle$, and $\mathit{Reach}(T) = \langle \hat{S}, \hat{D}, z\rangle$.

a) For every equivalence $R \subseteq \overset{S,D}{\sim}$ we have $T \sim T/R$.

b) $\mathit{Reach}(T/\overset{S,D}{\sim}) \cong \mathit{Reach}(T)/\overset{\hat{S},\hat{D}}{\sim}$.

Proof a) One easily checks that $B := \{\langle r, [s]_R\rangle \mid r \overset{S,D}{\sim} s\}$ is the needed strong bisimulation. b) Let $Reach(T/\overset{S,D}{\sim}) = \langle \hat{\hat{S}}, \hat{\hat{D}}, [z]_{\underset{\sim}{S,D}}\rangle$. Tedious but straightforward calculations show that

$$\varphi : \hat{S}/\overset{\hat{S},\hat{D}}{\sim} \longrightarrow \hat{\hat{S}}, \text{ where } \varphi\big([s]_{\underset{\sim}{\hat{S},\hat{D}}}\big) := [s]_{\underset{\sim}{S,D}} \text{ for } s \in \hat{S}$$

is the wanted isomorphism. □

The analogue of a) does not hold for $=_{\text{div}}$ and $=_{\text{fail}}$. Let us consider the case for $=_{\text{div}}$. For $T = \langle S, D, z\rangle$ define $\overset{S,D}{=}_{\text{div}} := \{\langle r, s\rangle \in S^2 \mid \langle S, D, r\rangle =_{\text{div}} \langle S, D, s\rangle\}$, and let $R \subseteq \overset{S,D}{=}_{\text{div}}$ be an equivalence relation. Then in general $T/R =_{\text{div}} T$ does not hold. For example let T be 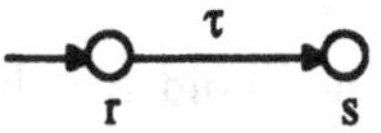

, then $r \overset{S,D}{=}_{\text{div}} s$, but T/R is

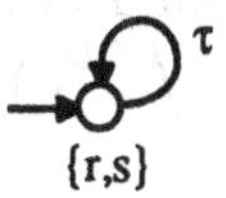

and $T \neq_{\text{div}} T/R$.

The same counterexample shows that the $=_{\text{fail}}$-analogue does not hold.

Theorem 1.38 (existence of the minimal strongly bisimular system)
Let $T = \langle S, D, z\rangle$ be a transition system, then

$$Reach(T/\overset{S,D}{\sim}) =: \langle \bar{S}, \bar{D}, \bar{z}\rangle =: \bar{T}$$

is the minimal strongly bisimular transition system of T in the following sense: For every transition system $T' = \langle S', D', z'\rangle$ with $T' \sim T$ there exists a surjective function $\beta : \hat{S} \to \bar{S}$ (where $\hat{S}$ is the set of states of $Reach(T')$) such that β is a strong bisimulation for T' and $\bar{T}$. Furthermore for every strong bisimulation B for T' and $\bar{T}$ we have $B \cap (\hat{S} \times \bar{S}) = \beta$.

Proof As $T' \sim T \overset{1.35,1.37}{\sim} \bar{T}$ there exists a strong bisimulation $\bar{B}$ for T' and $\bar{T}$. Let $\beta := \bar{B} \cap (\hat{S} \times \bar{S})$. By Proposition 1.37 clearly
(∗) $\forall s_1, s_2 \in \bar{S} : \langle \bar{S}, \bar{D}, s_1\rangle \sim \langle \bar{S}, \bar{D}, s_2\rangle \Rightarrow s_1 = s_2$. Hence β is uniquely defined (i.e. a partial function). The totality and the surjectivity of β follow by an induction on the length of the transition sequence leading to $s \in \hat{S}$, to $\bar{s} \in \bar{S}$, respectively.

Clearly β is a strong bisimulation for T' and $\bar{T}$. Let B be as stated, then $B \cap (\hat{S} \times \bar{S}) = \beta$ follows with the help of (∗). □

Corollary 1.39 Let $T' = \langle S', D', z'\rangle$ and $\bar{T} = \langle \bar{S}, \bar{D}, \bar{z}\rangle$ be as above.

1. If there exists a strong bisimulation B for T' and $\bar{T}$ which additionally is an injective function, then B is an isomorphism for T' and $\bar{T}$, i.e. $T' \cong \bar{T}$.

2. If $|\bar{S}| \geq |S'| \in I\!N \vee Reach(T') = T' \wedge \forall s_1, s_2 \in S' : s_1 \overset{S',D'}{\sim} s_2 \Rightarrow s_1 = s_2$, then $T' \cong \bar{T}$.

Proof 1. To show $T' = Reach(T')$ let $s' \in S'$. As B is a function there exists $\bar{s} \in \bar{S}$ such that $\langle s', \bar{s} \rangle \in B$. Clearly there exists a sequence $s_0 \ldots s_n$ for $n \geq 0$ such that $\bar{z} = s_0 -a_1\rightarrow_{\bar{D}} s_1 \ldots -a_n\rightarrow_{\bar{D}} s_n = \bar{s}$. As B is injective the sequence $B^{-1}(s_0) \ldots B^{-1}(s_n)$ is uniquely defined and as B is a strong bisimulation we have that $z' = B^{-1}(s_0) -a_1\rightarrow_{D'} B^{-1}(s_1) \ldots -a_n\rightarrow_{D'} B^{-1}(s_n) = s'$. Hence $T' = Reach(T')$. With the help of the above theorem we conclude that B is a bijective function. This and the fact that B is a strong bisimulation implies the claim.
2. Both conditions imply the premise of 1. □

The above corollary 2. does not hold for the $=_{tr}$-analogue: For $T = \langle S, D, z \rangle$ define $\overset{S,D}{=}_{tr} := \{\langle r, s \rangle \in S^2 \mid \langle S, D, r \rangle =_{tr} \langle S, D, s \rangle\}$, then in general for T' with $T' =_{tr} T$ and $|S_{Reach(T/\overset{S,D}{=}_{tr})}| \geq |S'| \in I\!N$ we do not have $T' \cong Reach(T/\overset{S,D}{=}_{tr})$.

Counterexamples 1. If T' is  and T is 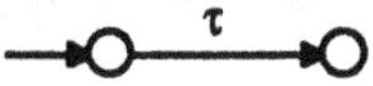

then $Reach(T/\overset{S,D}{=}_{tr})$ is 

. And we have $T' \ncong Reach(T/\overset{S,D}{=}_{tr})$.

2. If T' is 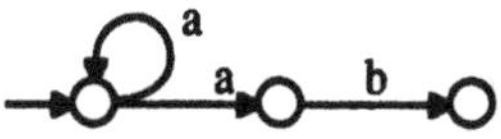

and T is 

then $Reach(T/\overset{S,D}{=}_{tr}) \cong T \ncong T'$. □

Proposition 1.40 For a finite transition system T its minimal strongly bisimular transition system is effectively constructable.

Proof In a first step T is reduced to its reachable subsystem, the procedure is well-known, see e.g. [Brauer 84, Verfahren 6.2.3, p. 314]. Let $\langle S, D, z \rangle = Reach(T)$. To construct $Reach(T)/\overset{S,D}{\sim}$, which according to Proposition 1.37 and Theorem 1.38 is the minimal strongly bisimular system of T, we calculate $\overset{S,D}{\sim}$ as follows.

$$
\begin{array}{l}
B := S^2 \\
\textbf{while } \exists \langle r, s \rangle \in B, a \in Act, r' \in S : \\
\qquad r -a\rightarrow_D r' \wedge \neg \exists s' \in S : s -a\rightarrow_D s' \wedge \langle r', s' \rangle \in B \\
\textbf{do } B := B - \{\langle r, s \rangle, \langle s, r \rangle\}.
\end{array}
$$

Clearly the condition is effectively checkable, as S and D are finite, and hence B is always finite. The procedure terminates, as S^2 is finite. Furthermore the following invariant is easily checked.

1) $id \subseteq B$,
2) B is symmetric, and
3) $\forall \langle r,s\rangle \in S^2 - B : \langle S,D,r\rangle \not\sim \langle S,D,s\rangle$.
When the procedure terminates B is a strong autobisimulation for $\langle S,D,z\rangle$: Due to 1) $\langle z,z\rangle \in B$. Now let $\langle r,s\rangle \in B, a \in Act$. If $r -a\rightarrow_D r'$, then $\exists s' \in S : s -a\rightarrow_D s' \wedge \langle r',s'\rangle \in B$, since otherwise $\langle r,s\rangle$ would not be in B.
If $s -a\rightarrow_D s'$, then due to 2) $\langle s,r\rangle \in B$, and as before $\exists r' \in S : r -a\rightarrow_D r' \wedge \langle s',r'\rangle \in B$. Again by 2) $\langle r',s'\rangle \in B$. Finally due to 3) $B = \overset{S,D}{\sim}$ (cf. Prop. 1.28). □

A similar unsophisticated procedure as that of the above proof is is well-known for reducing finite deterministic automata (see e.g. [Brauer 84, 2.4]). We did not aim at efficiency here.

Kanellakis and Smolka have shown that for finite transition systems T_1 and T_2 with n states and m transitions $T_1 \sim T_2$ can be decided in $O(m \cdot n)$ time. In the case that every state has at most c outgoing transitions the time complexity is given as $O(c^2 n \log n)$ [Kanellakis, Smolka 83, p. 235 Cor. 1.1]. On the other hand even for finite transition systems without τ-transitions deciding whether $T_1 =_{\mathrm{fail}} T_2$ is PSPACE-complete [Kanellakis, Smolka 83, p. 238 Th. 3], and the same is true for deciding $T_1 =_{\mathrm{tr}} T_2$ as is known from automata theory.

1.6 Correspondence with CCS

This section has the purpose to show that our operational semantics for the subset of terms of **A** corresponding to CCS is the "same" as the original one in [Milner 85]. There are the following differences:

1. Milner allows infinite summation and recursion.
2. He does not identify α-congruent terms.
3. His transition system is defined for closed terms only.
4. Milner defines transition rules for the parallel composition $(P \mid Q)$ directly, whereas we consider it as an abbreviation.

We have already discussed 1. The correspondence will be established for a version of CCS without infinite summation and recursion. The strongest conceivable correspondence would be some isomorphism result. But even for the reachable subsystems no such result holds due to 2. as the following example shows.

Example Let $P \equiv a(rec\, p.ap) + b(rec\, q.aq)$. Clearly $P \in clterms_{\mathrm{CCS}}$. Note that due to our convention of identifying α-congruent terms $rec\, p.ap \equiv rec\, q.aq$.

Reach$(\mathcal{T}[\![P]\!])$ may be pictured as

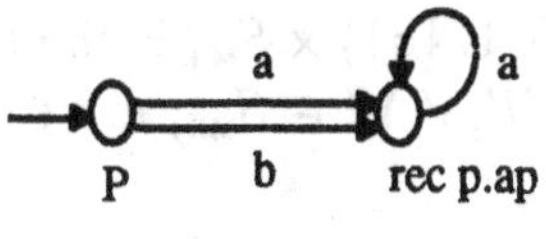

whereas the reachable subsystem of Milner's transition system for

$U \doteq a(rec\, p.ap) + b(rec\, q.aq)$ with $p \neq q$ is

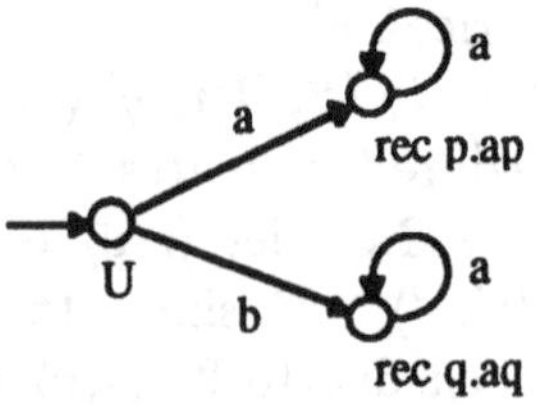

since α-congruent terms are not identified. The two transition systems are clearly not isomorphic. But they are strongly bisimular. □

Hence for the statement of the correspondence of Milner's and our semantics we will use "...is strongly bisimular to the original" for "...is the same as the original". And clearly such a correspondence suffices.

Milner's treatment of open terms differs (3.). He defines a transition system for closed terms only and extends the equivalence relation to open terms U and V with $FI(U) \cup FI(V) = \{p_1, \dots, p_n\}$ by defining (cf. [Milner 85, 2.2] for $\approx$)

$$U \sim V \quad \text{if for all closed terms } U_1, \dots, U_n$$
$$\mathcal{T}_{\text{Mil}}[\![U[U_1/p_1]\dots[U_n/p_n]]\!] \sim \mathcal{T}_{\text{Mil}}[\![V[U_1/p_1]\dots[U_n/p_n]]\!].$$

(Milner's transition system $\mathcal{T}_{\text{Mil}}$ is defined precisely below.) In our approach we define transition systems for open terms too, but we interpret free identifiers as *nil* (e.g. [Olderog 87] proceeds similarly).

Formally the precise correspondence is stated in Corollary 1.45 and 3. of Theorem 1.42 below. 2. is reflected in 1.42 1., 3. in 1.42 2., and 4. is taken into consideration in the proof of 1.42 2.

In order to formally relate Milner's transition system to ours, it is defined next. The states S_{Mil} in Milner's transition system are the closed terms produced by the syntax in 1.15 *without* identification of α-congruent terms. (In passing we note that this is also the "pure CCS" version of [Degano et al. 87] with the single exception that they allow singleton restriction only).

We use U, V, W to range over S_{Mil}. Throughout this subsection we have to distinguish carefully (plain) terms *without* identification of α-congruent terms and terms $P, Q \in$ *terms with* identification. The latter actually are α-congruence classes.

Definition 1.41 (Milner's transition system)
Let $S_{\text{Mil}} := \{U \mid U \in P \in clterms_{\text{CCS}}\}$, then for $U \in S_{\text{Mil}}$ the transition system for U according to [Milner 85] is

$$\mathcal{T}_{\text{Mil}}[\![U]\!] := \langle S_{\text{Mil}}, \mathbf{D}_{\text{Mil}}, U \rangle$$

where $\mathbf{D}_{\text{Mil}} \subseteq S_{\text{Mil}} \times (Vis \cup \{\tau\}) \times S_{\text{Mil}}$ is the least relation satisfying the following rules. For arbitrary $U, U', V, V' \in S_{\text{Mil}}$; $a, b \in Vis \cup \{\tau\}$; f and A as in Definition 1.15; and $r \in Idf$.

act$_{\text{Mil}}$) $\quad aU \xrightarrow{a}_{\text{Mil}} U$

en$_{\text{Mil}}$) $\quad \dfrac{U \xrightarrow{a}_{\text{Mil}} U'}{Uf \xrightarrow{af}_{\text{Mil}} U'f}$

es$_{\text{Mil}}$) $\quad \dfrac{U \xrightarrow{a}_{\text{Mil}} U' \wedge a \notin A}{U\text{-}A \xrightarrow{a}_{\text{Mil}} U'\text{-}A}$

um$_{\text{Mil}}$) $\quad \dfrac{U \xrightarrow{a}_{\text{Mil}} U'}{U+V \xrightarrow{a}_{\text{Mil}} U' \;\wedge\; V+U \xrightarrow{a}_{\text{Mil}} U'}$

syn$_{\text{Mil}}$) $\quad \dfrac{U \xrightarrow{a}_{\text{Mil}} U'}{U \mid V \xrightarrow{a}_{\text{Mil}} U' \mid V \;\wedge\; V \mid U \xrightarrow{a}_{\text{Mil}} V \mid U'}$

syn$_{\text{Mil}}$) $\quad \dfrac{a \in \mathit{Vis} \wedge U \xrightarrow{a}_{\text{Mil}} U' \wedge V \xrightarrow{\bar{a}}_{\text{Mil}} V'}{U \mid V \xrightarrow{\tau}_{\text{Mil}} U' \mid V'}$

ec$_{\text{Mil}}$) $\quad \dfrac{U \doteq \mathrm{rec}\, r.V \wedge V[U/r] \xrightarrow{a}_{\text{Mil}} U'}{U \xrightarrow{a}_{\text{Mil}} U'}$

(Note that syntactic substitution here is that of Definition 1.3.) □

eorem 1.42 Let $U \in P \in \mathit{clterms}_{\text{CCS}}$, and let $B \;:=\; \equiv_\alpha \cap (S_{\text{Mil}} \times S_{\text{Mil}})$.

1. B is a strong autobisimulation on $\mathcal{T}_{\text{Mil}}[\![U]\!]$, i.e. $B \subseteq \overset{S_{\text{Mil}},D_{\text{Mil}}}{\sim}$
2. $\mathcal{T}_{\text{Mil}}[\![U]\!]/B \;=\; \mathit{Reach}(\mathcal{T}[\![P]\!], \mathit{clterms}_{\text{CCS}})$
3. $\mathcal{T}_{\text{Mil}}[\![U]\!] \sim \mathcal{T}[\![P]\!]$

Proof Once 1. and 2. are proved, 3. follows immediately:

$$\begin{array}{lll} \mathcal{T}_{\text{Mil}}[\![U]\!] & \sim \mathcal{T}_{\text{Mil}}[\![U]\!]/B & \text{(by 1. and 1.37)} \\ & = \mathit{Reach}(\mathcal{T}[\![P]\!], \mathit{clterms}_{\text{CCS}}) & \text{(by 2.)} \\ & \sim \mathcal{T}[\![P]\!] & \text{(by 1.35).} \end{array}$$

To prove 1. and 2. let $\bar{U} \in \bar{P} \in \mathit{clterms}_{\text{CCS}}$.

1. Let $U, U', V \in S_{\text{Mil}}$, $a \in \{\tau\} \cup \mathit{Vis}$ and $U \equiv_\alpha V$ it suffices (since $\equiv_\alpha$ is symmetric) to show $U \xrightarrow{a}_{\text{Mil}} U' \Rightarrow \exists V' : V \xrightarrow{a}_{\text{Mil}} V' \wedge U' \equiv_\alpha V'$. We proceed by an induction on the length of the proof for $U \xrightarrow{a}_{\text{Mil}} U'$. In all cases but one this is trivial. E.g. if the last rule applied in the proof is

syn$_{\text{Mil}}$) Then $U \doteq U_1 \mid U_2$, $U' \doteq U_1' \mid U_2'$, $a = \tau$ and $U_1 \xrightarrow{b}_{\text{Mil}} U_1'$, $U_2 \xrightarrow{\bar{b}}_{\text{Mil}} U_2'$ for some $b \in \mathit{Vis}$. Furthermore $V \doteq V_1 \mid V_2$ for $V_i \equiv_\alpha U_i$. By ind. hyp. (twice) $\exists V_1', V_2' : V_1 \xrightarrow{b}_{\text{Mil}} V_1' \wedge V_2 \xrightarrow{\bar{b}}_{\text{Mil}} V_2' \wedge U_i' \equiv_\alpha V_i'$. By syn$_{\text{Mil}}$) $V \xrightarrow{\tau}_{\text{Mil}} V_1' \mid V_2'$ and clearly $U' \equiv_\alpha V_1' \mid V_2'$.

Only the case for recursion is non-trivial.

rec$_{\text{Mil}}$) Then $U \doteq rec\,r.W \wedge W[U/r] -a\rightarrow_{\text{Mil}} U'$. Since $U \equiv_\alpha V$ we have $V \doteq rec\,q.(W'[q/r])$ for some $q \notin FI(U)$ and $W' \equiv_\alpha W$.
$W'[q/r][V/q] \equiv_\alpha W[q/r][U/q]$ by Proposition 1.5 since $W' \equiv_\alpha W$ and $U \equiv_\alpha V$. And moreover $W[q/r][U/q] \equiv_\alpha W[U/r]$ by Proposition 1.11 1. if $q = r$, else by Proposition 1.11 4., since $q \neq r$ and $q \notin FI(U)$ implies $q \notin FI(W)$.
By ind. hyp. $\exists V' : W'[q/r][V/q] -a\rightarrow_{\text{Mil}} V' \wedge U' \equiv_\alpha V'$ hence by rec$_{\text{Mil}}$) $V -a\rightarrow_{\text{Mil}} V'$. □ 1.

2. Clearly $\bar{P} \in clterms_{\text{CCS}}$. Furthermore for any $P \in clterms_{\text{CCS}}$, any $a \in Act$, and any $Q \in terms$ $P -a\rightarrow Q$ implies $Q \in clterms_{\text{CCS}}$. Hence
$Reach(\mathcal{T}[\![\bar{P}]\!], clterms_{\text{CCS}}) = \left\langle clterms_{\text{CCS}}, \mathbf{D} \cap (clterms_{\text{CCS}} \times Act \times clterms_{\text{CCS}}), \bar{P}\right\rangle$.
On the other hand $\mathcal{T}_{\text{Mil}}[\![\bar{U}]\!]/B = \left\langle S_{\text{Mil}}/B, \hat{D}, [\bar{U}]_B\right\rangle = \langle clterms_{\text{CCS}}, \hat{D}, \bar{P}\rangle$, where $\hat{D} = \{\langle P, a, Q\rangle \mid \exists U \in P, V \in Q : U -a\rightarrow_{\text{Mil}} V\}$.
For equality we have to show for all $P, Q \in clterms_{\text{CCS}}$ and $a \in Act$:

$$P -a\rightarrow Q \text{ iff } \exists U \in P, V \in Q : U -a\rightarrow_{\text{Mil}} V.$$

"$\Leftarrow$" Let $U \in P \in clterms_{\text{CCS}}$, $V \in Q \in clterms_{\text{CCS}}$, $a \in Act$ and $U -a\rightarrow_{\text{Mil}} V$. We will show $P -a\rightarrow Q$ by an induction on the length of the proof for $U -a\rightarrow_{\text{Mil}} V$. If the last rule applied in the proof is ...

act$_{\text{Mil}}$) Then $U \doteq aV$, hence $P \equiv aP'$ with $V \in P'$. By act) $aP' -a\rightarrow P'$, and since $V \in Q \wedge V \in P'$ we conclude $P' \equiv Q$, i.e. $P -a\rightarrow Q$.

syn$_{\text{Mil}}$) Then $a = \tau$ and $U \doteq U_1 \mid U_2$, $V \doteq V_1 \mid V_2$ and for $b \in Vis$ $U_1 -b\rightarrow_{\text{Mil}} V_1$ and $U_2 -\bar{b}\rightarrow_{\text{Mil}} V_2$. By ind. hyp. (twice) for P_1, P_2, Q_1, Q_2 with $U_i \in P_i$, $V_i \in Q_i$: $P_1 -b\rightarrow Q_1$ and $P_2 -\bar{b}\rightarrow Q_2$. By syn) $P_1 \nmid P_2 -[b,\bar{b}]\rightarrow Q_1 \nmid Q_2$. And for g as in Definition 1.12 $([b,\bar{b}])g = \tau$. Thus by fun)
$P_1 \mid P_2 \equiv (P_1 \nmid P_2)g -\tau\rightarrow (Q_1 \nmid Q_2)g \equiv Q_1 \mid Q_2$. Clearly $U \in P_1 \mid P_2$, $V \in Q_1 \mid Q_2$, hence $P \equiv P_1 \mid P_2$, $Q \equiv Q_1 \mid Q_2$ and $P -a\rightarrow Q$.

rec$_{\text{Mil}}$) Then $U \doteq rec\,r.W$ and $W[U/r] -a\rightarrow_{\text{Mil}} V$. By ind. hyp. for $\bar{R}$ with $W[U/r] \in \bar{R}$ we know that $\bar{R} -a\rightarrow Q$. Let R be such that $W \in R$. By definition $\bar{R} \equiv R[P/r]$. Now since $W \in R$ $rec\,r.W \doteq U \in rec\,r.R$, and since $U \in P$ we have $P \equiv rec\,r.R$. By rec) $P -a\rightarrow Q$.

It is similarly easy to check the remaining cases ren$_{\text{Mil}}$), res$_{\text{Mil}}$), sum$_{\text{Mil}}$), and asyn$_{\text{Mil}}$). □ "$\Leftarrow$"

"$\Rightarrow$" Let $P, Q \in clterms_{\text{CCS}}$, $a \in Act$, and $P -a\rightarrow Q$. We prove $\exists U \in P, V \in Q : U -a\rightarrow_{\text{Mil}} V$ by induction on the length of the proof for $P -a\rightarrow Q$. If the last rule applied in the proof is ...

act) Then $P \equiv aQ$, and $a \in \{\tau\} \cup Vis$. Take any $V \in Q$ (exists !), and then let $U \doteq aV$. Clearly $U \in P$, and by act_{Mil}) $U -a\rightarrow_{\text{Mil}} V$.

fun) Then $P \equiv P'f$, $Q \equiv Q'f$ and for $b \in Act$ with $bf = a$: $P' -b\rightarrow Q'$. Now there are three cases:

1. $P', Q' \in clterms_{CCS}$ and f is as in Definition 1.15 (3).
2. $P', Q' \in clterms_{CCS}$ and $f = \{\langle c, \bot\rangle \mid c \in A\}$ for some A as in Def. 1.15 (4).
3. $P' \equiv P_1 \nmid P_2$, $Q' \equiv Q_1 \nmid Q_2$ for $P_1, P_2, Q_1, Q_2 \in clterms_{CCS}$ and $f = g$ (for g as in Def. 1.12), i.e. $P \equiv P_1 \mid P_2$ and $Q \equiv Q_1 \mid Q_2$.

Case 1: By ind. hyp. $\exists U' \in P', V' \in Q' : U' -b\rightarrow_{\text{Mil}} V'$ (in particular $b \in \{\tau\} \cup Vis$); by ren_{Mil}) $U'f -a\rightarrow_{\text{Mil}} V'f$, and clearly $U'f \in P$, $V'f \in Q$.
Case 2: Then $P'f \equiv P'{-}A$, $Q'f \equiv Q'{-}A$. By ind. hyp. $\exists U' \in P', V' \in Q'$: $U' -b\rightarrow_{\text{Mil}} V'$, and since $bf = a \neq \bot$ $b \notin A$ and $a = b$.
By res_{Mil}) $U'{-}A -a\rightarrow_{\text{Mil}} V'{-}A$. And we have $U'{-}A \in P$, $V'{-}A \in Q$.
Case 3: We distinguish two subcases.
3.1: The last rule applied to prove $P' -b\rightarrow Q'$ is asyn). Then w.l.o.g. $P_1 -b\rightarrow Q_1 \wedge P_2 \equiv Q_2$. By ind. hyp. $\exists U_1 \in P_1, V_1 \in Q_1 : U_1 -b\rightarrow_{\text{Mil}} V_1$ (in particular $b \in \{\tau\} \cup Vis$, hence $a = b$). Let $U_2 \in P_2 \equiv Q_2$. Then by asyn_{Mil}) $U_1 \mid U_2 -b\rightarrow_{\text{Mil}} V_1 \mid U_2$. Clearly $U_1 \mid U_2 \in P$ and $V_1 \mid U_2 \in Q$.
3.2: The last rule applied to prove $P' -b\rightarrow Q'$ is syn). Then $b = [c, d]$ for $c, d \in Vis$ and $P_1 -c\rightarrow Q_1 \wedge P_2 -d\rightarrow Q_2$. As $bg = a \neq \bot$, and $b \in EVis$ $\bar{c} = d$ and $a = \tau$. By ind. hyp. (twice) $\exists U_1 \in P_1, U_2 \in P_2, V_1 \in Q_1, V_2 \in Q_2 : U_1 -c\rightarrow_{\text{Mil}} V_1 \wedge U_2 -\bar{c}\rightarrow_{\text{Mil}} V_2$. By syn_{Mil}) $U_1 \mid U_2 -\tau\rightarrow_{\text{Mil}} V_1 \mid V_2$. Clearly $U_1 \mid U_2 \in P$, $V_1 \mid V_2 \in Q$.

sum) Trivial.

asyn) and syn) cannot be the last rule applied, since then we would have $P \equiv P_1 \nmid P_2 \notin clterms_{CCS}$.

rec) Then $P \equiv rec\, r.R$ and $R[P/r] -a\rightarrow Q$. Let $U \doteq rec\, r.W$ for any $W \in R$, clearly $U \in P$. Furthermore $W[U/r] \in R[P/r]$. By ind. hyp. $\exists \bar{W} \in R[P/r], \bar{V} \in Q : \bar{W} -a\rightarrow_{\text{Mil}} \bar{V}$. Then $W[U/r] \equiv_\alpha \bar{W}$. By this theorem 1. $\exists V : W[U/r] -a\rightarrow_{\text{Mil}} V \wedge V \equiv_\alpha \bar{V}$. Hence by rec_{Mil}) $U -a\rightarrow_{\text{Mil}} V$ and clearly $V \in Q$.
Theorem 1.42

Definition 1.43 For $P \in terms$ with $FI(P) = \{p_1, \dots, p_n\}$ define $\nu : terms \rightarrow clterms$, where $\nu(P) :\equiv P[nil/p_1] \dots [nil/p_n]$. □

Fact 1.44 For all $P \in terms$: $\quad \mathcal{T}[\![P]\!] \sim \mathcal{T}[\![\nu(P)]\!]$.

Proof $\quad B := \{\langle Q, \nu(Q)\rangle \mid Q \in terms\}$ is a strong bisimulation. □

Note that for $\mathcal{T}[\![P]\!]$ and $\mathcal{T}[\![\nu(P)]\!]$ in general no isomorphism result holds, as e.g. the reachable parts of $\mathcal{T}[\![ap + b\,nil]\!]$ and $\mathcal{T}[\![\nu(ap + b\,nil)]\!] = \mathcal{T}[\![a\,nil + b\,nil]\!]$ are not isomorphic.

Corollary 1.45 Let $P \in terms_{\text{CCS}}$, and $U \in \nu(P)$, then $\mathcal{T}_{\text{Mil}}[\![U]\!] \sim \mathcal{T}[\![P]\!]$.

Proof $\quad \mathcal{T}[\![P]\!] \overset{1.44}{\sim} \mathcal{T}[\![\nu(P)]\!] \overset{1.42}{\sim} \mathcal{T}_{\text{Mil}}[\![U]\!]$. □

Warning Note that some laws known from CCS do not generalize to **A**. For example in general $\mathcal{T}[\![nil \mid P]\!] \sim \mathcal{T}[\![P]\!]$ is *not true*.
Consider e.g. $P \equiv (a\,nil \between \bar{a}\,nil)\text{–}\{a, \bar{a}\}$. Then the reachable part of $\mathcal{T}[\![P]\!]$ is

$$\longrightarrow P \xrightarrow{[a,\bar{a}]} (nil \between nil)\text{–}\{a, \bar{a}\},$$

but that of $\mathcal{T}[\![nil \mid P]\!]$ is

$$\longrightarrow nil \mid P \xrightarrow{\tau} nil \mid ((nil \between nil)\text{–}\{a, \bar{a}\}),$$

since $\mid$ includes an action manipulation. Hence $\mathcal{T}[\![nil \mid P]\!] \not\sim \mathcal{T}[\![P]\!]$.
But for terms in $terms_{\text{CCS}}$ the laws known from CCS hold, due to 3. of the above theorem. E.g. for $P \in terms_{\text{CCS}}$ we have $\mathcal{T}[\![nil \mid P]\!] \sim \mathcal{T}[\![P]\!]$:
Let $U \in \nu(P)$, then $nil \mid U \in \nu(nil \mid P)$ and

$\mathcal{T}[\![P]\!]$	$\sim$	$\mathcal{T}_{\text{Mil}}[\![U]\!]$	by the above corollary
	$\sim$	$\mathcal{T}_{\text{Mil}}[\![nil \mid U]\!]$	known from CCS
	$\sim$	$\mathcal{T}[\![nil \mid P]\!]$	by the above corollary.

The proper termination property

In section 1.3 above we have stated how termination (by means of the special action $\surd$) and sequential composition can be added to **A** as derived operators. We noticed that in this case a term has a sensible interpretation only if it cannot perform any actions after a $\surd$, i.e. after 'termination'. We therefore define the following property.

Definition 1.46 Let $P \in terms$. P has the *proper termination property* if

$$\begin{aligned} &\forall w \in Act^*, Q \in terms: \\ &P \,\text{–}w\text{→}\, Q \;\Rightarrow\; w \in (Act - Ticks)^* \\ &\qquad\qquad\qquad \vee\; w = w'\surd \;\wedge\; w' \in (Act - Ticks)^* \;\wedge\; Q \not\rightarrow \;\wedge\; FI(Q) = \emptyset. \end{aligned}$$ □

We demand here for a term reached with $\surd$ that it has no free identifiers, as then even a recursive binding of any identifier cannot cause actions after a $\surd$.

Now it can be proved that the terms distinguished syntactically in Definition 1.17 4. have this property. The analogous result for a subset of CCS has been stated in [Milner 85, p. 225]. We will use this theorem in section 3.5.

Theorem 1.47 Every $P \in terms_{\surd}$ has the proper termination property.

Proof Left to the reader. □

1.7 An alternative rule for recursion

In this section we discuss an alternative inference rule for the derivation of transitions of terms of the form $rec\, r.R$. Below we will see that [Olderog, Hoare 86] have used this rule for their operational semantics. Also [De Nicola, Hennessy 87, Def. 2.2.1] use the same idea.

Definition 1.48 (the transition system $\mathcal{T}_\tau$) Let $P \in terms$, then

$$\mathcal{T}_\tau[\![P]\!] \; := \; \langle terms, \mathbf{D}_\tau, P\rangle$$

where $\mathbf{D}_\tau \subseteq terms \times Act \times terms$ is the least relation satisfying rules act), fun), sum), asyn), syn) as in Definition 1.24 and

rec$_\tau$)
$$\frac{P \equiv rec\, r.R}{P -\tau\!\rightarrow_\tau R[P/r]}$$

We write $P -a\!\rightarrow_\tau Q$ for $\langle P, a, Q\rangle \in \mathbf{D}_\tau$. □

Instead of rule rec) now the new rule rec$_\tau$) is used. For example the term $P \equiv rec\, p.p$ has as transition systems (we only draw the reachable subsystems)

$\mathcal{T}[\![P]\!] =$ 

and $\mathcal{T}_\tau[\![P]\!] =$ 

This example already demonstrates one advantage of the alternative rule, namely divergence is modelled more adequately.

A second point is that with the old rule rec) there may be an arbitrary high degree of parallelism right at the beginning, in other words arbitrary many parallel actions are enabled not only invisibly but "magically", i.e. without performing *any* action, not even the invisible one.

Of course in interleaving semantics this phenomenon shows up only indirectly as an infinite choice at the starting state of the transition system.

Example Let $P \equiv rec\, p.a\, nil \mid (b\, nil + p)$ for $a, b \in Alph$. Then (we use for this example the abbreviations $a. :\equiv a\, nil$, $b. :\equiv b\, nil$) the minimal strongly bisimular transition system of $\mathcal{T}[\![P]\!]$ is

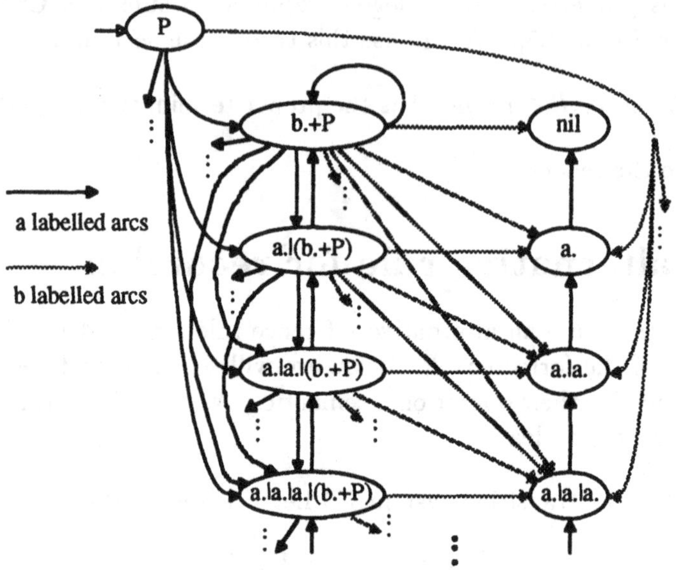

and the minimal strongly bisimular transition system of $\mathcal{T}_\tau[\![P]\!]$ is

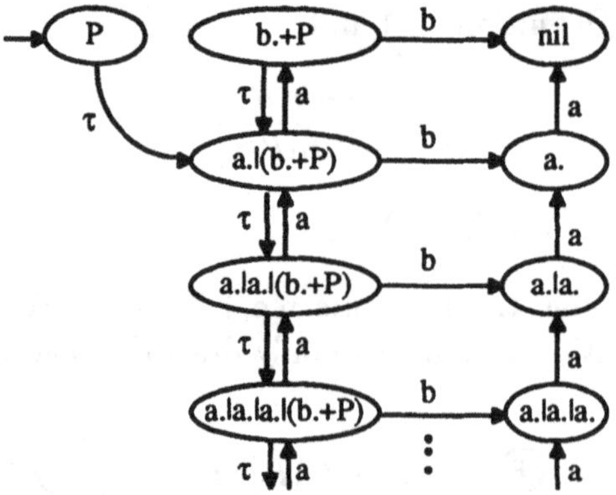

□

Formally we can prove that for any term the corresponding transition system is finitely branching.

Property 1.49 Let $P \in terms$, then $\mathcal{T}_\tau[\![P]\!]$ is finitely branching.

Proof $\mathcal{T}_\tau[\![P]\!] = \langle terms, \mathbf{D}_\tau, P\rangle$. We perform an induction on the structure of $Q \in terms$, to show that every state Q has only finitely many outgoing arcs.

$\underline{Q \equiv nil,\ Q \equiv p}$ for $p \in Idf$. Then Q has no outgoing arc, as there is no rule with a consequence of the form nil or p.

$\underline{Q \equiv aQ'}$ for $a \in \{\tau\} \cup Vis$. Then Q has one outgoing arc leading to Q', due to act).

$\underline{Q \equiv Q'f}$ for $f \in Fun$. Then Q has equally many or less outgoing arcs than Q', which by ind. hyp. has finitely many outgoing arcs.

$\underline{Q \equiv Q_1 + Q_2}$ has equally many (or less) outgoing arcs as Q_1 and Q_2 together. The claim follows by ind. hyp.

$\underline{Q \equiv Q_1 \nmid Q_2}$ Let n_i be the number of arcs starting from Q_i. Then the number of outgoing arcs of Q is bounded by $n_1 + n_2 + n_1 \cdot n_2$, which is finite, as by ind. hyp. $n_i \in I\!N$.

$\underline{Q \equiv rec\, r.R}$ Then Q has just one outgoing arc due to rec$_\tau$). □

Above we have seen that the alternative rule for recursion has nice properties, but in spite of investigating the two transition systems $\mathcal{T}[\![P]\!]$ and $\mathcal{T}_\tau[\![P]\!]$ for a term P separately, we use a trick which allows us to work with $\mathcal{T}[\![P]\!]$ only. The "trick" consists in distinguishing a certain subset of terms, namely $terms_\tau \subseteq terms$. And then the set

$$\{Reach(\mathcal{T}[\![P]\!]) \mid P \in terms_\tau\}$$

of transition systems is the same (up to isomorphism) as

$$\{Reach(\mathcal{T}_\tau[\![P]\!]) \mid P \in terms\}.$$

Hence investigating the subset $terms_\tau$ with rule rec) corresponds to investigating $terms$ with rule rec$_\tau$). Formally we have the following theorem.

Let $\sigma : terms \rightarrow terms_\tau$ be the syntactic transformation

$$\sigma(P) :\equiv \begin{cases} p & \text{if } P \equiv p \\ op(\sigma(P_1), \ldots, \sigma(P_n)) & \text{if } P \equiv op(P_1, \ldots, P_n) \\ rec\, r.\tau(\sigma(R)) & \text{if } P \equiv rec\, r.(R), \end{cases}$$

it simply prefixes every recursive body with the invisible action τ. Note that σ is bijective.

Theorem 1.50 Let $P \in terms$, then

a) $\mathcal{T}[\![\sigma(P)]\!] \sim \mathcal{T}_\tau[\![P]\!]$,

b) $Reach(\mathcal{T}[\![\sigma(P)]\!]) \cong Reach(\mathcal{T}_\tau[\![P]\!])$,

c) $Reach(\mathcal{T}[\![\sigma(P)]\!], terms_\tau) \cong \mathcal{T}_\tau[\![P]\!]$.

d) For all transition systems T
$\exists\, T_1 \in \{Reach(\mathcal{T}[\![P]\!]) \mid P \in terms_\tau\} : \; T_1 \cong T$
iff $\exists\, T_2 \in \{Reach(\mathcal{T}_\tau[\![P]\!]) \mid P \in terms\} : \; T_2 \cong T$.

Proof c) $\Rightarrow$ b) $\overset{1.33,1.35}{\Rightarrow}$ a).

d) "$\Leftarrow$" follows from b). "$\Rightarrow$" follows from b) and the fact that σ is surjective. Hence it suffices to prove c): Let $\bar{P} \in terms$, we will show $Reach(\mathcal{T}[\![\sigma(\bar{P})]\!], terms_\tau) \cong \mathcal{T}_\tau[\![\bar{P}]\!]$. As $\sigma(\bar{P}) \in terms_\tau \subseteq terms$, the l.h.s. is defined. An induction on the length of the proof of $P -a\rightarrow Q$ proves that $\forall P \in terms_\tau$: $P -a\rightarrow Q$ implies $Q \in terms_\tau$. Hence we conclude that

$$\begin{aligned} Reach(\mathcal{T}[\![\sigma(\bar{P})]\!], terms_\tau) &= \Big\langle terms_\tau, \mathbf{D} \cap (terms_\tau \times Act \times terms_\tau), \sigma(\bar{P})\Big\rangle \\ \mathcal{T}_\tau[\![\bar{P}]\!] &= \langle terms, \mathbf{D}_\tau, \bar{P}\rangle. \end{aligned}$$

We want to show that $\sigma : terms \rightarrow terms_\tau$ is the function needed for the claimed isomorphism. Clearly σ is a bijection between the states of the transition systems and preserves the starting state. We have to prove:

$$\forall P, Q \in terms : P -a\rightarrow_\tau Q \Leftrightarrow \sigma(P) -a\rightarrow \sigma(Q).$$

Let $P, Q \in terms$. "$\Rightarrow$" Induction on the length of the proof of $P -a\rightarrow_\tau Q$. All cases are trivial, except if the last rule applied is

rec$_\tau$) Then $P \equiv rec\, r.R$, $a = \tau$ and $Q \equiv R[P/r]$. By definition $\sigma(P) \equiv rec\, r.\tau\sigma(R)$. And clearly $\sigma(Q) \equiv \sigma(R[P/r]) \equiv \sigma(R)[\sigma(P)/r]$. Then $(\tau\sigma(R))[\sigma(P)/r] \equiv \tau\big(\sigma(R)[\sigma(P)/r]\big) \equiv \tau\sigma(Q)$. By rule act) $\tau\sigma(Q) -\tau\rightarrow \sigma(Q)$, hence by rule rec) $\sigma(P) \equiv rec\, r.\tau\sigma(R) -\tau\rightarrow \sigma(Q)$. Note that for this case we did not use the induction hypothesis. □ "$\Rightarrow$"

"$\Leftarrow$" Induction on the length of the proof of $\sigma(P) -a\rightarrow \sigma(Q)$. Trivial except

rec) Then $\sigma(P) \equiv rec\, r.\tau\sigma(R)$ and $P \equiv rec\, r.R$, and $\big(\tau\sigma(R)\big)[\sigma(P)/r] -a\rightarrow \sigma(Q)$. We have $(\tau\sigma(R))[\sigma(P)/r] \equiv \tau\big(\sigma(R)[\sigma(P)/r]\big)$. Hence $a = \tau$ and $\sigma(Q) \equiv \sigma(R)[\sigma(P)/r]$. Clearly $\sigma(R)[\sigma(P)/r] \equiv \sigma(R[P/r])$. And then, as σ is injective $Q \equiv R[P/r]$. By rule rec$_\tau$) $P -\tau\rightarrow_\tau R[P/r]$, i.e. $P -a\rightarrow_\tau Q$. Theorem 1.50 □

Let us emphasize that the above theorem b) has the consequence that mathematically it makes absolutely no difference to decide to work with the subset $terms_\tau = \sigma(terms)$ and the standard rule rec) for recursion or to decide to work with the set *terms* of all terms and the alternative rule rec$_\tau$). But both decisions comprise the wish to model recursive unwinding by the invisible action. Nevertheless they do not comprise a restriction with respect to the concurrency of any visible action.

Anticipating some later definitions concerning Petri nets let us illustrate the latter claim for the previous example term $P \equiv rec\, p.a\, nil \mid (b\, nil + p)$. We have that $Q :\equiv \sigma(P) \equiv rec\, p.\tau\big(a\, nil \mid (b\, nil + p)\big)$. A Petri net which represents P using rule rec_τ) and Q using rule rec), and which intuitively also models the inherent concurrency is

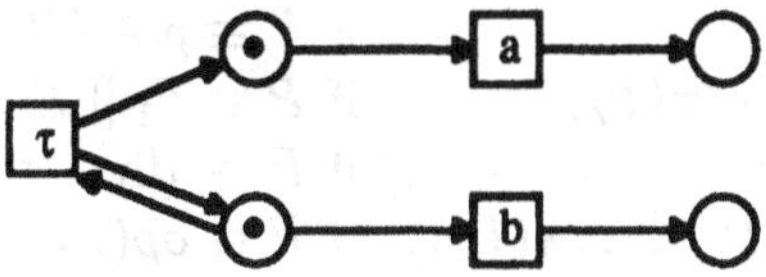

After a suitable sequence of τ's an arbitrary large a-step is possible. The occurrences of the τ-transition limit neither the mutual concurrency between different occurrences of the a-transition nor the mutual concurrency between occurrences of the a- and of the b-transition.

Note that there exists no finite Petri net which represents P using the standard rule rec) and which models the inherent parallelism as it would have to allow arbitrary large a-steps at the finite initial marking.

1.8 Correspondence with TCSP

We conclude this chapter with formally interrelating the version of TCSP in [Olderog, Hoare 86] and the respective subset of **A**.

The main differences are that in [Olderog, Hoare 86]

- only closed terms have an operational semantics
- the only action manipulation allowed is hiding, there are no renaming and restriction operators
- there is no sequential composition
- but the external choice ($[]$) is more general than we can model it in **A** with the help of $+$
- parallel composition ($\|_A$) is not treated as an abbreviation
- the underlying alphabet is finite.

Below we state the syntax of [Olderog, Hoare 86]. In [Olderog, Hoare 86] it is not said whether α-congruent terms are identified or not. We assume the former, otherwise a proof analogous to that of Theorem 1.42 would be needed.

The syntactic transformation π maps terms in $terms_{\text{OH}}$ to elements of $terms$, by changing $[]$ to $+$ and div to $rec\, p.p$.

Definition 1.51 1. Let $Alph_{\text{OH}}$ be a finite subset of $Alph$.

2. Let $terms_{\text{OH}}$ be the set of terms generated by the following syntax

$$P ::= nil \;\Big|\; div \;\Big|\; p \;\Big|\; aP \;\Big|\; P \setminus a \;\Big|\; P \textbf{ or } P \;\Big|\; P \,[]\, P \;\Big|\; P \,\|_A\, P \;\Big|\; rec\, p.P$$

where $p \in Idf$, $a \in Alph_{\text{OH}}$, and $A \subseteq Alph_{\text{OH}}$.

3. Define $\pi : terms_{\mathrm{OH}} \longrightarrow terms$

$$\pi(P) :\equiv \begin{cases} p & \text{if } P \equiv p \in Idf \\ \pi(P_1) + \pi(P_2) & \text{if } P \equiv P_1 \,[\,]\, P_2 \\ rec\, r.r & \text{if } P \equiv div \\ op(\pi(P_1), \ldots, \pi(P_n)) & \text{if } P \equiv op(P_1, \ldots, P_n) \wedge op \in Op_{\mathbf{A}} \\ rec\, r.\pi(R) & \text{if } P \equiv rec\, r.R, \end{cases}$$

where $Op_{\mathbf{A}}$ are the operators of $Sig_{\mathbf{A}}$ (cf. section 1.2). □

The transition system according to [Olderog, Hoare 86] is defined next. We hope the reader appreciates the small number of rules in Definition 1.24 having in mind the rather great expressiveness of **A**. Note that $\mathrm{rec}_{\mathrm{OH}}$) is the same as rec_τ).

Definition 1.52 (the transition system of Olderog and Hoare)
Let $P \in clterms_{\mathrm{OH}}$, then the transition system for P according to [Olderog, Hoare 86, Section 12] is $\mathcal{T}_{\mathrm{OH}}[\![P]\!] = \langle clterms_{\mathrm{OH}}, \mathbf{D}_{\mathrm{OH}}, P\rangle$, where $\mathbf{D}_{\mathrm{OH}} \subseteq clterms_{\mathrm{OH}} \times (Alph_{\mathrm{OH}} \cup \{\tau\}) \times clterms_{\mathrm{OH}}$ is the least relation satisfying the following rules. Let $P, P', Q, Q', R \in clterms_{\mathrm{OH}}$, $a \in Alph_{\mathrm{OH}}, b \in \{\tau\} \cup Alph_{\mathrm{OH}}$, $A \subseteq Alph_{\mathrm{OH}}$, and $r \in Idf$. We write $P -a\!\!\rightarrow_{\mathrm{OH}} Q$ for $\langle P, a, Q\rangle \in \mathbf{D}_{\mathrm{OH}}$.

$\mathrm{div}_{\mathrm{OH}}$) $\quad div -\tau\!\!\rightarrow_{\mathrm{OH}} div$

$\mathrm{act}_{\mathrm{OH}}$) $\quad aP -a\!\!\rightarrow_{\mathrm{OH}} P$

$\mathrm{hid1}_{\mathrm{OH}}$) $\quad \dfrac{P -b\!\!\rightarrow_{\mathrm{OH}} P' \wedge b \neq a}{P \setminus a -b\!\!\rightarrow_{\mathrm{OH}} P' \setminus a}$

$\mathrm{hid2}_{\mathrm{OH}}$) $\quad \dfrac{P -a\!\!\rightarrow_{\mathrm{OH}} P'}{P \setminus a -\tau\!\!\rightarrow_{\mathrm{OH}} P' \setminus a}$

$\mathrm{int}_{\mathrm{OH}}$) $\quad P \textbf{ or } Q -\tau\!\!\rightarrow_{\mathrm{OH}} P \wedge P \textbf{ or } Q -\tau\!\!\rightarrow_{\mathrm{OH}} Q$

$\mathrm{ext1}_{\mathrm{OH}}$) $\quad \dfrac{P -a\!\!\rightarrow_{\mathrm{OH}} P'}{P \,[\,]\, Q -a\!\!\rightarrow_{\mathrm{OH}} P' \wedge Q \,[\,]\, P -a\!\!\rightarrow_{\mathrm{OH}} P'}$

$\mathrm{ext2}_{\mathrm{OH}}$) $\quad \dfrac{P -\tau\!\!\rightarrow_{\mathrm{OH}} P'}{P \,[\,]\, Q -\tau\!\!\rightarrow_{\mathrm{OH}} P' \,[\,]\, Q \wedge Q \,[\,]\, P -\tau\!\!\rightarrow_{\mathrm{OH}} Q \,[\,]\, P'}$

$\mathrm{asyn}_{\mathrm{OH}}$) $\quad \dfrac{P -b\!\!\rightarrow_{\mathrm{OH}} P' \wedge b \notin A}{P \parallel_A Q -b\!\!\rightarrow_{\mathrm{OH}} P' \parallel_A Q \wedge Q \parallel_A P -b\!\!\rightarrow_{\mathrm{OH}} Q \parallel_A P'}$

$\mathrm{syn}_{\mathrm{OH}}$) $\quad \dfrac{P -a\!\!\rightarrow_{\mathrm{OH}} P' \wedge Q -a\!\!\rightarrow_{\mathrm{OH}} Q' \wedge a \in A}{P \parallel_A Q -a\!\!\rightarrow_{\mathrm{OH}} P' \parallel_A Q'}$

$\mathrm{rec}_{\mathrm{OH}}$) $\quad \dfrac{P \equiv rec\, r.R}{P -\tau\!\!\rightarrow_{\mathrm{OH}} R[P/r]}$ □

Chapter 2

Connections with formal language theory

In later chapters we want to study the (strongly bisimular) representation of a term as a finite automaton or as a finite Petri net (of some type). But we will see that there are terms of **A** which are not finitely representable as an automaton or as a place/transition system.

In order to get insight into the fundamental limits of the finite representability in this chapter we examine the relation to formal languages. Formal languages have a similar level of abstraction as traces for transition systems, in particular divergence and non-determinism are ignored. In the previous chapter we have seen that trace equivalence is very low in the hierarchy of equivalence notions, i.e. most equivalence notions are finer (in particular strong bisimularity is finer).

On the other hand if for some term there is no trace equivalent finite representation, there cannot be a finite representation for any finer equivalence notion. (Proof: Assume it exists, then Proposition 1.33 leads to a contradiction.)

This motivates why we investigate traces (formal languages) in order to study the inherent limits of the finite representability.

2.1 Terminating traces

There is one main difference between the set of traces of a transition system and a formal language (= set of traces over some finite alphabet): The former is always prefix closed.

Intuitively a formal language models termination which is not directly modelled in transition systems. But this gap is easily bridged by interpreting a special action $\surd \in Alph$ as termination, i.e. a state s with $s \xrightarrow{\surd}_D$ is considered as being a final state. Of course a state reached by $\surd$ should not have any outgoing arc, as there would be no sensible interpretation of an action which is performed after

The formal relationship of the version of TCSP in [Olderog, Hoare 86] and the respective subset of **A** is given next. Let us remark that π is not injective as $\pi(\mathit{div}) \equiv \pi(\mathit{rec}\, p.p)$ but $\mathit{div} \not\equiv \mathit{rec}\, p.p$. If we would take *div* as a syntactic abbreviation of *rec p.p* isomorphism results similar to Theorem 1.42 would hold.

Note that with the help of the consistency results in [Olderog, Hoare 86, Section 13] we also have a formal relation to all denotational semantics presented there.

Theorem 1.53 1. Let $P \in \mathit{clterms}_{\mathrm{OH}} \cap \pi^{-1}(\mathit{terms}_{\mathrm{TCSP}})$. Then

$$\mathcal{T}_{\mathrm{OH}}[\![P]\!] \sim \mathcal{T}_{\tau}[\![\pi(P)]\!] \sim \mathcal{T}[\![\sigma(\pi(P))]\!].$$

2. For $P \in \mathit{terms}_{\mathrm{OH}} \cap \pi^{-1}(\mathit{terms}_{\mathrm{TCSP}})$ and $Q \equiv \nu(P)$: $\mathcal{T}_{\mathrm{OH}}[\![Q]\!] \sim \mathcal{T}[\![\sigma(\pi(P))]\!]$ (where ν is extended for $\mathit{terms}_{\mathrm{OH}}$ in the obvious way).

Proof For 2. one easily checks that $\sigma(\pi(\nu(P))) \equiv \nu(\sigma(\pi(P)))$, and then $\mathcal{T}_{\mathrm{OH}}[\![Q]\!] \overset{1.}{\sim} \mathcal{T}[\![\nu(\sigma(\pi(P)))]\!] \overset{1.44}{\sim} \mathcal{T}[\![\sigma(\pi(P))]\!]$. Hence it remains to prove 1. The second bisimularity follows from Theorem 1.50. Let $\bar{P} \in X := \mathit{clterms}_{\mathrm{OH}} \cap \pi^{-1}(\mathit{terms}_{\mathrm{TCSP}})$. Let $B := \{\langle P, \pi(P)\rangle \mid P \in X\}$. With the help of

(*1) $P \in X \wedge P \xrightarrow{a}_{\mathrm{OH}} Q \Rightarrow Q \in X \wedge \pi(P) \xrightarrow{a}_{\tau} \pi(Q)$, and

(*2) $P \in X \wedge \pi(P) \xrightarrow{a}_{\tau} \tilde{Q} \Rightarrow \exists Q \in X : \pi(Q) \equiv \tilde{Q} \wedge P \xrightarrow{a}_{\mathrm{OH}} Q$

it is immediately clear that B is a strong bisimulation for $\mathcal{T}_{\mathrm{OH}}[\![\bar{P}]\!]$ and $\mathcal{T}_{\tau}[\![\pi(\bar{P})]\!]$.

The inductions on the length of the proof of $P \xrightarrow{a}_{\mathrm{OH}} Q$ respectively of $\pi(P) \xrightarrow{a}_{\tau} \tilde{Q}$ to prove (*1) and (*2) are left to the reader. Hint: Use a slightly more general induction hypothesis implying additionally ($\pi(P) \in \mathit{vterms} \Rightarrow a \neq \tau$), where *vterms* denotes the set of terms generated by the grammar in Definition 1.19 with starting symbol V. □

Conclusion to Chapter 1

This chapter has mainly collected from the literature the preliminaries needed for this work. New is the transference of Barendregt's technique of identifying α-congruent terms syntactically to abstract programming languages. Secondly, although it seems natural to form a quotient with respect to strong bisimularity, the theorem concerning the existence of the minimal strongly bisimular transition system appears to be new.

A small but useful point is Theorem 1.50 which reduces the investigation of an alternative rule for recursion, which models divergence adequately, to the investigation of a certain subset of terms using the standard rule.

termination. See Theorem 1.47 for a subset of terms whose transition systems have this property.

Definition 2.1 (terminating traces) For a transition system T

$$\surd traces(T) := \{w \in (Act - \{\surd\})^* \mid w\surd \in traces(T)\}. \qquad \square$$

A further difference between the traces and the √traces (pronounced 'tick-traces') of a transition system and a formal language is that in the traces of the latter only finitely many symbols occur (as the alphabet used there is finite), while this is not true for the former.

To get some acquaintance with the √traces of the transition system of terms of A we give some examples. The formal proofs are omitted. Very similar ones are carried out in detail for the counters below.

Examples Let $Alph \supseteq \mathbb{N} \cup \{\surd\}$. The first two examples show terms whose √traces are built from infinitely many different actions.

1. $P \equiv rec\, p.\big(0(pf) + skip\big)$ where $f : Act_\perp \to Act_\perp$ such that

$$af := \begin{cases} a+1 & \text{if } a \in \mathbb{N}, \\ a & \text{otherwise.} \end{cases}$$

One easily checks that $Reach(\mathcal{T}[\![P]\!])$ is

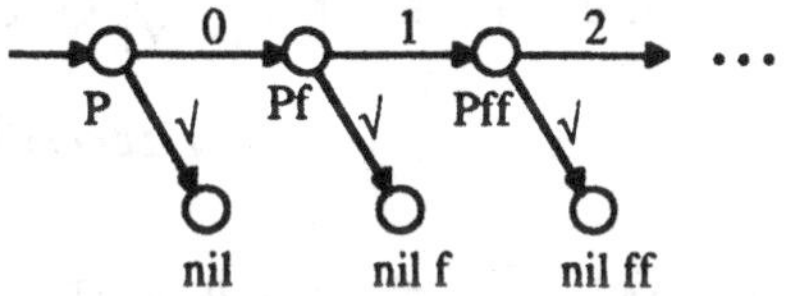

and then $\surd traces(\mathcal{T}[\![P]\!]) = \{\varepsilon, \langle 0\rangle, \langle 0,1\rangle, \langle 0,1,2\rangle, \ldots\}$. Note that $P \in terms_{TCSP} \cap terms_{\surd}$. If we use g instead of f, where $g : Act_\perp \to Act_\perp$ such that $ag := \begin{cases} a+1 & \text{if } a \in \mathbb{N} \\ \overline{\bar{a}+1} & \text{if } \bar{a} \in \mathbb{N} \\ a & \text{otherwise,} \end{cases}$

then $Q \equiv rec\, p.(0(pg) + skip) \in terms_{CCS} \cap terms_{\surd}$ and $Reach(\mathcal{T}[\![Q]\!])$ is isomorphic to the one presented above.

2. $P \equiv rec\, p.(pg + 0\, skip) \in terms_{CCS} \cap terms_{\surd}$, where g is as above.

$Reach(\mathcal{T}[\![P]\!])$ is

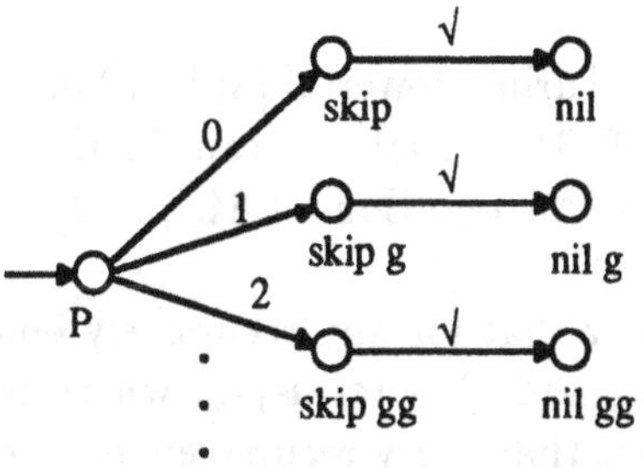

and the minimal strongly bisimular transition system for $\mathcal{T}[\![P]\!]$ is

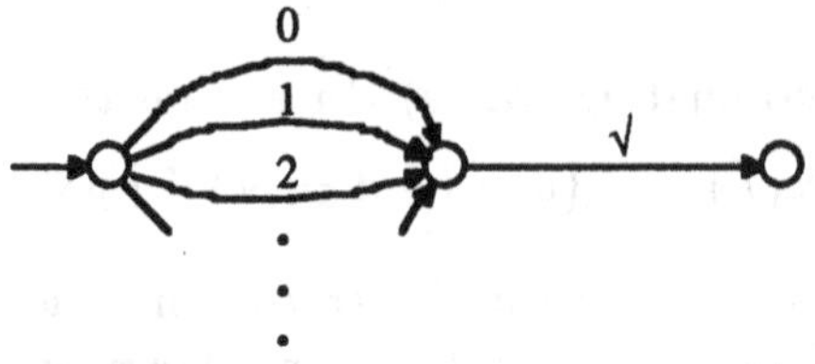

Clearly $\surd traces(\mathcal{T}[\![P]\!]) = \{\langle i \rangle \mid i \in \mathbb{N}\}$. This example term has a minimal transition system with finitely many states but nevertheless it is not finite.

3. $P :\equiv rec\, p.\big((adbdc\, skip \parallel_{\{d,\surd\}} p) \text{ or } dd\, skip\big) \in terms_{TCSP} \cap terms_{\surd}$

$$\surd traces(\mathcal{T}[\![P]\!]) = \{a^n db^n dc^n \mid n \in \mathbb{N}\}$$

4. $Q :\equiv rec\, p.((ap\, ;\, b\, skip) + skip) \in terms_{CCS} \cap terms_{TCSP} \cap terms_{\surd}$

$$\surd traces(\mathcal{T}[\![Q]\!]) = \{a^n b^n \mid n \in \mathbb{N}\}$$

5. Let $P :\equiv (rec\, p.(ap + skip))\, ;\, rec\, p.((bp\, ;\, c\, skip) + skip)$
$Q :\equiv rec\, p.((ap\, ;\, b\, skip) + skip)$
and $R :\equiv P \parallel_{\{a,b,\surd\}} Q \in terms_{TCSP} \cap terms_{\surd}$. Then

$$\surd traces(\mathcal{T}[\![R]\!]) = \{a^n b^n c^n \mid n \in \mathbb{N}\}.$$

6. Let $P :\equiv (rec\, p.(aa_1p + skip))\, ;\, rec\, p.((bb_1p\, ;\, c\, skip) + skip)$
$Q :\equiv rec\, p.((\bar{a}_1p\, ;\, \bar{b}_1\, skip) + skip)$
and $R :\equiv (P \mid_{\surd} Q) - \{a_1, \bar{a}_1, b_1, \bar{b}_1\} \in terms_{CCS} \cap terms_{\surd}$. Then

$$\surd traces(\mathcal{T}[\![R]\!]) = \{a^n b^n c^n \mid n \in \mathbb{N}\}$$

Examples □

2.2 Turing power

Folklore tells that CCS is Turing powerful [Milner 80, p. 48], [De Nicola, Hennessy 84, p. 101], [Goltz, Mycroft 84, p. 205] as it can simulate a counter. For MEIJE this has been made precise in [Austry, Boudol 84, p. 129] and for TCSP in [Taubner 87].

In this section we show that for any recursively enumerable language L there exist terms $P \in terms_{CCS}$ and $Q \in terms_{TCSP}$ whose terminating traces equal L. The proof exploits the fact that every recursively enumerable language is accepted by some Turing machine and (by a result due to Minsky) every Turing machine can be simulated by a three-counter-program.

Once we have three terms for the counters, say C_1, C_2, and C_3 it is easy to program the term R for the finite control which inputs the initial values of the counters and executes the counter program by communicating with the terms for the counters. E.g. for TCSP the term accepting L has the form

$$\Big((C_1 \parallel_{\emptyset} C_2 \parallel_{\emptyset} C_3) \parallel_A R\Big) \setminus A$$

where A is the set of actions used for the communication with the counters.

Hence the backbone of the proof of the Turing power is the exhibition of a term which satisfies the specification of a counter (to be given below). In fact, in the next section we will exhibit several terms for counters, some are coming from CCS, some from TCSP and we will aim at using as few different operators as possible. Doing so also shows which subsets of **A** are not representable by finite automata and finite place/transition systems, as neither finite automata nor finite place/transition systems can represent a counter. For the latter see chapter 5.

Theorem 2.2 (Turing power)

Given a finite alphabet Σ, then for some finite $Alph \supset \Sigma$ for every recursively enumerable language $L \subseteq \Sigma^*$ there effectively exists

$P \in clterms_{\text{CCS}}$ such that $\surd traces(\mathcal{T}[\![P]\!]) = L$, and

$Q \in clterms_{\text{TCSP}}$ such that $\surd traces(\mathcal{T}[\![Q]\!]) = L$.

Proof Follows from Lemma 2.4 and Propositions 2.5 and 2.7 below. □

Let us specify which terms are considered as counters. Actually the counters here are rather primitive, they allow only three operations:

increment	-	always possible,
decrement	-	possible only if the count is greater than zero,
zero	-	possible only if the count is zero.

Definition 2.3 (specification of a counter)

$C \in terms$ is called a *counter using* i, d, z if

$$\mathcal{T}[\![C]\!] =_{\text{tr}} \langle\ I\!N,\quad \begin{aligned} &\{\langle n, i, n+1\rangle \mid n \in I\!N\} \\ \cup\ &\{\langle n+1, d, n\rangle \mid n \in I\!N\} \\ \cup\ &\{\langle 0, z, 0\rangle\}, \end{aligned} \\ 0\ \rangle.$$

The transition system on the right-hand side graphically is the following

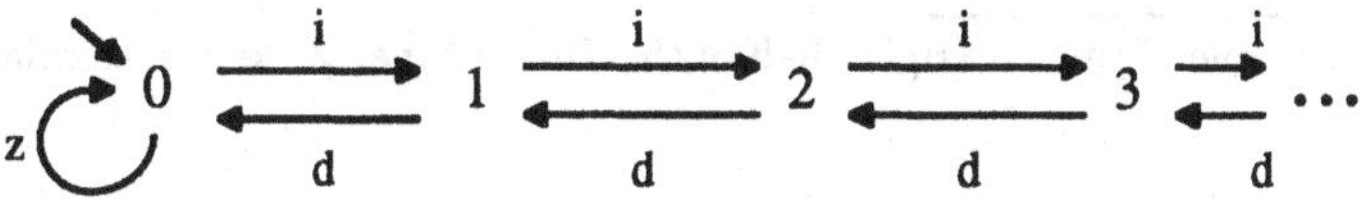

□

Lemma 2.4 Let $L \subseteq \Sigma^*$ be a language accepted by the Turing machine TM, for $j \in \{1,2,3\}$ let $C_j \in$ *terms* be counters using i_j, d_j, z_j then

1. if $C_1, C_2, C_3 \in clterms_{CCS}$ then there effectively exists $P \in clterms_{CCS}$ such that $\surd traces(\mathcal{T}[\![P]\!]) = L$,
2. if $C_1, C_2, C_3 \in clterms_{TCSP}$ then there effectively exists $Q \in clterms_{TCSP}$ such that $\surd traces(\mathcal{T}[\![Q]\!]) = L$.

Proof Without loss of generality we may assume that if some $w \in \Sigma^*$ is written on the tape of TM and TM is started with its read/write head positioned on the first blank to the right of w then TM halts if and only if $w \in L$ (see e.g. [Hopcroft, Ullman 79]). With [Minsky 67, Sections 11.1, 11.2, and 11.4] we conclude that there effectively exists a counter program (using[1] counters Z_1, Z_2, and Z_3)

$$\begin{array}{lcl} l_1 & : & s_1 \\ l_2 & : & s_2 \\ \vdots & & \\ l_{m-1} & : & s_{m-1} \\ l_m & : & \text{HALT} \end{array}$$

of $m \in I\!N$ labelled statements $l_i : s_i$, where l_i is the label and for $i \in \{1, \ldots, m-1\}$

$$\begin{array}{ll} \text{either} & s_i = \text{“}Z_j := Z_j + 1;\ \mathbf{goto}\ l_k\text{”} \\ \text{or} & s_i = \text{“}\mathbf{if}\ \ Z_j = 0\ \mathbf{then\ goto}\ l_k\ \mathbf{else}\ Z_j := Z_j - 1;\ \mathbf{goto}\ l_{k'}\ \mathbf{endif}\text{”} \end{array}$$

(for $j \in \{1,2,3\}$, and $k, k' \in \{1, \ldots, m\}$) and which, if started with $Z_1 = num(w)$ and $Z_2 = Z_3 = 0$, reaches its last statement l_m : HALT and halts if and only if w is accepted by TM, i.e. iff $w \in L$.

Here if $\Sigma = \{x_1, \ldots, x_{n-1}\}$ for $n \in I\!N_1$ the function $num : \Sigma^* \rightarrow I\!N$ is defined as

$$num(w) := \begin{cases} 0 & \text{if} \quad w = \varepsilon, \\ num(v) \cdot n + i & \text{if} \quad w = vx_i,\ i \in \{1, \ldots, n-1\}. \end{cases}$$

In words: Σ is mapped bijectively to the numbers $\{1, \ldots, n-1\}$ and $num(w)$ interprets the image of w under this mapping as a number with base n.

Now the final step of the proof is to build a term R which inputs any $w \in \Sigma^*$, puts $num(w)$ on C_1 (which plays the rôle of Z_1) and then ‘executes’ the counter program. For simplicity let us assume $\Sigma = \{1,2\}$. The general case can be derived easily. Let $\Sigma \cup \{i_j, d_j, z_j \mid 1 \leq j \leq 3\} \subset Alph$ and $\{p, p', p'', l_1, \ldots, l_m\} \subset Idf$.

[1] Z_1 (Z_2) plays the rôle of the left (right) half of the Turing tape. Z_3 serves auxiliary purposes.

For R we use a shorthand notation with a finite number (namely $m+3$) of equations, where the first equation is the start. They can easily be interpreted as one term of *clterms*, but the latter would be much harder to read. E.g.

$$\begin{array}{rcl} q_1 & = & aq_1 + bq_2 \\ q_2 & = & cq_1 + dq_2 \end{array}$$

stands for $rec\, q_1.aq_1 + b(rec\, q_2.cq_1 + dq_2)$. (Cf. e.g. [Milner 83, p. 274].)

Let

$$R \equiv \left(\begin{array}{ll} p & = (1i_2p' + 2i_2i_2p') \\ & \quad \textbf{or } l_1 \\ p' & = d_1i_2i_2i_2p' + z_1p'' \\ p'' & = d_2i_1p'' + z_2p \\ l_1 & = S_1 \\ & \vdots \\ l_{m-1} & = S_{m-1} \\ l_m & = skip \end{array} \right) \quad \begin{array}{l} \text{--Comments:} \\ \text{--initially } C_1 = C_2 = C_3 = 0 \\ \text{--input 1 or 2 to } C_2 \\ \text{--or start calculation} \\ \text{--}C_2 := C_2 + 3 \cdot C_1,\ C_1 := 0 \\ \text{--}C_1 := C_2,\ C_2 := 0 \end{array}$$

where for $i \in \{1, \ldots, m-1\}$

$$S_i \equiv \left\{ \begin{array}{lll} i_j l_k & \text{if } s_i = & \text{“}Z_j := Z_j + 1;\ \textbf{goto } l_k\text{”}, \\ z_j l_k + d_j l_{k'} & \text{if } s_i = & \text{“}\textbf{if } Z_j = 0 \textbf{ then goto } l_k \\ & & \quad \textbf{else } Z_j := Z_j - 1;\ \textbf{goto } l_{k'} \textbf{ endif}\text{”}. \end{array} \right.$$

We have $R \in clterms_{\text{CCS}} \cap clterms_{\text{TCSP}}$. Let $\bar{R}$ be as R but with $\bar{a}$ substituted for every usage of $a \in \{i_j, d_j, z_j \mid 1 \leq j \leq 3\}$. Then $\bar{R} \in clterms_{\text{CCS}}$.

We are now ready to state the terms P and Q accepting L. Let

$$Q \equiv \Big((C_1 \parallel_\emptyset C_2 \parallel_\emptyset C_3) \parallel_A R\Big) \setminus A$$

where $A = \{i_j, d_j, z_j \mid 1 \leq j \leq 3\}$, and let

$$P \equiv \Big((C_1 \mid C_2 \mid C_3) \mid \bar{R}\Big) \text{-} B$$

where $B = \{i_j, d_j, z_j, \bar{i}_j, \bar{d}_j, \bar{z}_j \mid 1 \leq j \leq 3\} = A \cup \bar{A}$.

Intuitively R (respectively $\bar{R}$) is capable of loading for any $w \in \Sigma^*$: $num(w)$ into the counter C_1 and then (with C_2, C_3 representing 0) offers exactly the choices of the counter program. The enforced communication of R with C_1, C_2, and C_3 in Q (respectively of $\bar{R}$ with C_1, C_2, and C_3 in P) makes sure that actually only those

choices taken by the counter program can be performed.
As the counter program, if started with $Z_1 = num(w)$ and $Z_2 = Z_3 = 0$ reaches l_m : HALT iff $w \in L$, we have that $\surd traces(\mathcal{T}[\![P]\!]) = \surd traces(\mathcal{T}[\![Q]\!]) = L$.
Furthermore if $C_1, C_2, C_3 \in clterms_{\mathrm{CCS}}$ then $P \in clterms_{\mathrm{CCS}}$, and if $C_1, C_2, C_3 \in clterms_{\mathrm{TCSP}}$ then $Q \in clterms_{\mathrm{TCSP}}$. Lemma 2.4

It is well-known [Minsky 67, Theorem 14.1-1] that a Turing machine can be simulated with two counters. One counter simulates the three counters used in the above proof by 'storing' their values as powers of primes, e.g. as $2^{Z_1}3^{Z_2}5^{Z_3}$. The other counter serves auxiliary purposes.

Nevertheless above we use three counters due to a notable difference. While Minsky's two-counter-program starts with $2^{num(w)}$ in its first counter the terms P and Q constructed in the above lemma start with all counters equalling zero. Before simulating the three-counter-program P and Q 'load' $num(w)$ into their first counter, i.e. they additionally carry out the coding of the input word as a number. If P and Q instead should simulate Minsky's two-counter-program they had to 'load' $2^{num(w)}$ into a counter. But we see no way how this loading could be accomplished with two counters.

However once we have a counter C using i, d, z further counters are easily derived by instantiating copies of C where i, d, z are replaced by i_j, d_j, z_j respectively.

2.3 Counters

In this section we present several terms which satisfy the specification of a counter given in Definition 2.3. To complete the proof of Theorem 2.2 we need a counter C using i, d, z being in $terms_{\mathrm{CCS}}$ respectively being in $terms_{\mathrm{TCSP}}$.

Example Let $C \equiv rec\, p.zp + (iC_1 \,;\, p)$
where $C_1 \equiv rec\, q.d\, skip + (iq \,;\, q)$.

Then $C \in clterms_{\mathrm{CCS}} \cap clterms_{\mathrm{TCSP}} \cap terms_{\surd}$. □

C is a counter using i, d, z ($C_1, C_2 \ldots$ are used to denote subterms of the counter C in this section). We omit the formal proof, as below we will present counters which are even simpler. They are simpler in the sense that for all action manipulation functions f occurring in them we have $\forall a \in Act : af \in \{a, \tau, \bot\}$, i.e. they do not need any renaming. Note that this is not true for the example counter above: For example $iq \,;\, q$ abbreviates $\big((iq)g_1 \mid \bar{\surd}_1 q\big) - \{\surd_1, \bar{\surd}_1\}$ where $g_1 = \{\surd \mapsto \surd_1, \bar{\surd} \mapsto \bar{\surd}_1\}$ and clearly $(\surd)g_1 \notin \{\surd, \tau, \bot\}$.

Proposition 2.5 (CCS counter without renaming)
Let $\{p, q, r, x\} \subset Idf$, $\{a, b, i, d, z\} \subset Alph$. Let

$$\begin{array}{rrcll} & C & \equiv & rec\, p.\ \ zp & +i\Big((C_1 \mid ap)\text{–}\{a, \bar{a}\}\Big) \\ \text{where} & C_1 & \equiv & rec\, q.\ \ d\bar{a}\, nil & +i\Big((C_2 \mid bq)\text{–}\{b, \bar{b}\}\Big) \\ \text{where} & C_2 & \equiv & rec\, r.\ \ d\bar{b}\, nil & +i\Big((q \mid ar)\text{–}\{a, \bar{a}\}\Big). \end{array}$$

Then $C \in clterms_{CCS}$ and C is a counter using i, d, z.

Proof The first fact is clear. Let $C_2' :\equiv C_2[C_1/q]$. We show that $(*)$ $Reach(\mathcal{T}[\![C]\!]/\sim_\$)$ (the minimal strongly bisimular transition system of $\mathcal{T}[\![C]\!]$) is

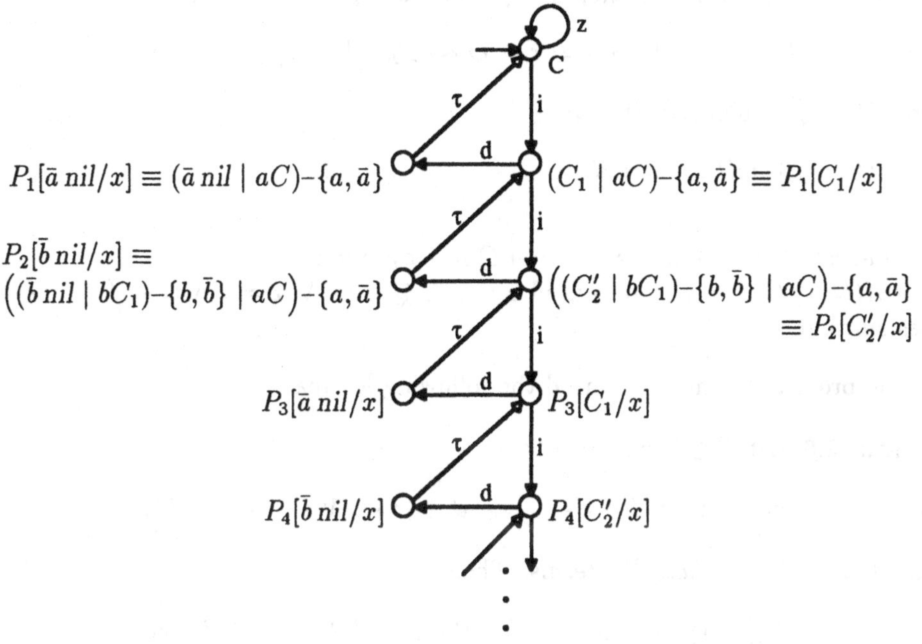

$$\begin{array}{llcl} \text{where} & P_1 & :\equiv & (x \mid aC)\text{–}\{a, \bar{a}\} \\ \text{and for } n \in I\!N_1 & P_{2n} & :\equiv & P_{2n-1}[(x \mid bC_1)\text{–}\{b, \bar{b}\}\ /\ x] \\ & P_{2n+1} & :\equiv & P_{2n}[(x \mid aC_2')\text{–}\{a, \bar{a}\}\ /\ x]. \end{array}$$

Then clearly C is a counter using i, d, z.

We use the convention for the graph of the minimal transition system that each state is labelled with a term of the bisimularity equivalence class of terms it represents. Furthermore an arrow

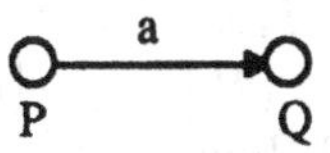

indicates for the representatives P and Q that $P \text{ –}a\text{→ } Q$ holds, while an arrow

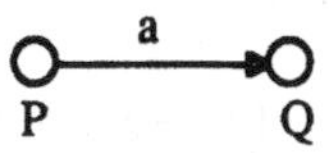

indicates that $\exists Q' : P \text{ –}a\text{→ } Q' \wedge Q' \sim_\$ Q$.

To show (*) it suffices to prove for all $n \in \mathbb{N}_1, c \in Act, Q \in terms$

1. $C -c\rightarrow Q \;\Leftrightarrow\; c = z \wedge Q \equiv C \;\vee\; c = i \wedge Q \equiv P_1[C_1/x]$
2. $P_{2n-1}[C_1/x] -c\rightarrow Q$
   $\Leftrightarrow\; c = d \wedge Q \equiv P_{2n-1}[\bar{a}\,nil/x] \;\vee\; c = i \wedge Q \equiv P_{2n}[C_2'/x]$
3. $P_{2n}[C_2'/x] -c\rightarrow Q$
   $\Leftrightarrow\; c = d \wedge Q \equiv P_{2n}[\bar{b}\,nil/x] \;\vee\; c = i \wedge Q \equiv P_{2n+1}[C_1/x]$
4. $P_{2n-1}[\bar{a}\,nil/x] -c\rightarrow Q$
   $\Rightarrow\; c = \tau \wedge$ (if $n = 1$ then $Q \sim_{\$} C$ else $Q \sim_{\$} P_{2n-2}[C_2'/x]$)
5. $P_{2n}[\bar{b}\,nil/x] -c\rightarrow Q \;\Rightarrow\; c = \tau \wedge Q \sim_{\$} P_{2n-1}[C_1/x]$
6. $\exists R : P_{2n-1}[\bar{a}\,nil/x] -\tau\rightarrow R$
7. $\exists R : P_{2n}[\bar{b}\,nil/x] -\tau\rightarrow R.$

1. Let $c \in Act, Q \in terms$. $C -c\rightarrow Q$ iff (by rule rec))
$zC + i((C_1 \mid aC)\text{-}\{a, \bar{a}\}) -c\rightarrow Q$ iff $c = z \wedge Q \equiv C \;\vee\; c = i \wedge Q \equiv P_1[C_1/x]$ by rules sum) and act).

For the proof of 2. and 3. we need the following lemma.

Lemma 2.6 Let $R \in terms$ such that

(†) $$\forall c' \in Act : \; R -c'\rightarrow \quad \Rightarrow\; c' \in \{\tau\} \cup Vis - \{a, \bar{a}, b, \bar{b}\},$$

and let $n \in \mathbb{N}_1, c \in Act, Q \in terms$. Then

$$P_n[R/x] -c\rightarrow Q \text{ iff } \exists R' : \; R -c\rightarrow R' \wedge Q \equiv P_n[R'/x].$$

Proof Induction on $n \in \mathbb{N}_1$.

<u>$n = 1$</u> $P_1[R/x] \equiv (R \mid aC)\text{-}\{a, \bar{a}\}$. Due to (†) $(R \mid aC)\text{-}\{a, \bar{a}\} -c\rightarrow Q$ iff $\exists R'$: $R -c\rightarrow R' \wedge Q \equiv (R' \mid aC)\text{-}\{a, \bar{a}\}$.
And we have $P_1[R'/x] \equiv (R' \mid aC)\text{-}\{a, \bar{a}\}$.

<u>$n \mapsto n+1$</u> Let us assume that $n+1$ is even, the case if $n+1$ is odd is analogous.
"$\Rightarrow$" Let $P_{n+1}[R/x] -c\rightarrow Q$. $P_{n+1}[R/x] \equiv P_n[(R \mid bC_1)\text{-}\{b, \bar{b}\}/x]$. As (†) holds we have $\forall c' \in Act : (R \mid bC_1)\text{-}\{b, \bar{b}\} -c'\rightarrow \quad \Rightarrow \quad c' \in \{\tau\} \cup Vis - \{a, \bar{a}, b, \bar{b}\}$. Hence by ind. hyp. $\exists R' : (R \mid bC_1)\text{-}\{b, \bar{b}\} -c\rightarrow R' \wedge Q \equiv P_n[R'/x]$.
Since by (†) $\neg(R -\bar{b}\rightarrow)$ we know for this R' that $\exists R'' : R -c\rightarrow R'' \wedge R' \equiv (R'' \mid bC_1)\text{-}\{b, \bar{b}\}$. Now as $Q \equiv P_n[R'/x] \equiv P_n[(R'' \mid bC_1)\text{-}\{b, \bar{b}\}/x]$

$\equiv P_{n+1}[R''/x]$ the claim follows.

"$\Leftarrow$" Let $R -c\rightarrow R' \wedge Q \equiv P_{n+1}[R'/x] \equiv P_n[(R' \mid bC_1)\text{-}\{b,\bar{b}\}/x]$. By (†) $c \in \{\tau\} \cup Vis - \{b,\bar{b}\}$, hence $\bar{R} :\equiv (R \mid bC_1)\text{-}\{b,\bar{b}\} -c\rightarrow (R' \mid bC_1)\text{-}\{b,\bar{b}\}$. As (†) holds $\forall c' \in Act : \bar{R} -c'\rightarrow \;\Rightarrow\; c' \in \{\tau\} \cup Vis\text{-}\{a,\bar{a},b,\bar{b}\}$. Hence by ind. hyp. $P_n[\bar{R}/x] -c\rightarrow Q$. Furthermore $P_n[\bar{R}/x] \equiv P_n[(R \mid bC_1)\text{-}\{b,\bar{b}\}/x] \equiv P_{n+1}[R/x]$. Lemma 2.6 □

2. Let $n \in \mathbb{N}_1, c \in Act, Q \in terms$. Clearly $\forall c' \in Act : C_1 -c'\rightarrow \;\Rightarrow\; c' \in \{d,i\} \subset Vis - \{a,\bar{a},b,\bar{b}\}$. Hence by the above lemma $P_{2n-1}[C_1/x] -c\rightarrow Q$ iff $\exists R : C_1 -c\rightarrow R \wedge Q \equiv P_{2n-1}[R/x]$. Furthermore we have for any R that $C_1 -c\rightarrow R$ iff $c = d \wedge R \equiv \bar{a}\,nil \vee c = i \wedge R \equiv (C_2' \mid bC_1)\text{-}\{b,\bar{b}\}$. We conclude

$$
\begin{aligned}
P_{2n-1}[C_1/x] -c\rightarrow Q \text{ iff } \quad & c = d \wedge Q \equiv P_{2n-1}[\bar{a}\,nil/x] \\
\vee\ & c = i \wedge Q \equiv P_{2n-1}[(C_2' \mid bC_1)\text{-}\{b,\bar{b}\}/x] \\
& \qquad\qquad \equiv P_{2n}[C_2'/x]
\end{aligned}
$$

3. is analogous.

For proving 4. through 7. we use the following facts.

(∗1) $C \sim_{\$} (\,nil \mid C)\text{-}\{a,\bar{a}\}$

(∗2) $C_1 \sim_{\$} (\,nil \mid C_1)\text{-}\{b,\bar{b}\}$

(∗3) $C_2' \sim_{\$} (\,nil \mid C_2')\text{-}\{a,\bar{a}\}$

(∗4) Let $R, R' \in terms$ and $R \sim_{\$} R'$. For all $n \in \mathbb{N}_1 : P_n[R/x] \sim_{\$} P_n[R'/x]$.

We sketch the proof of (∗2), the cases (∗1) and (∗3) are similar. One easily checks that for all $w \in Act^*$ $C_1 -w\rightarrow$ implies $w \in \left(\{\tau\} \cup Vis - \{b,\bar{b}\}\right)^*$. And with this fact it immediately follows that $B := \{\, \langle D, (\,nil \mid D)\text{-}\{b,\bar{b}\}\rangle \mid C_1 -w\rightarrow D \,\}$ is a strong bisimulation for $\mathcal{T}[\![C_1]\!]$ and $\mathcal{T}[\![(\,nil \mid C_1)\text{-}\{b,\bar{b}\}]\!]$.
(∗4) follows by an induction on n using Theorem 1.29.

4. and 6. If $n = 1$, then $P_{2n-1}[\bar{a}\,nil/x] \equiv (\bar{a}\,nil \mid aC)\text{-}\{a,\bar{a}\}$. And then $(\bar{a}\,nil \mid aC)\text{-}\{a,\bar{a}\} -c\rightarrow Q$ iff $c = \tau \wedge Q \equiv (\,nil \mid C)\text{-}\{a,\bar{a}\}$. (This already shows 6. for $n = 1$.) By (∗1) 4. follows.
Else if $n > 1$, then $P_{2n-1}[\bar{a}\,nil/x] \equiv P_{2n-2}[(\bar{a}\,nil \mid aC_2')\text{-}\{a,\bar{a}\}/x]$. Clearly $(\bar{a}\,nil \mid aC_2')\text{-}\{a,\bar{a}\} -c'\rightarrow Q'$ iff $c' = \tau \wedge Q' \equiv (\,nil \mid C_2')\text{-}\{a,\bar{a}\}$. Hence by Lemma 2.6 $P_{2n-1}[\bar{a}\,nil/x] -c\rightarrow Q$ iff $c = \tau \wedge Q \equiv P_{2n-2}[(\,nil \mid C_2')\text{-}\{a,\bar{a}\}/x]$ (this already proves 6.). By (∗3) and (∗4) $Q \sim_{\$} P_{2n-2}[C_2'/x]$ follows.

5. and 7. are proved similarly. Proposition 2.5 □

Proposition 2.7 (TCSP counter without renaming)
Let $\{p,q,r,x\} \subset Idf$, $\{a,b,i,d,z\} \subset Alph$. Let

$$\begin{array}{rrcll} & C & \equiv & rec\,p.zp & +i\Big((C_1 \parallel_a ap) \setminus a\Big) \\ \text{where} & C_1 & \equiv & rec\,q.da\,nil & +i\Big((C_2 \parallel_b bq) \setminus b\Big) \\ \text{where} & C_2 & \equiv & rec\,r.db\,nil & +i\Big((q \parallel_a ar) \setminus a\Big). \end{array}$$

Then $C \in clterms_{\mathrm{TCSP}}$ and C is a counter using i, d, z.

Proof Clearly $C \in clterms_{\mathrm{TCSP}}$. Let $C_2' :\equiv C_2[C_1/q]$. Similar to the proof of Proposition 2.5, one shows that $Reach(\mathcal{T}[\![C]\!]/\sim_\$)$ is

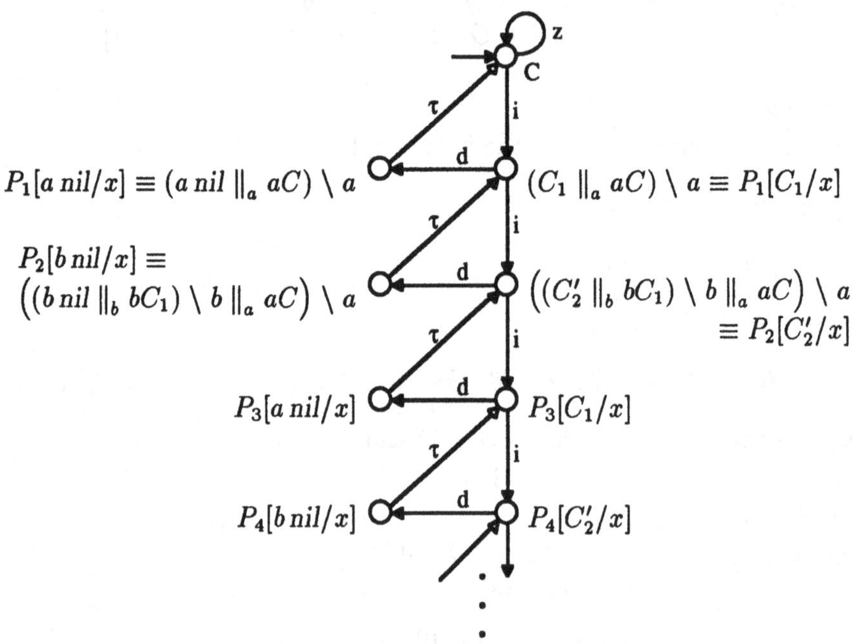

where $P_1 :\equiv (x \parallel_a aC) \setminus a$; and for $n \in \mathbb{N}_1$: $P_{2n} :\equiv P_{2n-1}[\,(x \parallel_b bC_1) \setminus b\ /\ x]$ and $P_{2n+1} :\equiv P_{2n}[\,(x \parallel_a aC_2') \setminus a\ /\ x]$. The details are omitted. □

Let us comment on the counters. Reconsider the example counter on page 52. If we expand that counter to the term it abbreviates, then we get

$$\begin{array}{rrcll} & C & \equiv & rec\,p.zp & +\Big((iC_1)g_1 \mid \bar{\surd}_1 p\Big)-\{\surd_1, \bar{\surd}_1\} \\ \text{where} & C_1 & \equiv & rec\,q.d\surd\,nil & +\Big((iq)g_1 \mid \bar{\surd}_1 q\Big)-\{\surd_1, \bar{\surd}_1\} \end{array}$$

where $g_1 = \{\surd \mapsto \surd_1, \bar{\surd} \mapsto \bar{\surd}_1\}$. This counter is precisely the counter presented in [Goltz, Mycroft 84, p. 205], only that there $\surd$ is named α and $\surd_1$ is named β.

Similarly in Proposition 2.5 the actions $a, \bar{a}, b, \bar{b}$ play the rôle of ticks. But due to the alternating use of them we avoid the need for renaming.

[Hoare 85, p. 33] gives an apparently very simple counter as follows.

$$\begin{aligned} C_0 &= zC_0 + iC_1 \\ C_{n+1} &= dC_n + iC_{n+2} \quad \text{for } n \in \mathbb{N}. \end{aligned}$$

But this specification has an infinite set of equations, it cannot be transferred back to one term of TCSP or **A**. That is why we reject this solution.

2.4 Decidability questions

We have seen that there are terms which cannot be represented as a finite automaton. It would be nice if we could state an algorithm which for a given term P outputs an equivalent finite transition system if it exists and otherwise outputs "no". Unfortunately no such algorithm exists. We introduce the following notions.

Definition 2.8 Let $P \in$ *terms*.

1. P is *$\surd$regular* if $\surd traces(\mathcal{T}[\![P]\!])$ is a regular set.
2. P is *regular* if $traces(\mathcal{T}[\![P]\!])$ is a regular set.
3. P is *representable by a finite transition system* if there exists a finite transition system T such that $T \sim \mathcal{T}[\![P]\!]$. □

Property 2.9 1. P is $\surd$regular iff there exists a finite transition system T such that $\surd traces(T) = \surd traces(\mathcal{T}[\![P]\!])$.

2. P is regular iff there exists a finite transition system T such that $T =_{tr} \mathcal{T}[\![P]\!]$.
3. P is representable by a finite transition system iff $Reach(\mathcal{T}[\![P]\!]/\sim_{\$})$ is finite.

Proof 1. "$\Rightarrow$" If P is $\surd$regular then $L := \surd traces(\mathcal{T}[\![P]\!])$ is a regular set, i.e. there exists a finite automaton A (with final states) which accepts L.
From A we derive a finite transition system T (without final states) by introducing a new state and a $\surd$-arc from every "final state" to this new state, and by changing ε-arcs to τ-arcs. Then $\surd traces(T) = L$.
"$\Leftarrow$" Let a finite T with $\surd traces(T) = \surd traces(\mathcal{T}[\![P]\!])$ be given. We construct a finite automaton A from T by considering states with an outgoing $\surd$-arc as being final, and by cancelling all $\surd$-arcs, and by changing all τ-arcs to ε-arcs. Then A accepts $\surd traces(\mathcal{T}[\![P]\!])$, hence it is regular and thus P is $\surd$regular.

2. Similar. Again τ-arcs in transition systems correspond to ε-arcs in automata. Furthermore as $traces(\mathcal{T}[\![P]\!])$ is prefix closed we may assume for the finite automaton accepting it that all states are final states.

3. "$\Leftarrow$" by Property 1.35 and Proposition 1.37. "$\Rightarrow$" by Theorem 1.38. □

Proposition 2.10 Let X be one of *terms*, $clterms_{\mathrm{TCSP}}$, $clterms_{\mathrm{CCS}}$ for *Alph* as in Theorem 2.2.

For $P \in X$ it is undecidable, whether P is $\surd$regular.

Proof Assume the contrary. By Theorem 2.2 for any recursively enumerable set $L \subseteq \Sigma^*$ there exists $P \in X$ such that $\surd traces(\mathcal{T}[\![P]\!]) = L$. Then the decision algorithm for "Is P $\surd$regular?" also decides whether L is regular, a contradiction to the well-known fact that regularity is not decidable for recursively enumerable languages. The latter is a corollary of Rice's Theorem, see e.g. [Hopcroft, Ullman 79, p. 189]. □

Although one expects the analogous problems "Is P regular?" and "Is P representable by a finite transition system?" to be undecidable too, the problems do not immediately reduce to that of the above proposition. E.g. although the existence of a finite T with $T \sim \mathcal{T}[\![P]\!]$ implies (by Proposition 1.33) $T =_{\mathrm{tr}} \mathcal{T}[\![P]\!]$ and hence $\surd$regularity of P, the converse is not true: The non-existence of a finite T with $T \sim \mathcal{T}[\![P]\!]$ does not imply the non-$\surd$regularity.

Example Let $P :\equiv rec\, p.\, skip + a(p\ ;\ skip) \equiv rec\, p.\surd nil + a\big((pg_1 \mid \bar{\surd}_1\surd nil){-}A\big)$ for $g_1 = \{\surd \mapsto \surd_1, \bar{\surd} \mapsto \bar{\surd}_1\}$ and $A = \{\surd_1, \bar{\surd}_1\}$. Then $Reach(\mathcal{T}[\![P]\!]/\sim_{\$})$ equals

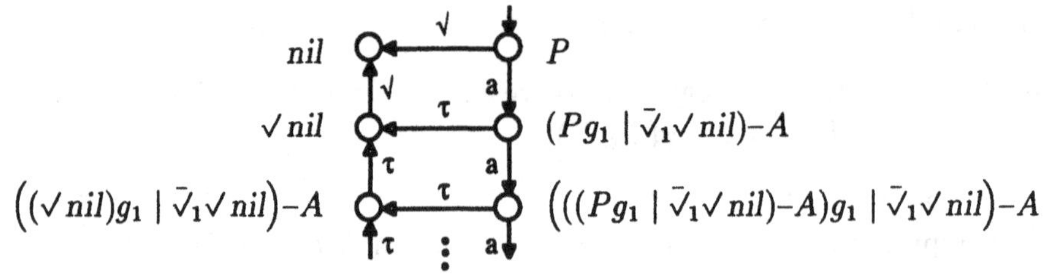

hence there exists no finite T such that $T \sim \mathcal{T}[\![P]\!]$. On the other hand let T be

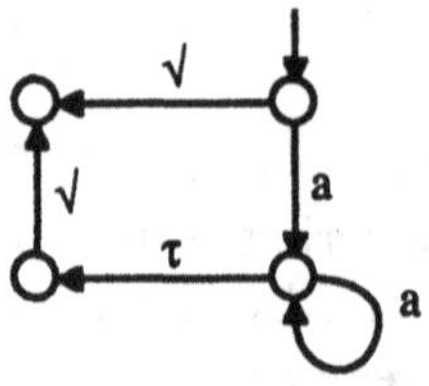

then $T \not\sim \mathcal{T}[\![P]\!]$ but $T \approx \mathcal{T}[\![P]\!]$, $T =_{\mathrm{fail}} \mathcal{T}[\![P]\!]$, $T =_{\mathrm{tr}} \mathcal{T}[\![P]\!]$. Hence in particular P is $\surd$regular. □

We prove the following.

Theorem 2.11 Let X be as in Proposition 2.10. Let eq be either $\sim$ or $=_{tr}$. Then there exists no algorithm which, for some $P \in X$ as input, outputs some finite transition system T with $T \; eq \; \mathcal{T}[\![P]\!]$ if such a T exists, and which outputs "no" otherwise.

Proof We will show that assuming the existence of such an algorithm leads to a decision algorithm for the emptiness of recursively enumerable languages, which is a contradiction (cf. [Hopcroft, Ullman 79, p. 189]).

We will use the following lemma.

Lemma 2.12 For every recursively enumerable language $L \subseteq \Sigma^*$ (given as a Turing machine) there effectively exists $Q_c \in clterms_{\text{CCS}}, Q_t \in clterms_{\text{TCSP}}$ such that for $Q \in \{Q_c, Q_t\}$

1. $\surd traces(\mathcal{T}[\![Q]\!]) = \emptyset$ if and only if $L = \emptyset$; and
2. $\surd traces(\mathcal{T}[\![Q]\!]) = \emptyset \;\Rightarrow$
   there exists a finite transition system T such that $T \sim \mathcal{T}[\![Q]\!]$.

Proof If $\Sigma = \{a_1, \ldots, a_n\}$ let $R \equiv rec\, r.(a_1 r + \bar{a}_1 r + \ldots + a_n r + \bar{a}_n r)$. Then for any $P \in terms_{\text{CCS}}$ clearly $(P \mid R)$–$(\Sigma \cup \bar{\Sigma}) \;\sim_\$\; P \setminus (\Sigma \cup \bar{\Sigma})$. The only difference is that the left-hand term is in $terms_{\text{CCS}}$ while the right-hand term is not. We are now ready to prove the lemma. Let

$Q_c :\equiv (P_c \mid R)$–$(\Sigma \cup \bar{\Sigma})$, where $P_c \in clterms_{\text{CCS}}$ is as the term "P" constructed in the proof of Lemma 2.4 and Prop. 2.5 for a Turing machine which halts on w if and only if $w \in L$ (such a Turing machine effectively exists), and

$Q_t :\equiv P_t \setminus \Sigma$, where $P_t \in clterms_{\text{TCSP}}$ is the corresponding TCSP-term "Q" constructed in Lemma 2.4 and Proposition 2.7.

Then for $Q \in \{Q_c, Q_t\}$ 1. follows immediately with Lemma 2.4. Furthermore $P \in \{P_c, P_t\}$ is constructed such that (*1) $\forall w \in Act^* : \; P \,-w\!\rightarrow \;\Rightarrow\; w \in (\Sigma \cup \{\tau, \surd\})^*$. And as the Turing machine P is constructed from halts only if it accepts, we even have (*2) $\forall w \in (Act - \{\surd\})^* : \; \forall P' : \; P \,-w\!\rightarrow P' \;\Rightarrow\; \exists a \in Act : \; P' \,-a\!\rightarrow$. From (*1) we conclude for Q (*3) $\forall w \in Act^* : \; Q \,-w\!\rightarrow \;\Rightarrow\; w \in \{\tau, \surd\}^*$, and from (*2) and (*3) we derive

(*4) $\quad \forall w \in (Act - \{\surd\})^* : \; \forall Q' : \; Q \,-w\!\rightarrow Q' \;\Rightarrow\; (Q' \,-\tau\!\rightarrow \;\vee\; Q' \,-\surd\!\rightarrow \;).$

Now to prove 2. let $\surd traces(\mathcal{T}[\![Q]\!]) = \emptyset$. Then with (*3) we conclude

(*5) $\quad \forall w \in Act^* : \; Q \,-w\!\rightarrow \;\Rightarrow\; w \in \{\tau\}^*.$

We prove $\mathcal{T}[\![Q]\!]$ $\sim$ 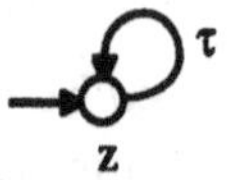

. To check that $B := \{\langle R, z\rangle \mid Q -w\rightarrow R\}$ is a strong bisimulation let $\langle R, z\rangle \in B$. If $R -a\rightarrow R'$ then by (*5) $a = \tau$. Clearly $z -\tau\rightarrow z \wedge \langle R', z\rangle \in B$. If $z -a\rightarrow z'$ then $a = \tau \wedge z' = z$. (*4) and (*5) imply $\exists R' : R -\tau\rightarrow R'$. Clearly then $\langle R', z\rangle \in B$. Lemma 2.12 □

Proof of Theorem 2.11 continued. Let X and *eq* as stated in the claim. Now let us assume there exists such an algorithm. Let L be any recursively enumerable language (given as a Turing machine). If $X = \mathit{clterms}_{\mathrm{CCS}}$ then let $Q \equiv Q_c$ otherwise let $Q \equiv Q_t$ as in the above lemma (they effectively exist). Then $Q \in X$. And by assumption we either know that (1) there exists no finite T such that T *eq* $\mathcal{T}[\![Q]\!]$, or (2) we effectively have some finite T such that T *eq* $\mathcal{T}[\![Q]\!]$.
In case of (1) we know that there exists no finite T such that $T \sim \mathcal{T}[\![Q]\!]$ (if $eq = =_{\mathrm{tr}}$ this follows by Proposition 1.33). By the above lemma we conclude that $L \neq \emptyset$.
In case of (2) we have a finite T with $\sqrt{}\mathit{traces}(T) = \sqrt{}\mathit{traces}(\mathcal{T}[\![Q]\!])$. And it is easily decidable whether $\sqrt{}\mathit{traces}(T) = \emptyset$. By the above lemma 1. we know whether $L = \emptyset$ or not. Hence we have a decision algorithm for emptiness of L, leading to a contradiction. Theorem 2.11 □

Conclusion to Chapter 2

Although the ability of certain abstract programming languages to model Turing machines is known by folklore, it is usually not proved. We carried out the proof here in order to see which operators are dispensable and which (combinations of) operators 'cause' the Turing power. In particular (and this is new) it is possible to program a counter without using any renaming.

Furthermore we have shown that there exists no effective procedure which for a given term outputs a finite transition system which is strongly bisimular with the transition system of the term, and which otherwise states its non-existence.

Chapter 3

Representation by finite automata

By a finite automaton we understand a finite alphabetic non-deterministic Rabin-Scott-automaton as defined in [Brauer 84, p. 224].

The differences to a finite transition system are the following:

- invisible transitions are labelled ε (or λ) instead of τ
- there are final states, and
- the (input) alphabet is finite.

But a finite transition system can easily be interpreted as a finite automaton by changing τ-transitions to ε-transitions and by considering only those actions in $Act - \{\tau\}$ which appear as labels of transitions as the alphabet of the automaton. If all states are taken as being final, then the language accepted by the automaton equals the traces of the transition system. Alternatively if additionally all $\surd$-transitions are cancelled, and only those states which had an outgoing $\surd$-transition are considered as being final, then the language accepted by the automaton equals the set of terminating traces of the transition system (cf. also the proof of Property 2.9).

In this chapter we will give a consistent syntax-driven construction of finite transition systems for certain terms. These transition systems can immediately be interpreted as finite automata as indicated above. Recall that consistency in this context means that the transition system constructed for some term P is strongly bisimular to the transition system $\mathcal{T}[\![P]\!]$.

As our construction is going to be syntax-driven, transition systems as defined in 1.20 are not sufficient. The construction for the recursion ($rec\, p.\cdot$) needs information on the free occurrences of p in the transition system already constructed. To this end in the following section we introduce so-called extended transition systems. The fundamental idea for the extension stems from Milner's charts [Milner 84], but in order to be able to cope with action manipulation functions we had to refine his charts.

Let us illustrate the basic idea with the example $P :\equiv rec\,p.a(pf)$, where $f = \{a \mapsto b\}$. The reachable part of the transition system for P is

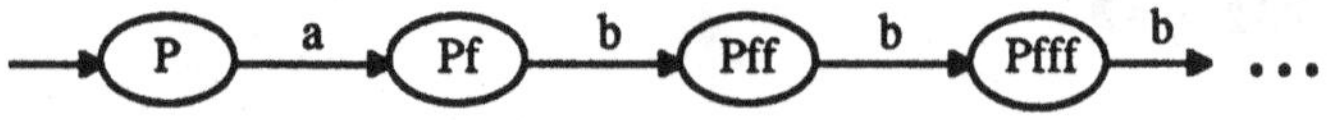

i.e. it is infinite.

Now the steps of our syntax-driven construction are as follows.

Step 1: For p we construct 

i.e. a transition system with just one state. This state has an extension, namely $\langle p, id \rangle$, where id is the identity on $Act_\perp$. It indicates that this state represents the free identifier p, and that, if this state is bound recursively the action manipulation id has to be carried out (here the manipulation is trivial).

Step 2: For pf we construct 

i.e. now some non-trivial manipulation appears.

Step 3: For $a(pf)$ we get 

Note that the starting state has no extension.

Step 4: The construction for $rec\,p.a(pf)$ leads to 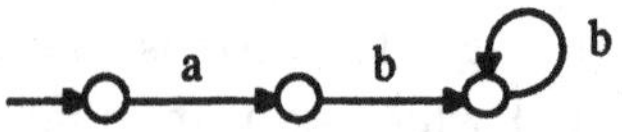

No state has an extension here, but for the construction the extension of the system in Step 3 has been used. (If the minimal transition system is wanted one can apply the algorithm of Proposition 1.40).

3.1 Extended transition systems

Definition 3.1 1. An *extended transition system* T is a quadruple $\langle S, D, E, z \rangle$,

where $\langle S, D, z \rangle$ is a transition system (cf. Definition 1.20) and $E \subseteq S \times Idf \times Fun_\perp$ is the set of *extensions*.

Here $Fun_\perp$ is the set of action manipulation functions enlarged by the special element $\perp$, i.e. $Fun_\perp := Fun \cup \{\perp\}$, with $\perp \notin Fun$.

2. We shall frequently use

$$\begin{array}{llll} D(s) & := & \{\langle a, s' \rangle \mid \langle s, a, s' \rangle \in D\} & \text{the outgoing arcs of } s, \\ E(s) & := & \{\langle p, f \rangle \mid \langle s, p, f \rangle \in E\} & \text{the extensions of } s, \\ E(s,p) & := & \{f \mid \langle s, p, f \rangle \in E\} & \text{the extensions of } s \text{ w.r.t. } p, \\ E(p) & := & \{f \mid \langle s, p, f \rangle \in E\} & \text{the functions appearing} \\ & & & \text{with the identifier } p. \end{array}$$

3. T is *finite* if S, D, and E are finite. □

An extension $\langle s, p, f\rangle$ is used to indicate that the state s represents the free identifier p which appears in the scope of the action manipulation function f. If $f = \bot$, then this indicates that a recursive binding cannot be handled by our construction; if the construction for *rec p.·* shall be applied, no state may have an extension $\langle p, \bot\rangle$. We say that $\langle s, p, \bot\rangle$ is a ***hot extension***.

Note that we get a 'chart' in the sense of [Milner 84, p. 442] if we project the extensions of an extended transition system to its first two components and leave everything else unchanged. In particular, if $E \subseteq S \times \mathit{Idf} \times \{id\}$, then 'extended transition system' and 'chart' are in a one-to-one correspondence.

We generalize the notions of a reachable subsystem and of strong bisimulation for extended transition systems. Milner's generalization of bisimulation for charts is analogous [Milner 84, p. 446].

Definition 3.2 (reachable subsystem) Let $T = \langle S, D, E, z\rangle$ be an extended transition system, and S' a set with $z \in S' \subseteq S$.

1. $\mathit{Reach}(T, S') := \big\langle \hat{S},\ D \cap (\hat{S} \times \mathit{Act} \times \hat{S}),\ E \cap (\hat{S} \times \mathit{Idf} \times \mathit{Fun}_\bot),\ z\big\rangle$,
   where $\hat{S}$ is the smallest set such that $S' \subseteq \hat{S}$ and
   $\langle r, a, s\rangle \in D$ for $r \in \hat{S}$ implies $s \in \hat{S}$.
2. $\mathit{Reach}(T) := \mathit{Reach}(T, \{z\})$. □

Definition 3.3 (strong bisimulation) Let $T_i = \langle S_i, D_i, E_i, z_i\rangle$ be extended transition systems and $s_i \in S_i$ for $i \in \{1, 2\}$, then $B \subseteq S_1 \times S_2$ is a *strong bisimulation for s_1 and s_2* if $\langle s_1, s_2\rangle \in B$ and $\forall \langle r, s\rangle \in B$, $a \in \mathit{Act}$:

$$\begin{array}{rl} \text{i)} & r -a\rightarrow_1 r' \;\Rightarrow\; \exists s' : s -a\rightarrow_2 s' \wedge \langle r', s'\rangle \in B \quad \text{and} \\ \text{ii)} & s -a\rightarrow_2 s' \;\Rightarrow\; \exists r' : r -a\rightarrow_1 r' \wedge \langle r', s'\rangle \in B \quad \text{and} \\ \text{iii)} & E_1(r) = E_2(s). \end{array}$$

The other notions and notations of Definition 1.26, such as $T_1 \sim T_2$, are carried over in the obvious way using the above definition of strong bisimulation. □

Clearly Property 1.35 holds analogously for extended transition systems.

Throughout this chapter we will not distinguish between isomorphic extended transition systems.

Definition 3.4 (isomorphic extended transition systems)
T_1 and T_2 are called *isomorphic*, if there exists a bijection $\varphi : S_1 \rightarrow S_2$ such that $\varphi(z_1) = z_2$, $\langle r, a, s\rangle \in D_1$ iff $\langle \varphi(r), a, \varphi(s)\rangle \in D_2$ and $\langle s, p, f\rangle \in E_1$ iff $\langle \varphi(s), p, f\rangle \in E_2$. □

3.2 Syntax-driven construction

In this section we define operators on extended transition systems, which correspond to the operators of **A**. We will use the same symbols, then by interpreting a term $P \in$ *terms* as the corresponding operators on extended transition systems we have a syntax-driven construction of the extended transition system for P, its result is denoted by $\mathcal{F}[P]$. This construction is not defined for all terms.

Definition 3.5 $\qquad nil := \langle\{z\}, \emptyset, \emptyset, z\rangle$ 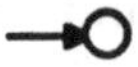

For $p \in Idf$ $\qquad p := \langle\{z\}, \emptyset, \{\langle z, p, id\rangle\}, z\rangle.$ 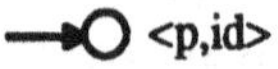

Let $T = \langle S, D, E, z\rangle$ be an extended transition system.

For $a \in \{\tau\} \cup Vis$ define $aT := \left\langle S \cup \{s\}, D \cup \{\langle s, a, z\rangle\}, E, s\right\rangle$
where $s \notin S$ is a new state.

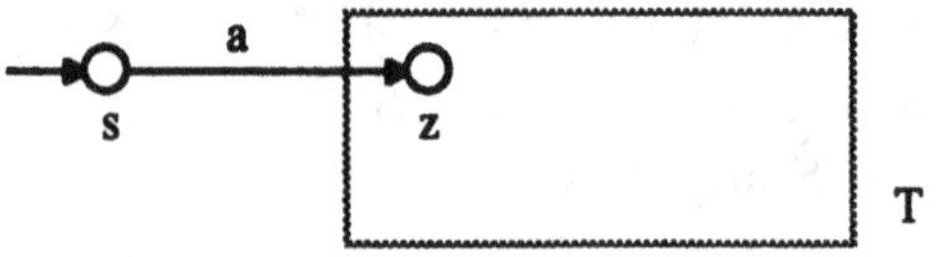

For $f \in Fun$ define $Tf := Reach(\langle S, D', E', z\rangle)$ where

$$\begin{array}{rlll} D' = & \{\langle r, af, s\rangle & \mid \langle r, a, s\rangle \in D \ \wedge \ af \neq \bot\} \\ E' = & \{\langle s, p, g \cdot f\rangle & \mid \langle s, p, g\rangle \in E \ \wedge \ g \neq \bot\} \\ & \cup \{\langle s, p, \bot\rangle & \mid \langle s, p, \bot\rangle \in E\}. \end{array}$$ □

Recall that action manipulation functions are written postfix even when applied to actions (af) or in function composition. I.e. $g \cdot f$ means that first g is applied and then f.

Example Let $f = \{a \mapsto b, b \mapsto \tau, c \mapsto \bot\}$, $g = \{d \mapsto a\}$.

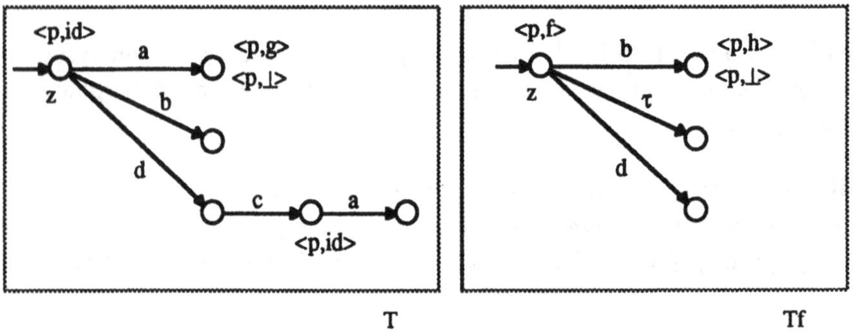

where $h = g \cdot f = \{a \mapsto b, b \mapsto \tau, c \mapsto \bot, d \mapsto b\}$. □

Definition 3.6 Let $T_i = \langle S_i, D_i, E_i, z_i\rangle$ for $i \in \{1,2\}$ be extended transition systems, and $S_1 \cap S_2 = \emptyset$.

$$T_1 + T_2 := Reach(\langle S_1 \cup S_2 \cup \{z\}, D_1 \cup D_2 \cup D, E_1 \cup E_2 \cup E, z\rangle)$$

where $z \notin S_1 \cup S_2$ and

$$\begin{array}{rcll} D & = & \{\langle z, a, s\rangle & \mid \langle a, s\rangle \in D_1(z_1) \cup D_2(z_2)\} \\ E & = & \{\langle z, p, f\rangle & \mid \langle p, f\rangle \in E_1(z_1) \cup E_2(z_2)\}. \end{array}$$ □

Example

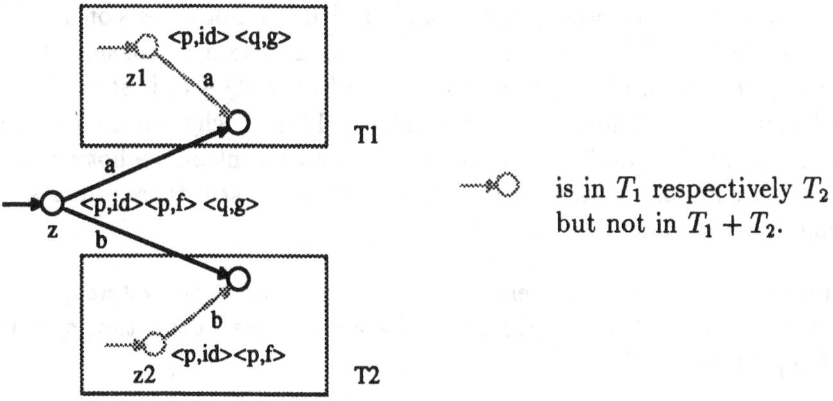

□

Definition 3.7 For T_1, T_2 as above $T_1 \ast T_2 := \big\langle S_1 \times S_2, D, E, \langle z_1, z_2\rangle\big\rangle$ where

$$\begin{array}{l} D = \Big\{ \Big\langle \langle r_1, r_2\rangle, a, \langle s_1, s_2\rangle \Big\rangle \mid \\ \qquad \langle r_1, a, s_1\rangle \in D_1 \wedge r_2 = s_2 \vee \langle r_2, a, s_2\rangle \in D_2 \wedge r_1 = s_1 \\ \qquad \vee \exists b_1, b_2 \in Vis : a = [b_1, b_2] \wedge \langle r_1, b_1, s_1\rangle \in D_1 \wedge \langle r_2, b_2, s_2\rangle \in D_2 \Big\} \\ E = \quad \Big\{ \Big\langle \langle s_1, s_2\rangle, p, f\Big\rangle \mid \langle p, f\rangle \in E_1(s_1) \cup E_2(s_2)\Big\} \\ \qquad \cup \Big\{ \Big\langle \langle s_1, s_2\rangle, p, \bot\Big\rangle \mid \quad E_1(s_1, p) \neq \emptyset \neq E_2(s_2) \cup D_2(s_2) \\ \qquad\qquad \vee E_2(s_2, p) \neq \emptyset \neq E_1(s_1) \cup D_1(s_1)\Big\}. \end{array}$$ □

Example Let $a, b \in Vis$.

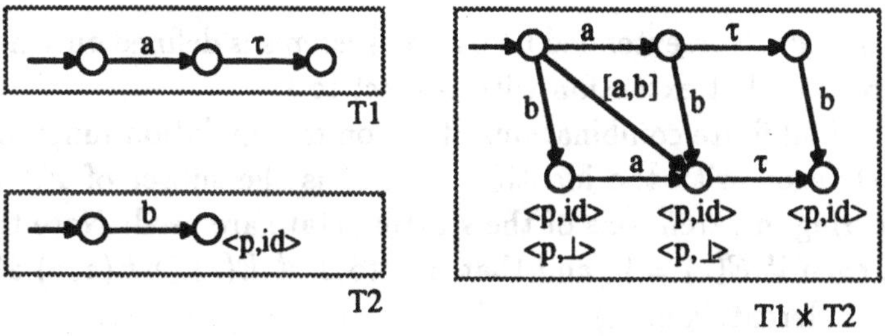

□

The purpose of a hot extension $\langle p, \bot \rangle$ is to abort our construction in the case that the application of the operator for the recursive binding could lead to an inconsistent representation. On page 69 this is explained with the example term $P \equiv rec\, p.b(a\, nil \mid p)$.

The parallel composition is the only operator where new hot extensions are produced. A new hot extension $\langle p, \bot \rangle$ is generated in the case that for some state of $T_1 \nmid T_2$ the corresponding state of one component has some p-extension while the state corresponding to the other component has some outgoing arc or some extension with respect to any identifier. In other words the state of the other component is not equivalent to *nil*.

A term with a subterm Q such that $\mathcal{F}[\![Q]\!]$ has a hot extension might be not representable by a finite transition system. As an example consider the term P above and $Q \equiv b(a\, nil \mid p)$. On the other hand $rec\, p.(Q - b)$ is strongly bisimular to *nil* and clearly is finitely representable. This is why we do not abort the construction at the parallel composition. Instead we introduce hot extensions for the parallel composition and check whether they are still there when a recursive binding is carried out.

Definition 3.8 (recursion operator for extended transition systems)

Let $r \in Idf$. Let $T = \langle S, D, E, z \rangle$ be an extended transition system where $\bot \notin E(r)$. Define

$$\begin{array}{lcll} F & := & \{id \cdot f_1 \cdot \ldots \cdot f_n & \mid n \geq 0,\ f_1, \ldots, f_n \in E(r)\}, \\ SF & := & \{id \cdot f_1 \cdot \ldots \cdot f_n & \mid n \geq 0,\ f_1, \ldots, f_n \in E(z, r)\}. \end{array}$$

For $f \in F$ let $\quad \langle S_f, D_f, E_f, z_f \rangle := Tf, \quad$ where for $f \neq g \quad S_f \cap S_g = \emptyset$.
Define

$$rec\, r.T \ := \ Reach\Big(\big\langle \mathbf{S}, \mathbf{D} \cup D_+, (\mathbf{E} \cup E_+) - (\mathbf{S} \times \{r\} \times Fun), z_{id} \big\rangle\Big)$$

where $\qquad \mathbf{S} = \bigcup_{f \in F} S_f, \qquad \mathbf{D} = \bigcup_{f \in F} D_f, \qquad \mathbf{E} = \bigcup_{f \in F} E_f$

$$\begin{array}{lrcl} \text{and} & D_+ & = & \{\langle s, a, s' \rangle \mid \bar{f} \in SF \ \wedge \ g \in \mathbf{E}(s, r) \ \wedge \ \langle z_{\bar{f} \cdot g}, a, s' \rangle \in \mathbf{D}\} \\ & E_+ & = & \{\langle s, p, h \rangle \mid \bar{f} \in SF \ \wedge \ g \in \mathbf{E}(s, r) \ \wedge \ \langle z_{\bar{f} \cdot g}, p, h \rangle \in \mathbf{E}\}. \ \Box \end{array}$$

The operator $rec\, r.T$ on extended transition systems is defined only if $\bot \notin E(r)$, i.e. only if there is no hot extension with respect to r.

F is the set of all finite combinations of action manipulation functions appearing in some extension with the identifier r. SF is the subset of F, where only functions appearing in extensions of the starting state are used. Note that always $id \in SF \subseteq F$, even if $E(r) = \emptyset$, and that due to $\bot \notin E(r) \supseteq E(z, r)$ all f_i above are in *Fun* (i.e. different from $\bot$).

Furthermore $\perp \notin F$, $\perp \notin SF$ and, as $\perp \notin E(r)$, for all $s \in \boldsymbol{S}$ we have $\perp \notin \mathbb{E}(s,r)$, hence the composition $\bar{f} \cdot g$ used in the definition of D_+ and E_+ is always defined.

Let us explain the definition of $rec\, p.T$ with an example. Consider

$$P \equiv rec\, p.a(pf),$$

where $f = \{a \mapsto b\}$. Then $T := \mathcal{F}[\![a(pf)]\!]$, i.e. $a(pf)$ interpreted as extended transition system yields

$T =$ 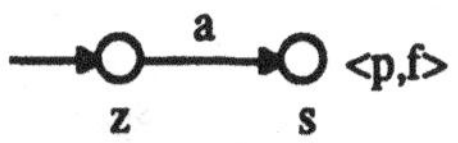

For this system $E(p) = \{f\}$ and $E(z,p) = \emptyset$. Hence $F = \{id, f\}$ and $SF = \{id\}$, as $f \cdot f = f$. For the recursion we need for every element g of F the extended transition system Tg. In our example

$T\,id =$ 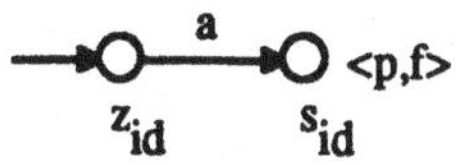

and $Tf =$ 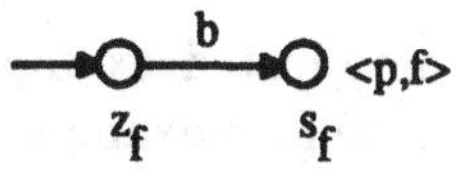

Now $rec\, p.T$ is built in four steps.
Firstly the disjoint union of these Tg is taken, leading to

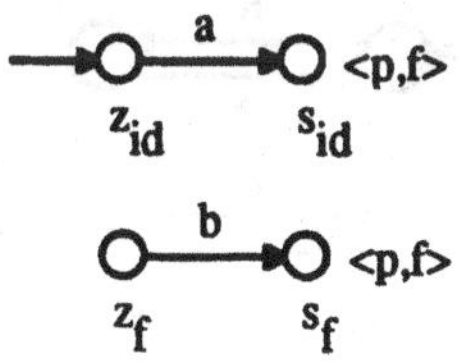

Secondly new arcs and extensions are introduced according to D_+ and E_+. In our example

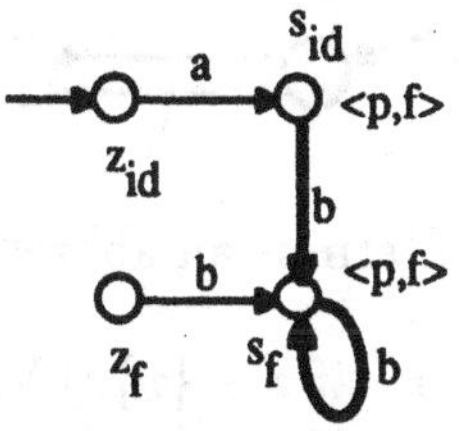

Note that in this example $E_+ = \emptyset$.

In a third step extensions referring to p are deleted:

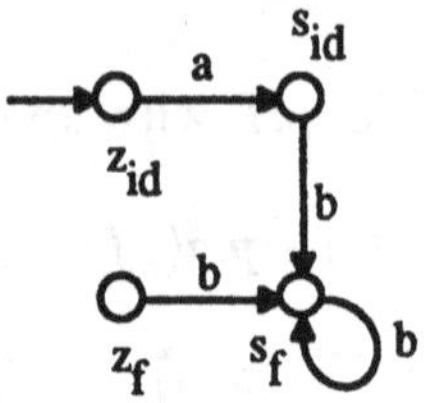

And finally the reachable subsystem is taken:

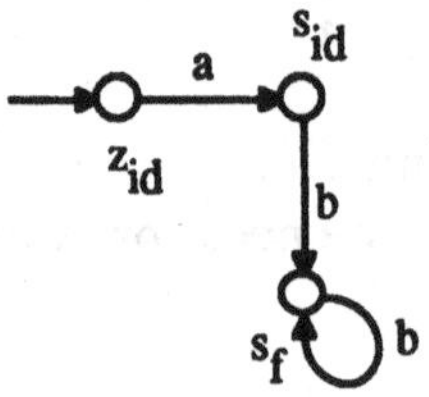

This ends our example.

Before giving more complicated examples for the intertwining of action manipulations and recursion, we give examples to convince the reader that the other operators yield those transition systems one would expect.

Example Let $P :\equiv rec\, p.abp$ and $Q :\equiv P\{b \mapsto c\}$.

1. $\mathcal{F}[\![P]\!] =$ 

$\mathcal{F}[\![Q]\!] =$ 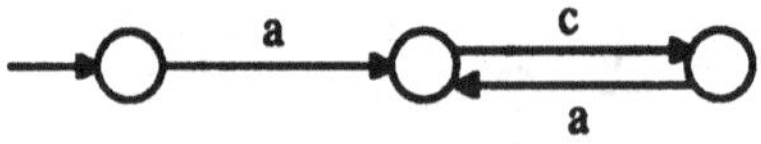

2. $\mathcal{F}[\![P+Q]\!] =$ 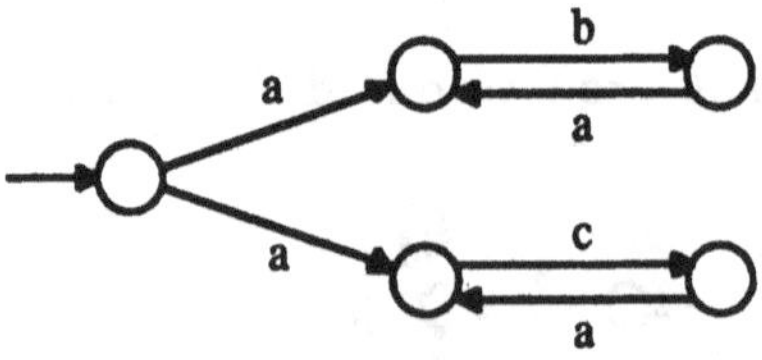

3. Now consider $P \parallel_a Q$. This term is an abbreviation for $(P \nmid Q)g$, where

$$(x)g = \begin{cases} x & \text{if } x \in \{\tau\} \cup Vis \ \wedge \ x \neq a, \\ a & \text{if } x = [a,a] \in EVis, \\ \perp & \text{otherwise.} \end{cases}$$

$\mathcal{F}[\![P \nmid Q]\!] =$

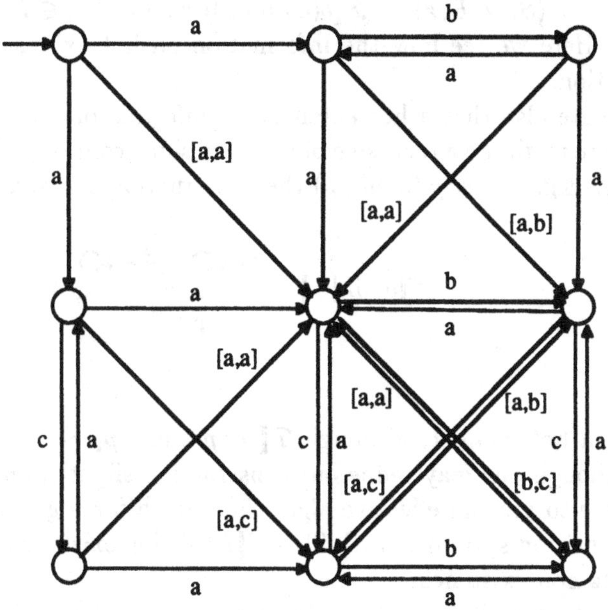

$\mathcal{F}[\![P \parallel_a Q]\!] =$

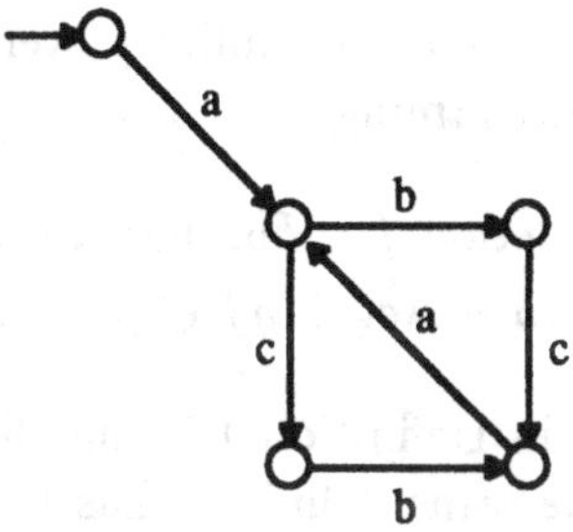

Note that it is not difficult to derive from the definitions of $\cdot \nmid \cdot$ and $\cdot f$ on extended transition systems definitions for operators which directly yield the result of $\cdot \parallel_A \cdot$ and $\cdot \mid \cdot$. □

In chapter 2 we have seen that there are terms, which are not finitely representable as transition systems. A very simple example is $P :\equiv rec\, p.b(a\, nil \mid p)$. The minimal transition system of P is

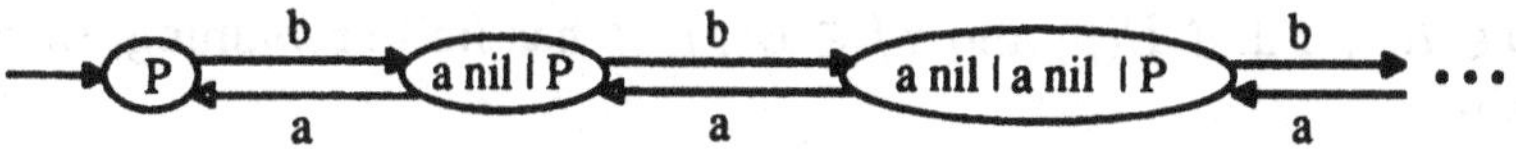

If we try to interpret P as extended transition system we have

$\mathcal{F}[\![b(a\, nil \mid p)]\!] =$

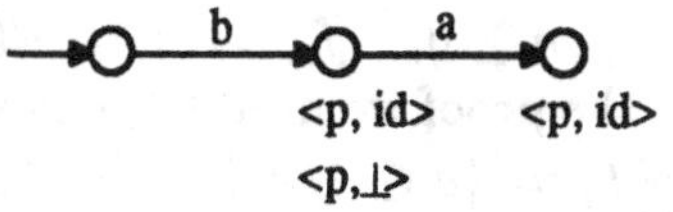

and then for $\langle S, D, E, z\rangle := \mathcal{F}[\![b(a\,nil \mid p)]\!]$ we have $\bot \in E(p)$. Hence $\mathcal{F}[\![P]\!]$ is not defined. Here we see how the information on hot extensions correctly stops the construction.

But note also that a hot extension is information which is treated pessimistically; there might be a recursive binding (in some context) which cannot be handled correctly. E.g. for $rec\, p.(a\, nil \mid p)$ the construction stops, as

$\mathcal{F}[\![a\, nil \mid p]\!] =$ 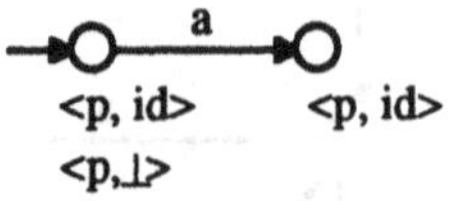

contains a hot context, although $\mathcal{T}[\![rec\, p.\, a\, nil \mid p]\!] \sim$ 

. But recall that, although one may refine our construction slightly, due to Theorem 2.11 it is impossible to give an effective algorithm which for a given term P outputs some finite transition system T with $T \sim \mathcal{T}[\![P]\!]$ if this exists and otherwise outputs the fact of its non-existence.

Other terms without a finite transition system have been given in the example starting on page 47. There the infinity stemmed from an action manipulation function with infinite renaming.

Definition 3.9 A function $f \in Fun$ has *finite renaming*, if

$$\{a \in Act \mid af \notin \{a, \tau, \bot\}\} \text{ is finite.}$$ □

For example g as in Definition 1.12 has finite renaming. And for every finite $A \subseteq Vis$ $\; g_A$ as in the same definition has finite renaming.

Next we show a sufficient condition for the finiteness of the result of the recursion operator on extended transition systems.

Theorem 3.10 Let T, T_1, T_2 be finite extended transition systems. Then

1. nil, p for $p \in Idf$, aT for $a \in \{\tau\} \cup Vis$, Tf for $f \in Fun$, $T_1 + T_2$, and $T_1 \nmid T_2$ are finite extended transition systems;
2. for $p \in Idf$, if $\bot \notin E(p)$ and $\forall f \in E(p) : f$ has finite renaming, then $rec\, p.T$ is finite.

Proof 1. is trivial. 2. Let $T = \langle S, D, E, z\rangle$ and $p \in Idf$. As $\bot \notin E(p)$ clearly $rec\, p.T$ is defined. And as T is finite it suffices to show that $F = \{id \cdot f_1 \cdot \ldots \cdot f_n \mid n \geq 0, \;\; f_1, \ldots, f_n \in E(p)\}$ is finite in order to prove that $rec\, p.T$ is finite. For the proof we need the following auxiliary sets and results. For $f \in Fun$ define $dom(f) := \{a \in Act \mid af \notin \{a, \tau, \bot\}\}$.

By assumption we have that (*1) $\forall f \in E(p): dom(f)$ is finite. Let $DOM := \bigcup_{f\in E(p)} dom(f)$ and $RAN := \{\perp, \tau\} \cup DOM \cup \bigcup_{f\in E(p)}\{af \mid a \in DOM\}$. As T is finite, $E(p)$ is finite. With (*1) we conclude that DOM and RAN are finite. Let $COM := Act_\perp - DOM$. Note that for all $f \in Fun$: (*2) $\perp f = \perp$ and $\tau f = \tau$. Hence $\{\perp, \tau\} \subseteq COM$. Furthermore
(*3) $\forall f \in E(p): \forall a \in COM: af \in \{a, \tau, \perp\} \subseteq COM$. Let $RES :=$

$$\{id\lceil_{COM} \cdot f_1\lceil_{COM} \cdot \ldots \cdot f_n\lceil_{COM} \mid n \geq 0,\ f_i \in E(p) \wedge (i \neq j \Rightarrow f_i \neq f_j)\}$$

be the set of finite compositions of pairwise different elements of $E(p)$ restricted to COM. As $E(p)$ is finite, RES is finite.
Due to (*2) and (*3) we have for $g = id\lceil_{COM} \cdot f_1\lceil_{COM} \cdot \ldots \cdot f_n\lceil_{COM} \in RES$:
(*4) $\forall i \in \{1, \ldots, n\}: g \cdot f_i\lceil_{COM} = g$, and (*5) $(COM)g \subseteq COM$.
We will now prove (*) $\forall f \in F: f\lceil_{DOM} \in RAN^{DOM} \wedge f\lceil_{COM} \in RES$ by an induction on n (in the definition of F).

<u>$n = 0$</u> Then $f = id$. As $DOM \subseteq RAN$ clearly $id\lceil_{DOM} \in RAN^{DOM}$ and clearly $id\lceil_{COM} \in RES$.

<u>$n \mapsto n+1$</u> Then $f = g \cdot h$ for $h \in E(p)$ and by ind. hyp. $g\lceil_{DOM} \in RAN^{DOM} \wedge g\lceil_{COM} \in RES$. To prove $f\lceil_{DOM} \in RAN^{DOM}$, let $a \in DOM$. Then $ag \in RAN$. If $ag \in DOM$ then $agh \in RAN$. Otherwise by (*3) $(ag)h \in \{ag, \tau, \perp\} \subseteq RAN$.

To prove $f\lceil_{COM} \in RES$ recall that $g\lceil_{COM} \in RES$, i.e. $\exists k \geq 0: \exists f_1, \ldots, f_k \in E(p): (i \neq j \Rightarrow f_i \neq f_j) \wedge g\lceil_{COM} = id\lceil_{COM} \cdot f_1\lceil_{COM} \cdot \ldots \cdot f_k\lceil_{COM}$.

If $h \notin \{f_1, \ldots, f_k\}$, clearly $g\lceil_{COM} \cdot h\lceil_{COM} \in RES$, otherwise $h \in \{f_1, \ldots, f_k\}$ then by (*4) $g\lceil_{COM} \cdot h\lceil_{COM} = g\lceil_{COM}$, and hence also $g\lceil_{COM} \cdot h\lceil_{COM} \in RES$. In both cases by (*5) $f\lceil_{COM} = g\lceil_{COM} \cdot h\lceil_{COM}$.

By (*) every element of F stems from one element of RAN^{DOM} and from one element of RES. As RAN^{DOM} and RES are finite, F is finite. Theorem 3.10 □

Property 3.11 For $P \in terms$, if $\mathcal{F}[\![P]\!]$ is defined, then

$$\mathcal{F}[\![P]\!] = Reach(\mathcal{F}[\![P]\!]).$$

Proof Induction on P. The only non-trivial case $P \equiv P_1 \nmid P_2$ is easily checked.
□

We conclude this section with examples which should convince the reader that the recursion operator on extended transition system has to be as defined in 3.8. The consistency is formally proved in section 3.4.

Examples 1. Let $P \equiv rec\, p.ab(p\{a \mapsto c\} + p\{b \mapsto c\})$.
Then $T := \mathcal{F}[\![ab(p\{a \mapsto c\} + p\{b \mapsto c\})]\!]$ is

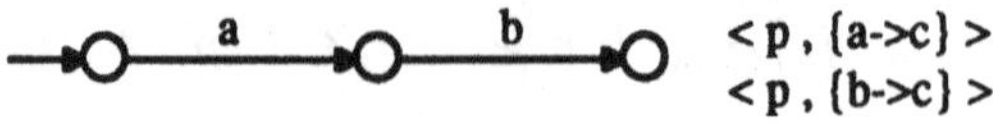

For $F = \{id, \{a \mapsto c\}, \{b \mapsto c\}, \{a \mapsto c, b \mapsto c\}\}$ and $SF = \{id\}$ the construction for $rec\, p.T$ before removing the p-extensions and the non-reachable part looks like:

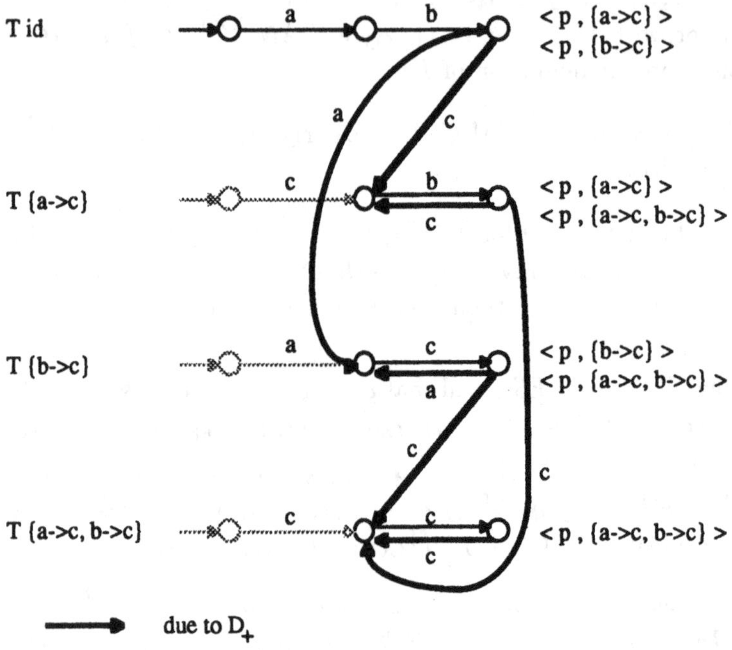

One easily checks that $P \xrightarrow{abcbcc}$, hence to be strongly bisimular it would not suffice to use $E(p)$ instead of F for the recursion operator.

2. Let $P \equiv rec\, p.\big(p\{b \mapsto c\} + a(p\{a \mapsto b\})\big)$. Let $f_1 = \{b \mapsto c\}$, $f_2 = \{a \mapsto b\}$.

$T := \mathcal{F}[\![pf_1 + a(pf_2)]\!] =$ 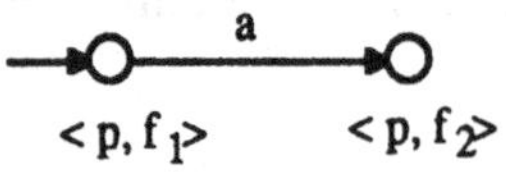

For this T we have $F = \{id, f_1, f_2, f_3, f_4\}$ and $SF = \{id, f_1\}$ where $f_3 = f_1 \cdot f_2 = \{a \mapsto b, b \mapsto c\}$ and $f_4 = f_2 \cdot f_1 = \{a \mapsto c, b \mapsto c\}$. The construction for $rec\, p.T$

before removing the p-extensions and the non-reachable part is as follows.

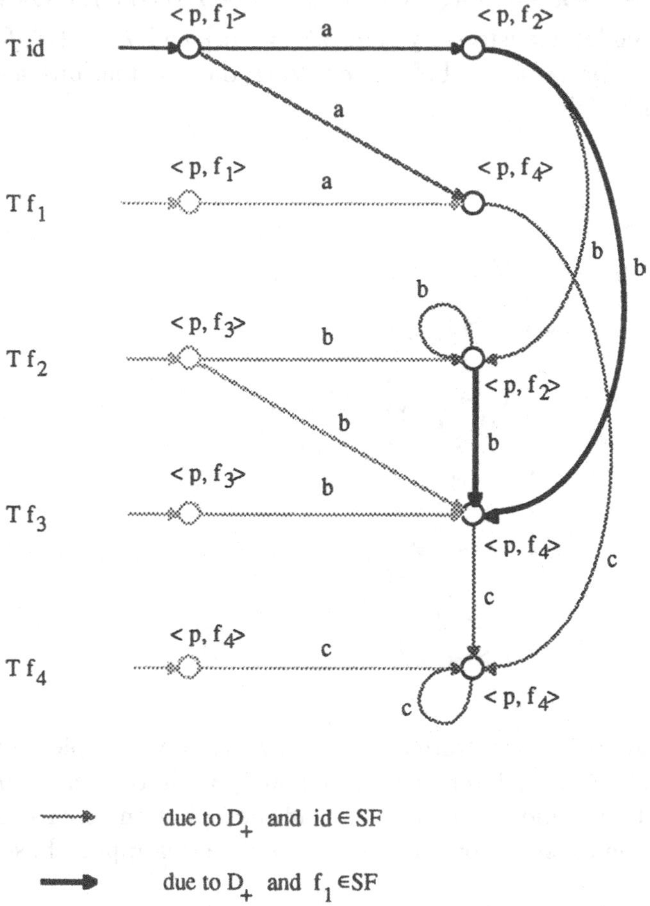

It is not hard to check that $P \overset{abc}{\longrightarrow}$. This illustrates that the transitions due to $f_1 \in SF$ and D_+ are actually necessary in our construction.

3. A similar example shows that SF and E_+ are needed as defined. Let

$$P \equiv \text{rec}\, q.a\, \text{rec}\, p.\big(q + (pf_1 + pf_2)\big),$$

where f_1 and f_2 are as above. Then

$$T := \mathcal{F}[\![q + (pf_1 + pf_2)]\!] \text{ is } \longrightarrow\!\!\bigcirc\ \langle q, id\rangle, \langle p, f_1\rangle, \langle p, f_2\rangle.$$

For this T we have $SF = F = \{id, f_1, f_2, f_3, f_4\}$, where the f_i are as in the previous example. And then $T' := \mathcal{F}[\![\text{rec}\, p.q + (pf_1 + pf_2)]\!]$ is

$$\longrightarrow\!\!\bigcirc\ \langle q, id\rangle, \langle q, f_1\rangle, \langle q, f_2\rangle, \langle q, f_3\rangle, \langle q, f_4\rangle.$$

Note that only the first three extensions are due to $id \in SF$.

Clearly aT' is 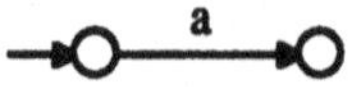

$\langle q, id\rangle, \langle q, f_1\rangle, \langle q, f_2\rangle, \langle q, f_3\rangle, \langle q, f_4\rangle$, but note that for this extended transition system $SF = \{id\}$ and $F = \{id, f_1, f_2, f_3, f_4\}$. The construction for $rec\, q.aT'$ before removing the q-extensions and the non-reachable part is as follows.

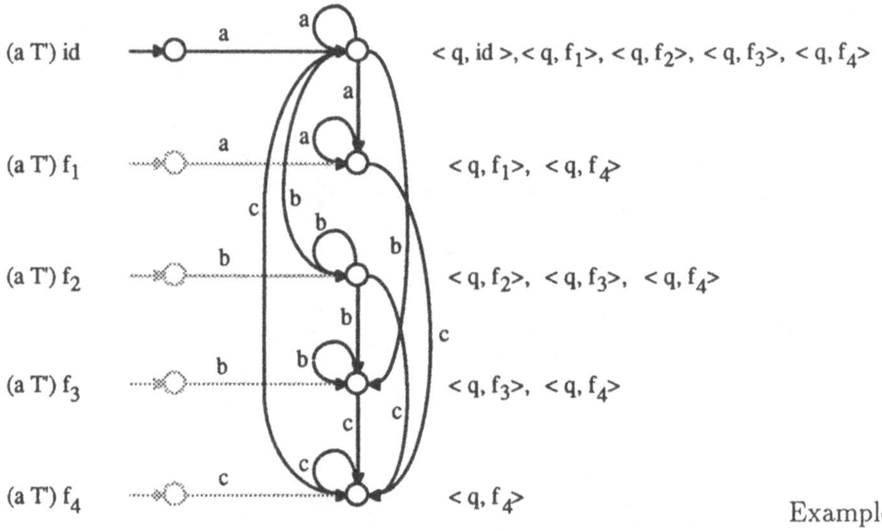

Examples □

The complications demonstrated in the previous two examples are caused by unguarded identifiers. If such terms are disallowed, SF in the definition for the recursion construction would be superfluous, and the definition much simpler. When giving the recursion construction on safe nets we take this approach, see Definition 4.15.

Although the result of the recursion operator applied to some extended transition system is finite under the conditions stated in Theorem 3.10 the result may be rather complex. In general for a system T with $|S| \in \mathbb{N}$ and $|F| \in \mathbb{N}$ (where F is as in Definition 3.8) the number of states of $rec\, p.T$ is of the order $|S| \cdot |F|$, and $|F|$ may be rather large. The following proposition shows that this complexity is actually needed and also shows the order of $|F|$.

Proposition 3.12 For $n \in \mathbb{N}$ there exists $P \equiv rec\, p.R \in terms$ such that $\mathcal{F}[\![R]\!]$ has $O(n)$ states, P and R have size[1] $O(n^2)$ and every transition system strongly bisimular with $\mathcal{T}[\![P]\!]$ has at least $(n+1)^{n+1}$ states.

[1]Let the size of a term be defined as the length of the derivation producing it syntactically.

Proof Let $n \in \mathbb{N}$. Let $\{a_1, \ldots, a_n, b_1, \ldots, b_n, c\} \subseteq Alph$. Define

$$\begin{aligned} P \equiv rec\,p.\Big(\quad & (rec\,q.a_1a_2\ldots a_n(q + c\,nil)) \\ & + p\{a_1 \mapsto b_1\} + p\{a_1 \mapsto b_2\} + \ldots + p\{a_1 \mapsto b_n\} \\ & \vdots \\ & + p\{a_n \mapsto b_1\} + p\{a_n \mapsto b_2\} + \ldots + p\{a_n \mapsto b_n\} \Big) \end{aligned}$$

and let R be the body of P, i.e. $P \equiv rec\,p.R$. Clearly P and R have size $O(n^2)$. Then $T := \langle S, D, E, z\rangle := \mathcal{F}[\![R]\!]$ is

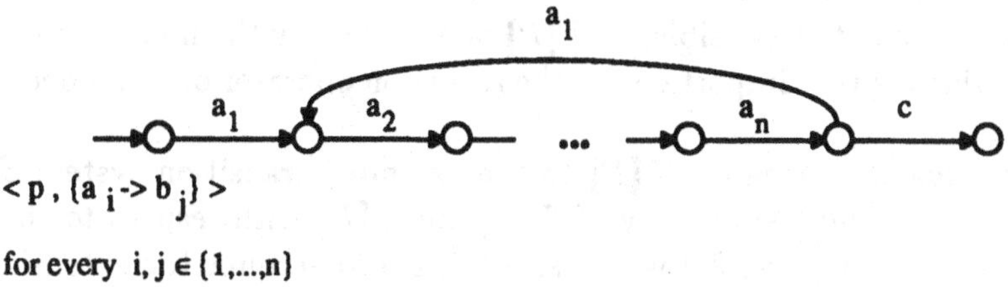

T has $O(n)$ states and $O(n^2)$ extensions. Let $A = \{a_1, \ldots, a_n\}$, $B = \{b_1, \ldots, b_n\}$, then for T according to Definition 3.8 we have
$F = SF = \{f \in A^{A \cup B} \mid af \in A \Rightarrow af = a\}$. This set has $(n+1)^n$ elements. We can sketch $rec\,p.T = \mathcal{F}[\![P]\!]$ as follows.

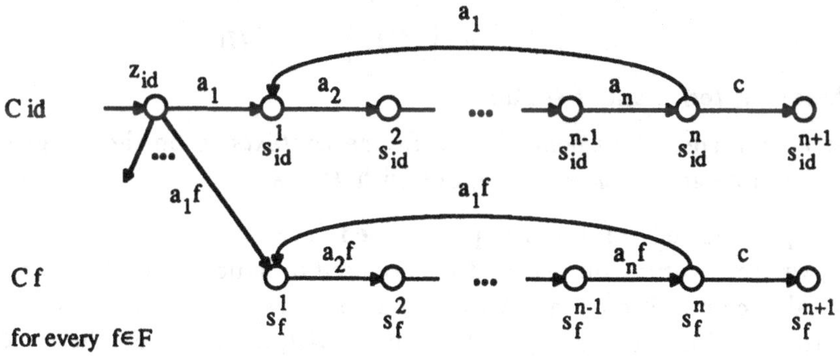

$\mathcal{F}[\![P]\!] =: \langle S', D', E', z'\rangle$ has $O(|S| \cdot |F|) = O\big((n+1)^{n+1}\big)$ states. By our general consistency result given in section 3.4 we have $\mathcal{T}[\![P]\!] \sim \langle S', D', z'\rangle$. We now prove that every transition system strongly bisimular with $\mathcal{T}[\![P]\!]$ (and hence with $\langle S', D', z'\rangle$) has at least $(n+1)^{n+1}$ states. To prove this it suffices to show that no pair $\langle s^i_f, s^j_g\rangle$ of states of $\mathcal{F}[\![P]\!]$ with $i, j \in \{1, \ldots, n\}$, $f, g \in F$ and $i \neq j \vee f \neq g$ is strongly bisimular.
Let $s^i_f, s^j_g \in S'$ such that $i, j \in \{1, \ldots, n\}$, $f, g \in F$, and such that $s^i_f \sim s^j_g$. Then $s^i_f \; -wc\!\rightarrow_{D'}$, where $w = (a_{i+1})f(a_{i+2})f \ldots (a_n)f$. As $s^i_f \sim s^j_g$ also $s^j_g \; -wc\!\rightarrow_{D'}$, and hence $i = j$.

Furthermore s_f^i $-(w\,(a_1)f\ldots(a_n)f\,c)\!\rightarrow_{D'}$, and again as $s_f^i \sim s_g^i$ also s_g^i $-(w\,(a_1)f\ldots(a_n)f\,c)\!\rightarrow_{D'}$. The only possibility that this is true is if $\forall i \in \{1,\ldots,n\}: a_i f = a_i g$. Hence $f = g$, and we have $s_f^i = s_g^j$. □

3.3 The extended transition system for a term

This and the next section are devoted to the proof of the consistency of the operators on extended transition systems given in the previous section. I.e. we want to show that for every term P, if $\mathcal{F}[\![P]\!]$ is defined and equals $\langle S, D, E, z\rangle$ then $\langle S, D, z\rangle \sim \mathcal{T}[\![P]\!]$. We want to perform an induction on the structure of P, but this is not immediately possible, as $\mathcal{T}[\![P]\!]$ does not carry the information of the extensions, which is very important for the recursion operator on extended transition systems.

Our approach is to refine $\mathcal{T}[\![P]\!]$ to the extended transition system $\mathcal{E}[\![P]\!]$, and then to prove strong bisimularity of $\mathcal{F}[\![P]\!]$ and $\mathcal{E}[\![P]\!]$ with respect to the stronger notion given in Definition 3.3 which also takes into account the extensions. Then $\langle S, D, z\rangle \sim \mathcal{T}[\![P]\!]$ follows trivially.

In this section we define $\mathcal{E}[\![P]\!]$ and prove several properties of it, which are used in the proof of $\mathcal{F}[\![P]\!] \sim \mathcal{E}[\![P]\!]$ in the next section.

Definition 3.13 (contexted terms, contexts)

1. Define *conterms* to be the set of terms generated by the following grammar.

$$C ::= P \;\big|\; Cf \;\big|\; C\llcorner \;\big|\; C\lrcorner$$

   where $P \in$ *terms* and $f \in$ *Fun*.

2. Let κ be a special element of *Idf*. Define *contexts* to be the set generated by the same grammar as above, but with $P \equiv \kappa$. □

Here $\llcorner$ (pronounced "el") and $\lrcorner$ (pronounced "reverse el") are two new unary operators written postfix. Intuitively they are used to indicate that their argument is in a parallel composition context with some partner on the side the operator is pointing to, i.e. C in $C\llcorner$ is in a parallel context with a partner on the right-hand side, whereas in $C\lrcorner$ it is in a context with a partner on the left-hand side. We interpret contexts as functions in *Fun* as follows.

Definition 3.14 Define $\mathcal{L}[\![\cdot]\!]$: *contexts* → *Fun* such that

$$\mathcal{L}[\![C]\!] := \begin{cases} id & \text{if } C \equiv \kappa, \\ \mathcal{L}[\![C']\!]\cdot f & \text{if } C \equiv C'f, \\ \mathcal{L}[\![C']\!] & \text{if } C \equiv C'\llcorner \text{ or } C \equiv C'\lrcorner. \end{cases}$$

Recall that elements of *Fun* are written postfix, in particular $a\mathcal{L}[\![C']\!]\cdot f = \big((a)\mathcal{L}[\![C']\!]\big)f$. □

Definition 3.15 For $P \in conterms$, $C \in contexts$

$$PC \;:\equiv\; C[P/\kappa]. \qquad \Box$$

For example $(a\,nil)(\kappa f \llcorner) \equiv (\kappa f \llcorner)[a\,nil/\kappa] \equiv (a\,nil) f \llcorner$.

Fact 3.16 $conterms = \{PC \mid P \in terms, C \in contexts\} \supset terms \cup contexts$ $\Box$

See also the overview on page 165.

Fact 3.17 Let $P \in conterms$, $C, K \in contexts$, and $f \in Fun$. Then

1. $PC \in conterms$, $CK \in contexts$
2. $P(Cf) \equiv (PC)f$, $P(C\llcorner) \equiv (PC)\llcorner$, and $P(C\lrcorner) \equiv (PC)\lrcorner$
3. $P(CK) \equiv (PC)K$
4. $\mathcal{L}[\![CK]\!] \equiv \mathcal{L}[\![C]\!] \cdot \mathcal{L}[\![K]\!]$ $\Box$

2. and 3. allow us to omit parentheses unambiguously.

Next we define the so-called *context relation*. We write $P \rhd_p \kappa$ to express that in the term P the free identifier p 'can be chosen' without performing any action (see rules idf) and idfsum) below). If such a choice of a free identifier without performing an action can be done only while crossing the scope of an action manipulation function or the scope of some parallel composition, this fact is noted in the context (see rule idffun) and idfpar)). For example $p+(qf) \rhd_p \kappa$, $p+(qf) \rhd_q \kappa f$, and $p \nmid a\,nil \rhd_p \kappa\llcorner$.

The rule for recursion is more complicated. It allows to pile contexts, which may be reached in the body of the recursion via the recursively bound identifier, on top of the context reached via another identifier. E.g. for $P \equiv rec\,r.(r\{a \mapsto b\} + p)$ we have $P \rhd_p \kappa$, $P \rhd_p \kappa\{a \mapsto b\}$, $P \rhd_p \kappa\{a \mapsto b\}\{a \mapsto b\}$, ...

Note that $P \rhd_p C$ is independent of the α-congruent representative chosen for P, as then always $p \in FI(P)$, which is proved in Proposition 3.22 2.

Definition 3.18 (context relation $\rhd$)

$\rhd \subseteq terms \times Idf \times contexts$ is defined to be the least relation satisfying the rules below. $\langle P, p, C\rangle \in \rhd$ is written $P \rhd_p C$. For every $P, Q, R \in terms$, $C, C_i \in contexts$, $f \in Fun$, $p, r \in Idf$ and $n \in I\!N$ there exist rules

idf) $\quad p \rhd_p \kappa$

idffun) $$\frac{P \rhd_p C}{Pf \rhd_p Cf}$$

idfsum) $$\frac{P \rhd_p C}{P + Q \rhd_p C \;\wedge\; Q + P \rhd_p C}$$

idfpar) $$\frac{P \rhd_p C}{P \nmid Q \rhd_p C\lfloor \;\wedge\; Q \nmid P \rhd_p C\rfloor}$$

idfrec) $$\frac{r \neq p \;\wedge\; R \rhd_p C \;\wedge\; R \rhd_r C_1 \;\wedge \ldots \wedge\; R \rhd_r C_n}{rec\, r.R \rhd_p CC_1 \ldots C_n}$$

We use the following shorthands.

$$P \rhd_p \;:\Leftrightarrow\; \exists C:\; P \rhd_p C \qquad P \not\rhd_p \;:\Leftrightarrow\; \neg(P \rhd_p)$$
$$P \rhd \;:\Leftrightarrow\; \exists p:\; P \rhd_p \qquad P \not\rhd \;:\Leftrightarrow\; \neg(P \rhd)$$
□

The next relation indicates which hot contexts can be reached in a term. The only operator which causes new hot contexts is the parallel composition (see rule hotpar) below). If one component can reach a context via p, and the other component is capable of performing an action or of reaching a context, then the parallel composition leads to a hot context via p. For example $(p \nmid a\,nil) \blacktriangleright p$, but $(p \nmid nil) \not\blacktriangleright p$. The other rules just express that hot contexts of the component(s) are also hot contexts of the compound term. The particular form of the rule hotrec) has been chosen in order to be able to carry out the proofs of this and the next section. Again $P \blacktriangleright p$ does not depend on the α-congruent representative chosen for P.

Definition 3.19 (hot context relation $\blacktriangleright$)

$\blacktriangleright \subseteq terms \times Idf$ is defined to be the least relation satisfying the rules below. $\langle P, p\rangle \in \blacktriangleright$ is written $P \blacktriangleright p$.
For every $P, Q, R \in terms$, $p, r \in Idf$ and $f \in Fun$ there exist rules

hotfun) $$\frac{P \blacktriangleright p}{Pf \blacktriangleright p}$$

hotsum) $$\frac{P \blacktriangleright p}{P + Q \blacktriangleright p \;\wedge\; Q + P \blacktriangleright p}$$

hotpar) $$\frac{P \blacktriangleright p \vee P \rhd_p \;\wedge\; (Q \rightarrow \;\vee\; Q \rhd)}{P \nmid Q \blacktriangleright p \;\wedge\; Q \nmid P \blacktriangleright p}$$

hotrec) $$\frac{p \neq r \;\wedge\; (R \blacktriangleright p \;\vee\; R \rhd_p \wedge R \blacktriangleright r)}{rec\, r.R \blacktriangleright p}$$

We use the following shorthands.

$$P \not\blacktriangleright p :\Leftrightarrow \neg(P \blacktriangleright p), \quad P \blacktriangleright :\Leftrightarrow \exists p:\; P \blacktriangleright p, \quad \text{and } P \not\blacktriangleright :\Leftrightarrow \neg(P \blacktriangleright).$$
□

The extended transition system $\mathcal{E}[P]$ of a term P is the transition system $\mathcal{T}[P]$ plus a new component for the extensions. For the latter a context is interpreted as an element of *Fun* according to Definition 3.14, and hot contexts are interpreted as hot extensions.

Definition 3.20 (the extended transition system of a term) For $P \in terms$

$$\mathcal{E}[\![P]\!] := \langle terms, \mathbf{D}, \mathbf{E}, P\rangle$$

where $\mathbf{D}$ is as in Definition 1.24, and

$$\mathbf{E} := \{\langle Q, p, \mathcal{L}[\![C]\!]\rangle \mid Q \rhd_p C\} \cup \{\langle Q, p, \bot\rangle \mid Q \blacktriangleright p\}. \qquad \square$$

The rest of this section shows a number of properties of the extended transition system of terms which are used for the proof of the consistency in the next section. The reader not interested in proofs should continue reading on page 86.

Lemma 3.21 Let $P, Q, R \in terms$, $a \in Act$, $p \in Idf$. Then

$$P \xrightarrow{-a\rightarrow} Q \;\Rightarrow\; P[R/p] \xrightarrow{-a\rightarrow} Q[R/p].$$

Proof Induction on the length of the proof of $P -a\rightarrow Q$. If the last rule applied is one of act), fun), sum), asyn), and syn) the implication is easily derived, else it is ...

<u>rec)</u> Then $P \equiv rec\, r.P'$ and $P'[P/r] -a\rightarrow Q$. By Fact 1.9 we may assume $r \notin \{p\} \cup FI(R)$ and we have $P[R/p] \equiv rec\, r.(P'[R/p])$. By ind. hyp. $P'[P/r][R/p] -a\rightarrow Q[R/p]$. By Proposition 1.11 $P'[P/r][R/p] \equiv P'[R/p][\,P[R/p]\,/r]$. Hence by rec) $P[R/p] -a\rightarrow Q[R/p]$. $\square$

Proposition 3.22 Let $P, Q \in terms$, $C \in contexts$, and $p, q \in Idf$. Then

1. $P \blacktriangleright p \;\Rightarrow\; P \rhd_p$
2. $P \rhd_p \;\Rightarrow\; p \in FI(P)$
3. $P[Q/q] \rhd_p C$ with length of proof l
   iff
   $p \neq q \;\wedge\; P \rhd_p C$ with length of proof l
   $\vee$
   $\exists C_1, C_2 :\; C \equiv C_1C_2 \;\wedge\; Q \rhd_p C_1 \;\wedge\; P \rhd_q C_2$
4. $P[Q/q]\!\rightarrow \;\vee\; P[Q/q] \rhd \quad\Rightarrow\quad P\!\rightarrow \;\vee\; P \rhd$
5. If $P \not\blacktriangleright q$, then
   $P[Q/q] \blacktriangleright p$ iff $(p \neq q \;\wedge\; P \blacktriangleright p) \;\vee\; (P \rhd_q \;\wedge\; Q \blacktriangleright p)$

Proof 1. and 2. are easily checked by an induction on the length of the proof of $P \blacktriangleright p$ respectively of $P \rhd_p$.

3. If $P \equiv q$, then $P[Q/q] \equiv Q$, and $\forall C' : P \rhd_q C' \Rightarrow C' \equiv \kappa$, and $C \equiv C\kappa$. The claim follows. Now assume $P \not\equiv q$.

"$\Rightarrow$" Let $P[Q/q] \rhd_p C$ with proof length l. We perform an induction on l. If the last rule applied is ...

idf) Then $P[Q/q] \equiv p$ and $C \equiv \kappa$. As $P \not\equiv q$ we conclude $P \equiv p$. Hence $P \triangleright_p C$ with the same length of proof and $p \neq q$.

idfpar) Then $P[Q/q] \equiv P_1 \nmid P_2$, and as $P \not\equiv q$, $P \equiv P_1' \nmid P_2'$, such that $\forall i \in \{1,2\} : P_i \equiv P_i'[Q/q]$, and w.l.o.g. $P_1 \triangleright_p C'$ with length $l-1$ and $C \equiv C'\llcorner$. If by ind. hyp. $p \neq q$ and $P_1' \triangleright_p C'$ with length $l-1$, then by idfpar) $P \triangleright_p C$ with length l. Otherwise by ind. hyp. $Q \triangleright_p C_1 \wedge P_1' \triangleright_q C_2 \wedge C' \equiv C_1C_2$ for some C_1, C_2. Then by idfpar) $P \triangleright_q C_2\llcorner$ and $C \equiv C_1C_2\llcorner$.

idffun) idfsum) are similarly easy.

idfrec) Then $P[Q/q] \equiv rec\, r.R$. By Fact 1.9 we may assume that $r \notin \{q\} \cup FI(Q)$. As $P \not\equiv q$ we conclude that $P \equiv rec\, r.R'$ and $R \equiv R'[Q/q]$. By idfrec) $r \neq p$, $R'[Q/q] \triangleright_p C'$, and for some $n \geq 0 : R'[Q/q] \triangleright_r C_1, \ldots, R'[Q/q] \triangleright_r C_n$, such that $C \equiv C'C_1 \ldots C_n$. The sum of the lengths of all these proofs equals $l-1$.
Now as $r \notin FI(Q)$ by 2. $Q \not\triangleright_r$, hence by ind. hyp. for all $i \in \{1, \ldots, n\}$: $r \neq q \wedge R' \triangleright_r C_i$ (with the same length of proof as $R'[Q/q] \triangleright_r C_i$).
Furthermore by ind. hyp. $p \neq q \wedge R' \triangleright_p C'$ (with the same proof length as $R'[Q/q] \triangleright_p C'$) or $\exists \bar{C}_1, \bar{C}_2 : C' \equiv \bar{C}_1\bar{C}_2 \wedge Q \triangleright_p \bar{C}_1 \wedge R' \triangleright_q \bar{C}_2$.
In the first case by idfrec) $P \triangleright_p C'C_1 \ldots C_n \equiv C$ with length l. In the second case by idfrec) $P \triangleright_q \bar{C}_2C_1 \ldots C_n$ (recall that $r \neq q$). And then $C \equiv C'C_1 \ldots C_n \equiv \bar{C}_1\bar{C}_2C_1 \ldots C_n$. □ "⇒"

"⇐" We distinguish two cases. If $p \neq q \wedge P \triangleright_p C$ with length l, a very simple induction on l proves the result. Otherwise if $C \equiv C_1C_2 \wedge Q \triangleright_p C_1 \wedge P \triangleright_q C_2$, an induction on the length of the proof of $P \triangleright_q C_2$ shows the result. We show the only interesting case, namely if the last rule applied is ...

idfrec) Then $P \equiv rec\, r.R$. By 1.9 we may assume $r \notin \{q\} \cup FI(Q)$. By idfrec) $R \triangleright_q C'$, $R \triangleright_r C_1', \ldots, R \triangleright_r C_n'$ and $C_2 \equiv C'C_1' \ldots C_n'$. By ind. hyp. $R[Q/q] \triangleright_p C_1C'$, and by the above case (as $r \neq q$)
$R[Q/q] \triangleright_r C_i'$ for all i. By 2. $Q \triangleright_p$ implies $p \in FI(Q)$, hence $r \neq p$. Thus $P[Q/q] \overset{1.10}{\equiv} rec\, r.(R[Q/q]) \triangleright_p C_1C'C_1' \ldots C_n' \equiv C$. □ 3.

4. Let us first prove (∗)

$$\forall a, \tilde{Q} : P \not\triangleright_q \wedge P[Q/q] -a\rightarrow \tilde{Q} \Rightarrow \exists Q' : \tilde{Q} \equiv Q'[Q/q] \wedge P -a\rightarrow Q',$$

by an induction on the length of the proof of $P[Q/q] -a\rightarrow \tilde{Q}$. Note that $P \not\triangleright_q$ implies $P \not\equiv q$. Again we state the details only for the case that the last rule applied is rec) Then as $P \not\equiv q$, $P[Q/q] \equiv rec\, r.(R[Q/q])$ and by 1.9 we may assume $r \notin \{q\} \cup FI(Q)$. Then $P \equiv rec\, r.R$, and $R[Q/q][P[Q/q]/r] -a\rightarrow \tilde{Q}$. By 1.11 $R[Q/q][P[Q/q]/r] \equiv R[P/r][Q/q]$. As $P \not\triangleright_q$ and $r \neq q$ by idfrec) $R \not\triangleright_q$. By 3. $R[P/r] \not\triangleright_q$. Hence by ind. hyp. $\exists Q' : R[P/r] -a\rightarrow Q'$ and $\tilde{Q} \equiv Q'[Q/q]$. $P -a\rightarrow Q'$ follows.

Now to prove the claim, let $P[Q/q]\rightarrow \ \vee\ P[Q/q] \triangleright$. If $P \not\triangleright$ then by 3. $P[Q/q] \not\triangleright$, hence $P[Q/q]\rightarrow$. And then (*) implies $P\rightarrow$. □ 4.

5. Let $P \not\blacktriangleright q$. If $P \equiv q$ the claim holds trivially. Now assume $P \not\equiv q$.
"⇒" Induction on the length of the proof of $P[Q/q] \blacktriangleright p$. If the last rule applied is ... (hotfun) and hotsum) are left to the reader)

hotpar) Then as $P \not\equiv q$, $P \equiv P_1 \nmid P_2$, $P[Q/q] \equiv P_1[Q/q] \nmid P_2[Q/q]$ and w.l.o.g. $P_1[Q/q] \blacktriangleright p \ \vee\ P_1[Q/q] \triangleright_p \wedge (P_2[Q/q]\rightarrow \ \vee\ P_2[Q/q] \triangleright)$.
As $P \not\blacktriangleright q$ we know that $P_1 \not\blacktriangleright q$.
If $P_1[Q/q] \blacktriangleright p$, then by ind. hyp. $p \neq q \wedge P_1 \blacktriangleright p \ \vee\ P_1 \triangleright_q \wedge Q \blacktriangleright p$. With hotpar) respectively idfpar) the claim follows.
Otherwise $P_1[Q/q] \triangleright_p \wedge (P_2[Q/q]\rightarrow \ \vee\ P_2[Q/q] \triangleright)$. By 4. $P_2\rightarrow \ \vee\ P_2 \triangleright$. As $P \not\blacktriangleright q$ we know $P_1 \not\triangleright_q$. Hence by 3. $P_1 \triangleright_p \wedge p \neq q$. And $P \blacktriangleright p$ follows from hotpar). Note that we did not use the ind. hyp. for this subcase.

hotrec) Then as $P \not\equiv q$, $P \equiv rec\, r.R$, and by 1.9 we may assume $r \notin \{q\} \cup FI(Q)$, hence $P[Q/q] \equiv rec\, r.(R[Q/q])$. As $P \not\blacktriangleright q$ we know

$$(*1) \qquad R \not\blacktriangleright q \wedge (R \not\triangleright_q \ \vee R \not\blacktriangleright r).$$

If $p \neq r \wedge R[Q/q] \blacktriangleright p$, then by ind. hyp. $p \neq q \wedge R \blacktriangleright p \ \vee\ R \triangleright_q \wedge Q \blacktriangleright p$. In the first case hotrec) implies $P \blacktriangleright p$. In the second case idfrec) implies $P \triangleright_q$ (recall that $r \neq q$), and the claim follows.
Else by $P[Q/q] \blacktriangleright p$ we conclude

$$(*2) \qquad p \neq r \wedge R[Q/q] \triangleright_p \wedge R[Q/q] \blacktriangleright r.$$

Note that due to $r \notin FI(Q)$, 1. and 2. we know that $Q \not\blacktriangleright r$. Hence applying the ind. hyp. to $R[Q/q] \blacktriangleright r$ ((*1) allows us to do so) implies $R \blacktriangleright r$. With (*1) follows $R \not\triangleright_q$, hence 3. and (*2) imply $p \neq q \wedge R \triangleright_p$, hence by hotrec) $P \blacktriangleright p$. □ "⇒"

"⇐" We distinguish two cases. If $P \not\blacktriangleright q$ and $p \neq q \wedge P \blacktriangleright p$, we perform an induction on the length of the proof of $P \blacktriangleright p$. If the last rule is ...

hotfun), hotsum) the claim is easily proved.

hotpar) Then $P \equiv P_1 \nmid P_2$ and w.l.o.g. $P_1 \blacktriangleright p \;\vee\; P_1 \rhd_p \wedge (P_2 \!\rightarrow\; \vee\; P_2 \rhd)$, and $P_1 \not\blacktriangleright q$. If $P_1 \blacktriangleright p$, then by ind. hyp. $P_1[Q/q] \blacktriangleright p$, and the claim follows. Else $P_1 \rhd_p$ and $p \neq q$ imply by 3. $P_1[Q/q] \rhd_p$. And furthermore if $P_2 \!\rightarrow$ then by 3.21 $P_2[Q/q]\!\rightarrow$, else $P_2 \rhd$. And then $P \not\blacktriangleright q$ and $P_1 \rhd_p$ imply $P_2 \not\rhd_q$. Hence $\exists r \neq q : P_2 \rhd_r$. By 3. $P_2[Q/q] \rhd_r$. And then hotpar) implies $P_1[Q/q] \nmid P_2[Q/q] \blacktriangleright p$, which proves the claim.

hotrec) Then $P \equiv rec\, r.R$ for some $r \notin \{q\} \cup FI(Q)$, and $p \neq r \;\wedge\; (R \blacktriangleright p \;\vee\; R \rhd_p \;\wedge R \blacktriangleright r)$. Furthermore $P \not\blacktriangleright q \;\wedge\; r \neq q$ imply $R \not\blacktriangleright q$. If $R \blacktriangleright p$, then by ind. hyp. $R[Q/q] \blacktriangleright p$, hence as $p \neq r$ by hotrec) $rec\, r.(R[Q/q]) \blacktriangleright p$.
Else $R \rhd_p$ and $p \neq q$ imply by 3. $R[Q/q] \rhd_p$, and $R \blacktriangleright r \;\wedge\; r \neq q$ imply by ind. hyp. $R[Q/q] \blacktriangleright r$. Hence hotrec) implies the result.

Otherwise if $P \not\blacktriangleright q \;\wedge\; P \rhd_q \;\wedge Q \blacktriangleright p$ an induction on the length of the proof of $P \rhd_q$ shows the claim. If the last rule applied is ...

idf), idffun), idfsum), idfpar) the proof is trivial.

idfrec) Then $P \equiv rec\, r.R$ and by 1.9 we may assume $r \notin \{q\} \cup FI(Q)$, and we have $r \neq q \;\wedge\; R \rhd_q$. Furthermore $P \not\blacktriangleright q$ and $r \neq q$ imply $R \not\blacktriangleright q$. By ind. hyp. $R[Q/q] \blacktriangleright p$. By 1., 2. and $Q \blacktriangleright p$ we have $p \in FI(Q)$, hence $r \neq p$. Hence hotrec) implies $rec\, r.(R[Q/q]) \blacktriangleright p$, and the claim follows.

Proposition 3.22 □

Definition 3.23 (nil insertions) Let $nilterms := \{P \in terms \mid P \not\rightarrow \;\wedge\; P \not\rhd\}$. Define $ni : conterms \rightarrow \mathcal{P}(terms)$

$$ni(P) := \begin{cases} \{P\} & \text{if } P \in terms \\ \{Qf \mid Q \in ni(P')\} & \text{if } P \equiv P'f \wedge P \notin terms \\ \{Q_1 \nmid Q_2 \mid Q_1 \in ni(P') \;\wedge\; Q_2 \in nilterms\} & \text{if } P \equiv P'\llcorner \\ \{Q_1 \nmid Q_2 \mid Q_1 \in nilterms \;\wedge\; Q_2 \in ni(P')\} & \text{if } P \equiv P'\lrcorner. \end{cases}$$ □

Proposition 3.24 Let $P, Q, Q' \in terms$, $C, C' \in contexts$, $p \in Idf$.

1. $Q \in ni(PC) \;\wedge\; Q' \in ni(QC') \;\Rightarrow\; Q' \in ni(PCC')$
2. For $Q \in ni(PC')$: a) $Q \blacktriangleright p$ iff $P \blacktriangleright p$
   b) $Q \rhd_p C$ iff $\exists C_1 \in contexts : P \rhd_p C_1 \wedge C \equiv C_1 C'$

Proof By an induction on the structure of C'. We give the details for the following case, the others are similar.

<u>$C' \equiv \bar{C}\lfloor$</u> 1. Let $Q \in ni(PC) \wedge Q' \in ni(QC') = ni(Q\bar{C}\lfloor)$. Then for some $R_1 \in ni(Q\bar{C})$, $R_2 \in$ *nilterms*: $Q' \equiv R_1 \mathbin{\ast\!\!\!|} R_2$. By ind. hyp. $R_1 \in ni(PC\bar{C})$, hence $Q' \equiv R_1 \mathbin{\ast\!\!\!|} R_2 \in ni(PC\bar{C}\lfloor) = ni(PCC')$.
2. Let $Q \in ni(PC') = ni(P\bar{C}\lfloor)$. Then for some $R_1 \in ni(P\bar{C})$, $R_2 \in$ *nilterms*: $Q \equiv R_1 \mathbin{\ast\!\!\!|} R_2$. a) As $R_2 \not\triangleright$ by 3.22 1. $R_2 \not\blacktriangleright$. And then by hotpar) $R_1 \mathbin{\ast\!\!\!|} R_2 \blacktriangleright p$ iff $R_1 \blacktriangleright p$ iff (by ind. hyp.) $P \blacktriangleright p$.
b) "$\Rightarrow$" $Q \triangleright_p C$ implies by idfpar) and $R_2 \in$ *nilterms* for some C_2: $R_1 \triangleright_p C_2 \wedge C \equiv C_2\lfloor$. By ind. hyp. for some $C_1 : P \triangleright_p C_1 \wedge C_2 \equiv C_1\bar{C}$, and we have $C \equiv C_1\bar{C}\lfloor \equiv C_1C'$. "$\Leftarrow$" Let $C \equiv C_1C' \wedge P \triangleright_p C_1$. Then $C \equiv C_1\bar{C}\lfloor$. By ind. hyp. $R_1 \triangleright_p C_1\bar{C}$. By idfpar) $Q \triangleright_p C_1\bar{C}\lfloor \equiv C$. □

Proposition 3.25
Let $P, P', Q, Q', \tilde{Q}, R \in$ *terms*, $C \in$ *contexts*, $p, r \in$ *Idf*, $a, b \in$ *Act*. Then

1. $P -b\rightarrow Q \wedge a = b\mathcal{L}[\![C]\!] \wedge P' \in ni(PC)$
$\Rightarrow \exists Q' \in ni(QC) : P' -a\rightarrow Q'$.
2. $P' \in ni(PC) \wedge P' -a\rightarrow Q'$
$\Rightarrow \exists b \in Act, Q \in terms : Q' \in ni(QC) \wedge b\mathcal{L}[\![C]\!] = a \wedge P -b\rightarrow Q$.
3. $P \not\blacktriangleright p \wedge P \triangleright_p C \wedge Q -a\rightarrow Q' \wedge a\mathcal{L}[\![C]\!] \neq \bot$
$\Rightarrow \exists \tilde{Q} \in ni(Q'C) : P[Q/p] -a\mathcal{L}[\![C]\!]\rightarrow \tilde{Q}$.
4. $R \not\blacktriangleright r \wedge P \equiv rec\, r.R \wedge P -a\rightarrow Q$
$\wedge\, \exists n \in I\!N : \forall i \in \{1, \ldots, n\} : \exists C_i : R \triangleright_r C_i \wedge a\mathcal{L}[\![\kappa C_1 \ldots C_n]\!] = b \neq \bot$
$\Rightarrow \exists \tilde{Q} \in ni(Q\kappa C_1 \ldots C_n) : P -b\rightarrow \tilde{Q}$.
5. $P \not\blacktriangleright p \wedge P[Q/p] -a\rightarrow \tilde{Q}$ (with proof of length l)

$$\begin{array}{rl} \Rightarrow & \exists Q' \in terms : \tilde{Q} \equiv Q'[Q/p] \wedge P -a\rightarrow Q' \\ \vee & \exists Q' \in terms, C \in contexts, b \in Act : \\ & \quad \tilde{Q} \in ni(Q'C) \wedge P \triangleright_p C \wedge a = b\mathcal{L}[\![C]\!] \\ & \quad \wedge\, Q -b\rightarrow Q' \text{ (with proof length } l' \leq l) \end{array}$$

6. $R \not\blacktriangleright r \wedge P \equiv rec\, r.R \wedge P -a\rightarrow Q$
$\Rightarrow \exists n \in I\!N, Q' \in terms, b \in Act : \forall i \in \{1, \ldots, n\} : \exists C_i \in contexts :$
$R \triangleright_r C_i \wedge Q \in ni(Q'[P/r]\kappa C_1 \ldots C_n)$
$\wedge\, a = b\mathcal{L}[\![\kappa C_1 \ldots C_n]\!] \wedge R -b\rightarrow Q'$.

Proof 1. and 2. Induction on the structure of C.
3. Induction on the length of the proof of $P \triangleright_p C$. The interesting cases are if the last rule applied is ...

<u>idfpar)</u> Then $P \equiv P_1 \ddagger P_2$ and w.l.o.g. $C \equiv C'\mathrm{l}$, $P_1 \triangleright_p C'$, and $a\mathcal{L}[\![C]\!] = a\mathcal{L}[\![C']\!] \neq \bot$. Furthermore $P \not\triangleright p$ implies $P_1 \not\triangleright p$.
By ind. hyp. $\exists\tilde{Q} \in ni(Q'C') : P_1[Q/p] - a\mathcal{L}[\![C']\!] \rightarrow \tilde{Q}$. By asyn)
$P[Q/p] \equiv P_1[Q/p] \ddagger P_2[Q/p] - a\mathcal{L}[\![C]\!] \rightarrow \tilde{Q} \ddagger P_2[Q/p]$. $P_1 \triangleright_p$ and $P \not\triangleright p$ imply via hotpar) $P_2 \not\rightarrow \quad \wedge\ P_2 \not\triangleright$. 3.22 4. implies $P_2[Q/p] \in nilterms$.
Hence $\tilde{Q} \ddagger P_2[Q/p] \in ni(Q'C'\mathrm{l})$.

<u>idfrec)</u> Then $P \equiv rec\, r.R$, $r \neq p\ \wedge\ R \triangleright_p C'\ \wedge\ \exists n : \forall i \in \{1,\ldots,n\} : R \triangleright_r C_i\ \wedge\ C \equiv C'C_1\ldots C_n$. By 1.9 we may assume $r \notin FI(Q)$.
We show with an inner induction on n that

$$\exists\tilde{Q} \in ni(Q'C'C_1\ldots C_n) : P[Q/p] - a\mathcal{L}[\![C'C_1\ldots C_n]\!] \rightarrow \tilde{Q}.$$

<u>$n = 0$</u> Then $C \equiv C'$. As $r \neq p\ \wedge\ R \triangleright_p C$ Proposition 3.22 3. implies $R[P/r] \triangleright_p C$ with the same proof length as $R \triangleright_p C$, which in turn is less than the length of the proof of $P \triangleright_p C$. Moreover $P \not\triangleright p \wedge r \neq p \wedge R \triangleright_p$ implies by hotrec) $R \not\triangleright p \wedge R \not\triangleright r$. Then 3.22 5. implies $R[P/r] \not\triangleright p$.
Hence by the outer ind. hyp. $\exists\tilde{Q} \in ni(Q'C) : R[P/r][Q/p] - a\mathcal{L}[\![C]\!] \rightarrow \tilde{Q}$.
The substitution lemma implies $R[P/r][Q/p] \equiv R[Q/p][\,P[Q/p]/r\,]$.
And by rec) $P[Q/p] \equiv rec\, r.(R[Q/p]) - a\mathcal{L}[\![C]\!] \rightarrow \tilde{Q}$.

<u>$n \mapsto n+1$</u> Then by the inner ind. hyp. $\exists\tilde{Q} \in ni(Q'C'C_1\ldots C_n)$: $P[Q/p] - a\mathcal{L}[\![C'C_1\ldots C_n]\!] \rightarrow \tilde{Q}$. Note that $\bot \neq a\mathcal{L}[\![C]\!] = a\mathcal{L}[\![C'C_1\ldots C_n]\!] \cdot \mathcal{L}[\![C_{n+1}]\!]$. As $R \triangleright_r C_{n+1}$ and $r \neq p$ by 3.22 3. $R[Q/p] \triangleright_r C_{n+1}$ with the same length of proof as $R \triangleright_r C_{n+1}$, which in turn is less than that of $P \triangleright_p C$. Moreover $P \not\triangleright p\ \wedge\ p \neq r\ \wedge\ R \triangleright_p$ implies $R \not\triangleright p\ \wedge\ R \not\triangleright r$. As $r \notin FI(Q)$ 3.22 1. and 2. imply $Q \not\triangleright r$.
Hence 3.22 5. implies $R[Q/p] \not\triangleright r$. We are now ready to apply the outer ind. hyp., it leads to $\exists\tilde{\tilde{Q}} \in ni(\tilde{Q}C_{n+1})$:
$R[Q/p][\,P[Q/p]/r\,] - (a\mathcal{L}[\![C'C_1\ldots C_n]\!] \cdot \mathcal{L}[\![C_{n+1}]\!]) \rightarrow \tilde{\tilde{Q}}$.
And by rec) $P[Q/p] - a\mathcal{L}[\![C]\!] \rightarrow \tilde{\tilde{Q}}$. Furthermore 3.24 1. implies
$\tilde{\tilde{Q}} \in ni(Q'C'C_1\ldots C_nC_{n+1}) = ni(Q'C)$. □ 3.

4. We perform an induction on n.

<u>$n = 0$</u> Then $a = b$. Choose $\tilde{Q} \equiv Q$ and the claim follows.

<u>$n \mapsto n+1$</u> By ind. hyp. $\exists\tilde{Q} \in ni(Q\kappa C_1\ldots C_n) : P - a\mathcal{L}[\![\kappa C_1\ldots C_n]\!] \rightarrow \tilde{Q}$. As $R \not\triangleright r \wedge R \triangleright_r C_{n+1}\ \wedge\ a\mathcal{L}[\![\kappa C_1\ldots C_nC_{n+1}]\!] \neq \bot$ by 3. $\exists\tilde{\tilde{Q}} \in ni(\tilde{Q}C_{n+1})$: $R[P/r] - a\mathcal{L}[\![\kappa C_1\ldots C_{n+1}]\!] \rightarrow \tilde{\tilde{Q}}$. By 3.24 1. $\tilde{\tilde{Q}} \in ni(Q\kappa C_1\ldots C_nC_{n+1})$, and rec) implies the claim. □ 4.

5. If $P \equiv p$, then $P \triangleright_p \kappa$ and for $Q' \equiv \tilde{Q}$ the second alternative holds. Else $P \not\equiv p$. We perform an induction on l. If the last rule applied is …

act) Then (as $P \not\equiv p$) $P \equiv aP'$, $\tilde{Q} \equiv P'[Q/p]$ and the first alternative holds.

fun) Then (as $P \not\equiv p$) $P \equiv P'f$, $\tilde{Q} \equiv \tilde{\tilde{Q}}f$ and for some $b \in Act$ $P'[Q/p] -b\rightarrow \tilde{\tilde{Q}}$ with proof of length $l-1$ and $bf = a$. Moreover $P \not\triangleright p$ implies $P' \not\triangleright p$.
If $\exists Q' : \tilde{\tilde{Q}} \equiv Q'[Q/p] \;\wedge\; P' -b\rightarrow Q'$, then $P -a\rightarrow Q'f$ and $\tilde{Q} \equiv Q'f[Q/p]$.
Else by ind. hyp. $\exists Q', C, c : \tilde{\tilde{Q}} \in ni(Q'C) \wedge P' \triangleright_p C \wedge b = c\mathcal{L}[\![C]\!] \wedge Q -c\rightarrow Q'$ with length less than l. And then $P \triangleright_p Cf \;\wedge\; \tilde{Q} \in ni(Q'Cf)$.

sum) trivial.

asyn) Then (due to $P \not\equiv p$) $P \equiv P_1 \nmid P_2$ and w.l.o.g. $P_1[Q/p] -a\rightarrow \tilde{Q}_1$ (with length $l-1$) and $\tilde{Q} \equiv \tilde{Q}_1 \nmid P_2[Q/p]$. $P \not\triangleright p$ implies $P_1 \not\triangleright p$. If $\exists Q' : \tilde{Q}_1 \equiv Q'[Q/p] \;\wedge\; P_1 -a\rightarrow Q'$, then $P_1 \nmid P_2 -a\rightarrow Q' \nmid P_2$ and $\tilde{Q} \equiv (Q' \nmid P_2)[Q/p]$. Else by ind. hyp. $\exists Q', C, b : \tilde{Q}_1 \in ni(Q'C) \wedge P_1 \triangleright_p C \wedge a = b\mathcal{L}[\![C]\!] \wedge Q -b\rightarrow Q'$ with length less than l. And then $P \triangleright_p C\llcorner$. Furthermore $P \not\triangleright p \wedge P_1 \triangleright_p$ implies $P_2 \not\rightarrow \;\wedge\; P_2 \not\triangleright$. By 3.22 4. $P_2[Q/p] \in$ *nilterms*, hence $\tilde{Q} \equiv \tilde{Q}_1 \nmid P_2[Q/p] \in ni(Q'C\llcorner)$. And we have $a = b\mathcal{L}[\![C\llcorner]\!]$.

syn) Then $P \equiv P_1 \nmid P_2$, $\tilde{Q} \equiv \tilde{Q}_1 \nmid \tilde{Q}_2$ and for $b_1, b_2 \in Vis$:$\forall i : P_i[Q/p] -b_i\rightarrow \tilde{Q}_i$ and $a = [b_1, b_2]$. $P \not\triangleright p$ implies $P_1 \not\triangleright p \;\wedge\; P_2 \not\triangleright p$, furthermore $P \not\triangleright p$ implies $\neg(P_1 \triangleright_p \;\wedge\; P_2 \triangleright_p)$. W.l.o.g. assume $P_1 \not\triangleright_p$. Then by ind. hyp. $\exists Q_1' : \tilde{Q}_1 \equiv Q_1'[Q/p] \;\wedge\; P_1 -b_1\rightarrow Q_1'$. In particular $P_1 \rightarrow$, and then $P \not\triangleright p$ implies $P_2 \not\triangleright_p$. Again by ind. hyp. $\exists Q_2' : \tilde{Q}_2 \equiv Q_2'[Q/p] \wedge P_2 -b_2\rightarrow Q_2'$. And then clearly $\tilde{Q} \equiv (Q_1' \nmid Q_2')[Q/p]$ and $P -a\rightarrow Q_1' \nmid Q_2'$.

rec) Then $P \equiv rec\, r.R$ and w.l.o.g. $r \notin \{p\} \cup FI(Q)$. $P \not\triangleright p$ implies $R \not\triangleright p$ $\wedge\, (R \not\triangleright_p \;\vee R \not\triangleright r)$. If $R \not\triangleright_p$, then $P \not\triangleright_p$. Then by (*) in the proof of 3.22 4. $\exists Q' : \tilde{Q} \equiv Q'[Q/p] \;\wedge\; P -a\rightarrow Q'$.
Else $R \not\triangleright r$. By 3.22 5. $R[P/r] \not\triangleright p$. Furthermore $P[Q/p] -a\rightarrow \tilde{Q}$ implies $R[Q/p][\,P[Q/p]/r\,] -a\rightarrow \tilde{Q}$ with length $l-1$. By the substitution lemma 1.11 $R[Q/p][\,P[Q/p]/r\,] \equiv R[P/r][Q/p]$. Hence we may apply the ind. hyp. to $R[P/r]$. And this leads to $\exists Q' : \tilde{Q} \equiv Q'[Q/p] \wedge R[P/r] -a\rightarrow Q' \vee \exists Q', C, b :$ $\tilde{Q} \in ni(Q'C) \;\wedge\; R[P/r] \triangleright_p C \;\wedge\; a = b\mathcal{L}[\![C]\!] \;\wedge\; Q -b\rightarrow Q'$ with proof of length less than l. In the first case $P -a\rightarrow Q'$, in the second case by 3.22 3. $R \triangleright_p C \;\vee\; C \equiv C_1C_2 \;\wedge\; R \triangleright_r C_2 \;\wedge\; P \triangleright_p C_1$. And as $P \triangleright_p C_1$ implies $R \triangleright_p C' \wedge$ for some $n :$ $R \triangleright_r C_i'$ such that $C_1 \equiv C'C_1' \ldots C_n'$, in both cases idfrec) implies $P \triangleright_p C$. □ 5.

6. $P -a\rightarrow Q$ implies $R[P/r] -a\rightarrow Q$. We perform an induction on the length l of the proof of $R[P/r] -a\rightarrow Q$.

$l = 0$ Then the only rule applied is act), and $R[P/r] \equiv aQ$, and $R \equiv aQ'$, and $Q \equiv Q'[P/r]$, hence the claim is true for $n = 0$.

<u>$l \mapsto l+1$</u> By 5. $\exists Q' : Q \equiv Q'[P/r] \ \wedge \ R -a\rightarrow Q'$ or $\exists Q', C, b : Q \in ni(Q'C) \ \wedge \ R \rhd_r C \ \wedge \ a = b\mathcal{L}[\![C]\!] \ \wedge \ P -b\rightarrow Q'$ with proof length $l' \leq l+1$. In the first case the claim follows for $n = 0$. Otherwise rec) implies $R[P/r] -b\rightarrow Q'$ with proof length $l'-1 < l+1$. Then by ind. hyp. $\exists Q'', c, n \geq 0 : \forall i \in \{1, \ldots, n\} : \exists C_i : R \rhd_r C_i \ \wedge \ Q' \in ni(Q''[P/r]\kappa C_1 \ldots C_n) \ \wedge \ b = c\mathcal{L}[\![\kappa C_1 \ldots C_n]\!] \ \wedge \ R -c\rightarrow Q''$. And then $a = c\mathcal{L}[\![\kappa C_1 \ldots C_n]\!] \cdot \mathcal{L}[\![C]\!]$ and by 3.24 1.
$Q \in ni(Q''[P/r]\kappa C_1 \ldots C_n C)$, which proves the claim. □ 6.

Proposition 3.25 □

3.4 Consistency

This section is solely devoted to the proof of the following theorem.

Theorem 3.26 Let $P \in terms$ and $\mathcal{F}[\![P]\!]$ be defined. Then

$$\mathcal{F}[\![P]\!] \sim \mathcal{E}[\![P]\!].$$

With this result we immediately have the following.

Corollary 3.27 For P as above, let $\mathcal{F}[\![P]\!] = \langle S, D, E, z\rangle$, then

$$\langle S, D, z\rangle \sim \langle terms, \mathbf{D}, P\rangle = \mathcal{T}[\![P]\!].$$ □

In other words, when disregarding the extensions of $\mathcal{F}[\![P]\!]$ it is as transition system strongly bisimular to the transition system for P given in chapter 1, i.e. if $\mathcal{F}[\![P]\!]$ is defined it is consistent with the interleaving operational semantics of P.

Proof of Theorem 3.26 We perform an induction on the structure of P. The case $P \equiv rec\, r.R$ is rather involved and highly depends on the properties shown in the previous section.
In the following let $\mathcal{F}[\![P]\!] = \langle S_P, D_P, E_P, z_P\rangle$, $\mathcal{F}[\![P_i]\!] = \langle S_i, D_i, E_i, z_i\rangle$ and so forth. And let $\mathcal{E}[\![P]\!] = \langle terms, \mathbf{D}, \mathbf{E}, P\rangle$ as defined in 3.20.

<u>$P \equiv nil$</u> Then $\{\langle z_P, P\rangle\}$ is a strong bisimulation for $\mathcal{F}[\![P]\!]$ and $\mathcal{E}[\![P]\!]$.

<u>$P \equiv p$</u> for $p \in Idf$. Then $\{\langle z_P, P\rangle\}$ is a strong bisimulation for $\mathcal{F}[\![P]\!]$ and $\mathcal{E}[\![P]\!]$, in particular $E_P(z_P) = \{\langle p, id\rangle\} = \{\langle p, \mathcal{L}[\![\kappa]\!]\rangle\} = \mathbf{E}(P)$.

<u>$P \equiv aP'$</u> for $a \in \{\tau\} \cup Vis$. If $\mathcal{F}[\![P]\!]$ is defined, then $\mathcal{F}[\![P']\!]$ is defined, and then by ind. hyp. there exists a strong bisimulation B' for $\mathcal{F}[\![P']\!]$ and $\mathcal{E}[\![P']\!]$. Then $B := \{\langle z_P, P\rangle\} \cup B'$ is a strong bisimulation for $\mathcal{F}[\![P]\!]$ and $\mathcal{E}[\![P]\!]$.

<u>$P \equiv P'f$</u> for $f \in Fun$. Similarly to the above case the needed strong bisimulation is $B := \{\langle s, Qf\rangle \mid s \in S_P \ \wedge \ \langle s, Q\rangle \in B'\}$.

$\underline{P \equiv P_1 + P_2}$ If $\mathcal{F}[\![P]\!]$ is defined, so are $\mathcal{F}[\![P_1]\!]$ and $\mathcal{F}[\![P_2]\!]$. By ind. hyp. there exist strong bisimulations B_i (for $i \in \{1,2\}$) for $\mathcal{F}[\![P_i]\!]$ and $\mathcal{E}[\![P_i]\!]$.

$$B := \{\langle z_P, P\rangle\} \cup \{\langle s, Q\rangle \mid s \in S_P \wedge \langle s, Q\rangle \in B_1 \cup B_2\}$$

is easily checked to be the wanted strong bisimulation.

$\underline{P \equiv P_1 \nmid P_2}$ Let B_i be as above and define

$$B := \Big\{\big\langle\langle s_1, s_2\rangle, Q_1 \nmid Q_2\big\rangle \,\Big|\, \langle s_1, Q_1\rangle \in B_1 \wedge \langle s_2, Q_2\rangle \in B_2\Big\}.$$

We show that B is a strong bisimulation for $\mathcal{F}[\![P]\!]$ and $\mathcal{E}[\![P]\!]$. We have that $z_P = \langle z_1, z_2\rangle$ and $\langle z_1, P_1\rangle \in B_1, \langle z_2, P_2\rangle \in B_2$, hence $\langle z_P, P\rangle \in B$. Now let $\langle s, Q\rangle \in B$, i.e. $s = \langle s_1, s_2\rangle \in S_P, Q \equiv Q_1 \nmid Q_2$ and $\forall i : \langle s_i, Q_i\rangle \in B_i$.

i) If $\langle s, a, s'\rangle \in D_P$, then $s' = \langle s_1', s_2'\rangle \in S_P$ and we distinguish three cases.
1. $\langle s_1, a, s_1'\rangle \in D_1 \wedge s_2 = s_2'$, then as B_1 is a strong bisimulation $\exists Q_1' : Q_1 -a\rightarrow Q_1{}' \wedge \langle s_1', Q_1'\rangle \in B_1$. By asyn) $Q \equiv Q_1 \nmid Q_2 -a\rightarrow Q_1' \nmid Q_2$ and clearly $\big\langle\langle s_1', s_2\rangle, Q_1' \nmid Q_2\big\rangle \in B$.
2. $\langle s_2, a, s_2'\rangle \in D_2 \wedge s_1 = s_1'$ is symmetrical.
3. $\exists b_1, b_2 \in \mathit{Vis} : a = [b_1, b_2] \wedge \forall i : \langle s_i, b_i, s_i'\rangle \in D_i$. Then as B_1, B_2 are strong bisimulations there exist Q_1', Q_2' such that $\forall i : Q_i -b_i\rightarrow Q_i' \wedge \langle s_i', Q_i'\rangle \in B_i$. By syn) $Q -a\rightarrow Q_1' \nmid Q_2'$ and clearly $\big\langle\langle s_1', s_2'\rangle, Q_1' \nmid Q_2'\big\rangle \in B$.

ii) If $Q -a\rightarrow \tilde{Q}$, then there are also three cases.
1. $\tilde{Q} \equiv Q_1' \nmid Q_2$ and $Q_1 -a\rightarrow Q_1'$. Using B_1 we conclude $\exists s_1' \in S_1 : \langle s_1, a, s_1'\rangle \in D_1 \wedge \langle s_1', Q_1'\rangle \in B_1$. Then $\big\langle\langle s_1, s_2\rangle, a, \langle s_1', s_2\rangle\big\rangle \in D_P$ and $\big\langle\langle s_1', s_2\rangle, Q_1' \nmid Q_2\big\rangle \in B$. 2. $\tilde{Q} \equiv Q_1 \nmid Q_2'$ and $Q_2 -a\rightarrow Q_2'$ is symmetrical.
3. $\tilde{Q} \equiv Q_1' \nmid Q_2'$ and $\exists b_1, b_2 \in \mathit{Vis} : a = [b_1, b_2] \wedge \forall i : Q_i -b_i\rightarrow Q_i'$. Then as B_1, B_2 are strong bisimulations, there exist $s_1' \in S_1, s_2' \in S_2 : \forall i : s_i -b_i\rightarrow s_i' \wedge \langle s_i', Q_i'\rangle \in B_i$. And then $\big\langle\langle s_1, s_2\rangle, a, \langle s_1', s_2'\rangle\big\rangle \in D_P$ and $\big\langle\langle s_1', s_2'\rangle, Q_1' \nmid Q_2'\big\rangle \in B$.

iii) $E_P(s) = E_1(s_1) \cup E_2(s_2) \cup \{\langle p, \perp\rangle \mid E_1(s_1, p) \neq \emptyset \neq E_2(s_2) \cup D_2(s_2) \vee E_2(s_2, p) \neq \emptyset \neq E_1(s_1) \cup D_1(s_1)\}$

$$\overset{(*)}{=} \{\langle p, \mathcal{L}[\![C]\!]\rangle \mid Q_1 \rhd_p C \vee Q_2 \rhd_p C\}$$
$$\cup\ \{\langle p, \perp\rangle \mid Q_1 \blacktriangleright p \vee Q_2 \blacktriangleright p \vee Q_1 \rhd_p \wedge (Q_2 \rightarrow \vee Q_2 \rhd) \vee Q_2 \rhd_p \wedge (Q_1 \rightarrow \vee Q_1 \rhd)\}$$
$$= \{\langle p, \mathcal{L}[\![C]\!]\rangle \mid Q_1 \nmid Q_2 \rhd_p C\} \cup \{\langle p, \perp\rangle \mid Q_1 \nmid Q_2 \blacktriangleright p\} = \mathbf{E}(Q).$$

The equality $(*)$ holds by ind. hyp. and the fact that by Proposition 3.22 1. $Q_i \blacktriangleright p \Rightarrow Q_i \rhd_p$.

<u>$P \equiv \text{rec}\, r.R$</u> As $\mathcal{F}[\![P]\!]$ is defined, $\mathcal{F}[\![R]\!] =: \langle S, D, E, z\rangle =: T$ is defined and $\perp \notin E(r)$. Then $\mathcal{F}[\![P]\!] = \text{rec}\, r.T =$

$$Reach\Big(\langle\, \boldsymbol{S}, \boldsymbol{D} \cup D_+,\ (\boldsymbol{E} \cup E_+) - (\boldsymbol{S} \times \{r\} \times Fun),\ z_{id}\, \rangle\Big) \;=:\; \langle \hat{S}, \hat{D}, \hat{E}, z_{id}\rangle.$$

Throughout this proof we use the denotations as in Definition 3.8 of the recursion operator. Note that we have $\langle S, D, E, z\rangle = \langle S_{id}, D_{id}, E_{id}, z_{id}\rangle$.
By induction hypothesis there exists a strong bisimulation B_R for $\mathcal{F}[\![R]\!]$ and $\mathcal{E}[\![R]\!]$. Define

$$B_P := \{\langle z_{id}, P\rangle\} \cup \Big\{\langle s_f, \hat{Q}\rangle \mid \langle s, Q\rangle \in B_R \wedge s_f \in \hat{S} \wedge \mathcal{L}[\![C]\!] = f \wedge \hat{Q} \in ni(Q[P/r]C)\Big\}.$$

For the definition of *ni* see 3.23. We will show that B_P is a strong bisimulation for $\mathcal{F}[\![P]\!]$ and $\mathcal{E}[\![P]\!]$ according to Definition 3.3.
Clearly $\langle z_{id}, P\rangle \in B_P$. Next we prove conditions i) - iii) of Definition 3.3. To this end let $\langle \hat{s}, \hat{Q}\rangle \in B_P$ and $a \in Act$.

i) We have to show $\langle \hat{s}, a, \tilde{s}\rangle \in \hat{D} \;\Rightarrow\; \exists \tilde{Q} \in \textit{terms} : \hat{Q} -a\rightarrow \tilde{Q} \;\wedge\; \langle \tilde{s}, \tilde{Q}\rangle \in B_P$.

Case 1: $\langle \hat{s}, \hat{Q}\rangle = \langle z_{id}, P\rangle$
Let $\langle z_{id}, a, \tilde{s}\rangle \in \hat{D}$. If $\langle z_{id}, a, \tilde{s}\rangle \in \boldsymbol{D}$, then $\tilde{s} = s'_{id} \in S_{id}$ and $\langle z_{id}, a, s'_{id}\rangle \in D_{id}$, hence $\langle z, a, s'\rangle \in D$. By ind. hyp. $\langle z, R\rangle \in B_R$ and $\exists Q' : R -a\rightarrow Q' \;\wedge\; \langle s', Q'\rangle \in B_R$. By Proposition 3.21 $R[P/r] -a\rightarrow Q'[P/r]$, by rule rec) $P -a\rightarrow Q'[P/r]$. Clearly $\mathcal{L}[\![\kappa]\!] = id, Q'[P/r] \in ni(Q'[P/r]\kappa)$, and $s'_{id} \in \hat{S}$, hence $\langle s'_{id}, Q'[P/r]\rangle \in B_P$.
Else if $\langle z_{id}, a, \tilde{s}\rangle \in D_+$, then for $\bar{f} \in SF, g \in E_{id}(z_{id}, r)$ and $\tilde{s} = s'_{\bar{f}\cdot g}$ we have $\langle z_{\bar{f}\cdot g}, a, s'_{\bar{f}\cdot g}\rangle \in D_{\bar{f}\cdot g}$.
Furthermore $\bar{f} = id \cdot f_1 \cdot \ldots \cdot f_n$ for $n \geq 0$, and $f_i \in E(z, r) \overset{\text{i.h.}}{=} \mathbf{E}(R, r)$, hence there exist C_i such that $\mathcal{L}[\![C_i]\!] = f_i$ and $R \triangleright_r C_i$ (recall that $\perp \notin E(z, r)$ and hence $R \not\triangleright r$). Also $g \in E(z, r) \overset{\text{i.h.}}{=} \mathbf{E}(R, r)$, hence $\exists C' : \mathcal{L}[\![C']\!] = g \;\wedge\; R \triangleright_r C'$.
By definition of $T\bar{f}\cdot g$ there exists $b \in Act$ such that $(b)\bar{f}\cdot g = a$ and $\langle z, b, s'\rangle \in D$. By ind. hyp. $\exists Q' : R -b\rightarrow Q' \;\wedge\; \langle s', Q'\rangle \in B_R$. By Proposition 3.21 $R[P/r] -b\rightarrow Q'[P/r]$, by rec) $P -b\rightarrow Q'[P/r]$. We have $b\mathcal{L}[\![\kappa C_1 \ldots C_n C']\!] = (b)\bar{f}\cdot g = a$. As $R \not\triangleright r$ by Proposition 3.25 4. $\exists \tilde{Q} \in ni(Q'[P/r]\kappa C_1 \ldots C_n C') : P -a\rightarrow \tilde{Q}$. Hence $\langle \tilde{s}, \tilde{Q}\rangle \in B_P$.

Case 2:
$\langle \hat{s}, \hat{Q}\rangle = \langle s_f, \hat{Q}\rangle$ for $f \in F$ and $\hat{Q} \in ni(Q[P/r]C)$ for $\langle s, Q\rangle \in B_R, \mathcal{L}[\![C]\!] = f$
Let $\langle s_f, a, \tilde{s}\rangle \in \hat{D}$. If $\langle s_f, a, \tilde{s}\rangle \in \boldsymbol{D}$, then $\tilde{s} = s'_f \in \hat{S} \cap S_f$, and $\langle s_f, a, s'_f\rangle \in D_f$. Then $\exists b : bf = a \wedge \langle s, b, s'\rangle \in D$. By ind. hyp. $\exists Q' : Q -b\rightarrow Q' \wedge \langle s', Q'\rangle \in B_R$. By Prop. 3.21 $Q[P/r] -b\rightarrow Q'[P/r]$ by Prop. 3.25 1. $\exists \tilde{Q} \in ni(Q'[P/r]C) : \hat{Q} -a\rightarrow \tilde{Q}$. Furthermore $\langle s'_f, \tilde{Q}\rangle \in B_P$.
Else if $\langle s_f, a, \tilde{s}\rangle \in D_+$, then for $\bar{f} \in SF, g \in E_f(s_f, r)$ and $\tilde{s} = s'_{\bar{f}\cdot g}$ we have

$\langle z_{\bar{f}\cdot g}, a, s'_{\bar{f}\cdot g}\rangle \in D_{\bar{f}\cdot g}$. This implies $\exists b \in Act : (b)\bar{f}\cdot g = a \;\wedge\; \langle z, b, s'\rangle \in D$. By ind. hyp. $\exists Q' : R -b\rightarrow Q' \;\wedge\; \langle s', Q'\rangle \in B_R$. By Prop. 3.21 and rec) $P -b\rightarrow Q'[P/r]$. Furthermore $\bar{f} \in SF$ implies for some $n \geq 0$ that $\bar{f} = id \cdot f_1 \cdot \ldots \cdot f_n$ for some $f_i \in E(z,r) \overset{\text{i.h.}}{=} \mathbf{E}(R,r)$. Hence there exists C_i such that $\mathcal{L}[\![C_i]\!] = f_i \;\wedge\; R \rhd_r C_i$. Recall that $R \not\rhd r$. By Prop. 3.25 4. $\exists \tilde{Q} \in ni(Q'[P/r]\kappa C_1 \ldots C_n) : P -b\bar{f}\rightarrow \tilde{Q}$. As $\bot \neq g \in E_f(s_f, r)$ we have $g = g'f$ for some $g' \neq \bot$ and $\langle s, r, g'\rangle \in E$. By ind. hyp. $\exists C' : Q \rhd_r C' \;\wedge\; \mathcal{L}[\![C']\!] = g'$. As $\bot \neq a = b\bar{f}\cdot g = b\bar{f}\cdot g' \cdot f$ we know that $b\bar{f}\cdot g' \neq \bot$. By ind. hyp. $\mathbf{E}(Q,r) = E(s,r) \not\ni \bot$, hence $Q \not\rhd r$. We are now ready to apply Prop. 3.25 3. which leads to $\exists \tilde{\tilde{Q}} \in ni(\tilde{Q}C') : Q[P/r] -(b\bar{f}\cdot g')\rightarrow \tilde{\tilde{Q}}$. Prop. 3.24 1. implies $\tilde{\tilde{Q}} \in ni(Q'[P/r]\kappa C_1 \ldots C_n C')$. Applying again Prop. 3.25 1. leads to $\exists \tilde{Q}' \in ni(\tilde{\tilde{Q}}C) : \hat{Q} -a\rightarrow \tilde{Q}'$. By Prop. 3.24 1. $\tilde{Q}' \in ni(Q'[P/r]\kappa C_1 \ldots C_n C' C)$. And as $\mathcal{L}[\![\kappa C_1 \ldots C_n C' C]\!] = \bar{f}\cdot g' \cdot f = \bar{f}\cdot g$ we have that $\langle s'_{\bar{f}\cdot g}, \tilde{Q}'\rangle \in B_P$.

ii) We have to show $\hat{Q} -a\rightarrow \tilde{Q} \;\Rightarrow\; \exists \tilde{s} \in \hat{S} : \langle \hat{s}, a, \tilde{s}\rangle \in \hat{D} \;\wedge\; \langle \tilde{s}, \tilde{Q}\rangle \in B_P$.

Case 1: $\langle \hat{s}, \hat{Q}\rangle = \langle z_{id}, P\rangle$

Let $P -a\rightarrow \tilde{Q}$. By ind. hyp. $\mathbf{E}(R,r) = E(z,r) \not\ni \bot$, hence $R \not\rhd r$. By Prop. 3.25 6. for some $n \geq 0$ there exist C_i, Q', and $b \in Act$ such that $R \rhd_r C_i \;\wedge\; \tilde{Q} \in ni(Q'[P/r]\kappa C_1 \ldots C_n) \;\wedge\; a = b\mathcal{L}[\![\kappa C_1 \ldots C_n]\!] \;\wedge\; R -b\rightarrow Q'$. By ind. hyp. $\exists s' : \langle z, b, s'\rangle \in D \;\wedge\; \langle s', Q'\rangle \in B_R$.
If $n = 0$, then $a = b$ and $\langle z_{id}, a, s'_{id}\rangle \in D_{id} \cap \hat{D}$, then as $\mathcal{L}[\![\kappa]\!] = id$ we conclude $\langle s'_{id}, \tilde{Q}\rangle \in B_P$. Else $n > 0$. Then for all i : $\mathcal{L}[\![C_i]\!] \in \mathbf{E}(R,r) \overset{\text{i.h.}}{=} E(z,r) = E_{id}(z_{id}, r)$. Let $g := \mathcal{L}[\![C_n]\!]$ (exists as $n > 0$!) and $\bar{f} := \mathcal{L}[\![\kappa C_1 \ldots C_{n-1}]\!]$. Clearly $g \in E_{id}(z_{id}, r)$ and $\bar{f} \in SF$. Furthermore $(b)\bar{f}\cdot g = a$, hence $\langle z_{\bar{f}\cdot g}, a, s'_{\bar{f}\cdot g}\rangle \in D_{\bar{f}\cdot g} \subseteq \mathbb{D}$. Thus $\langle z_{id}, a, s'_{\bar{f}\cdot g}\rangle \in D_{+} \cap \hat{D}$. $\langle s'_{\bar{f}\cdot g}, \tilde{Q}\rangle \in B_P$ follows.

Case 2:
$\langle \hat{s}, \hat{Q}\rangle = \langle s_f, \hat{Q}\rangle$ for $f \in F$ and $\hat{Q} \in ni(Q[P/r]C)$ for $\langle s, Q\rangle \in B_R, \mathcal{L}[\![C]\!] = f$

Let $\hat{Q} -a\rightarrow \tilde{\tilde{Q}}$. By Prop. 3.25 2. there exist $b \in Act, \tilde{Q}$ such that $\tilde{\tilde{Q}} \in ni(\tilde{Q}C) \;\wedge\; Q[P/r] -b\rightarrow \tilde{Q} \;\wedge\; b\mathcal{L}[\![C]\!] = a$.
If $\exists Q' : \tilde{Q} \equiv Q'[P/r] \wedge Q -b\rightarrow Q'$, then by ind. hyp. $\exists s' : \langle s, b, s'\rangle \in D \wedge \langle s', Q'\rangle \in B_R$. And then $\langle s_f, a, s'_f\rangle \in D_f \cap \hat{D}$, and $\langle s'_f, \tilde{\tilde{Q}}\rangle \in B_P$.
Else $\neg\exists Q' : \tilde{Q} \equiv Q'[P/r] \;\wedge\; Q -b\rightarrow Q'$. By ind. hyp. $\mathbf{E}(Q,r) = E(s,r) \not\ni \bot$, hence $Q \not\rhd r$. By Prop. 3.25 5. there exist Q', C', and $c \in Act$ such that $\tilde{Q} \in ni(Q'C') \;\wedge\; Q \rhd_r C' \;\wedge\; b = c\mathcal{L}[\![C']\!] \;\wedge\; P -c\rightarrow Q'$. As we also have $R \not\rhd r$, by Prop. 3.25 6. for some $n \geq 0$ there exist C_i, Q'', and $d \in Act$, such that $R \rhd_r C_i \;\wedge\; Q' \in ni(Q''[P/r]\kappa C_1 \ldots C_n) \;\wedge\; c = d\mathcal{L}[\![\kappa C_1 \ldots C_n]\!] \;\wedge\; R -d\rightarrow Q''$.
Applying Prop. 3.24 1. twice leads to (*1) $\tilde{\tilde{Q}} \in ni(Q''[P/r]\kappa C_1 \ldots C_n C' C)$.
By ind. hyp. $\mathcal{L}[\![C_i]\!] \in E(z,r)$, hence (*2) $\bar{f} := \mathcal{L}[\![\kappa C_1 \ldots C_n]\!] \in SF$.
As $Q \rhd_r C'$ by ind. hyp. (*3) $g := \mathcal{L}[\![C']\!] \in E(s,r) \subseteq F$.

By definition of Tf we have (*4) $g \cdot f \in E_f(s_f, r)$
As $\langle z, R\rangle \in B_R$ and $R -d\rightarrow Q''$ by ind. hyp.

$$\exists s' \in S: \ \langle z, d, s'\rangle \in D \ \wedge \ \langle s', Q''\rangle \in B_R. \qquad (*5)$$

We have $(d)\bar{f} \cdot g \cdot f = a$, and by (*2, *3) and $f \in F$ we conclude $\bar{f} \cdot g \cdot f \in F$. Hence (*5) implies $\langle z_{\bar{f}\cdot g\cdot f}, a, s'_{\bar{f}\cdot g\cdot f}\rangle \in D_{\bar{f}\cdot g\cdot f} \subseteq \mathbb{D}$.
(*4) and (*2) imply then $\langle s_f, a, s'_{\bar{f}\cdot g\cdot f}\rangle \in D_+ \cap \hat{D}$. Furthermore, as $\bar{f} \cdot g \cdot f = \mathcal{L}[\![\kappa C_1 \ldots C_n C' C]\!]$, with (*1) $\langle s'_{\bar{f}\cdot g\cdot f}, \tilde{\tilde{Q}}\rangle \in B_P$ follows.

iii) We will show $\hat{E}(\hat{s}) = \mathbf{E}(\hat{Q})$.

Case 1: $\langle \hat{s}, \hat{Q}\rangle = \langle z_{id}, P\rangle$
Always have in mind that $\perp \notin SF \ni id$.

$$\begin{aligned}
\hat{E}(z_{id}) \ = \ & \{\langle p,h\rangle \mid p \neq r \ \wedge \ \langle p,h\rangle \in E_{id}(z_{id})\} \\
& \cup \{\langle p,h\rangle \mid p \neq r \ \wedge \ \bar{f} \in SF \ \wedge \ g \in E_{id}(z_{id}, r) \ \wedge \ \langle p,h\rangle \in E_{\bar{f}\cdot g}(z_{\bar{f}\cdot g})\} \\
= \ & \{\langle p,h\rangle \mid p \neq r \ \wedge \ \langle p,h\rangle \in E(z)\} \\
& \cup \{\langle p,h\rangle \mid p \neq r \ \wedge \ h = h'f \ \wedge \ h' \neq \perp \ \wedge \ f \in SF \ \wedge \ \langle p,h'\rangle \in E(z)\} \\
= \ & \{\langle p,\perp\rangle \mid p \neq r \ \wedge \ \langle p,\perp\rangle \in E(z)\} \\
& \cup \{\langle p, h' \cdot f\rangle \mid p \neq r \ \wedge \ h' \neq \perp \ \wedge \ \langle p,h'\rangle \in E(z) \ \wedge \ f \in SF\} \\
\overset{\text{i.h.}}{=} \ & \{\langle p,\perp\rangle \mid p \neq r \ \wedge \ R \blacktriangleright p\} \\
& \cup \ \{\langle p, \mathcal{L}[\![CC_1 \ldots C_n]\!]\rangle \mid \ p \neq r \ \wedge \ R \rhd_p C \\
& \qquad \text{and for } n \geq 0: \forall i \in \{1, \ldots, n\}: R \rhd_r C_i\} \\
\overset{(*)}{=} \ & \{\langle p,\perp\rangle \mid P \blacktriangleright p\} \cup \{\langle p, \mathcal{L}[\![C]\!]\rangle \mid P \ \rhd_p C\} = \mathbf{E}(P).
\end{aligned}$$

For (*) we have used idfrec) and hotrec), for "$\supseteq$" recall that by ind. hyp. $\langle r, \perp\rangle \notin E(z) = \mathbf{E}(R)$, hence $R \not\blacktriangleright r$.

Case 2:
$\langle \hat{s}, \hat{Q}\rangle = \langle s_f, \hat{Q}\rangle$ for $f \in F$ and $\hat{Q} \in ni(Q[P/r]C)$ for $\langle s, Q\rangle \in B_R, \mathcal{L}[\![C]\!] = f$
Recall that for all $f \in F$, for all $s \in S: \perp \notin E_f(s_f, r)$, and in particular this implies (with the ind. hyp.) $Q \not\blacktriangleright r$.

$$\begin{aligned}
\hat{E}(s_f) = \ & \{\langle p,h\rangle \mid p \neq r \ \wedge \ \langle p,h\rangle \in E_f(s_f)\} \\
& \cup \{\langle p,h\rangle \mid p \neq r \ \wedge \ \bar{f} \in SF \ \wedge \ g \in E_f(s_f, r) \ \wedge \ \langle z_{\bar{f}\cdot g}, p, h\rangle \in E_{\bar{f}\cdot g}\}
\end{aligned}$$

$$\begin{aligned}
= \ & \{\langle p,\perp\rangle \mid p \neq r \ \wedge \ (\langle p,\perp\rangle \in E(s) \ \vee \ \langle p,\perp\rangle \in E(z) \ \wedge \ E(s,r) \neq \emptyset)\} \\
& \cup \{\langle p,h\rangle \ \mid p \neq r \ \wedge \ h = h' \cdot f \ \wedge \ h' \neq \perp \ \wedge \ \langle p,h\rangle \in E(s)\} \\
& \cup \{\langle p,h\rangle \ \mid p \neq r \wedge h = h' \cdot \bar{f} \cdot g' \cdot f \ \wedge \ h' \neq \perp \ \wedge \ \bar{f} \in SF \\
& \qquad \wedge \ g' \in E(s,r) \ \wedge \ \langle p,h'\rangle \in E(z)\}
\end{aligned}$$

$$\begin{aligned}
\overset{\text{i.h.}}{=} \ & \{\langle p,\perp\rangle \mid p \neq r \ \wedge \ (Q \blacktriangleright p \ \vee \ R \blacktriangleright p \ \wedge \ Q \rhd_r)\} \\
& \cup \{\langle p, \mathcal{L}[\![C'C]\!]\rangle \mid p \neq r \ \wedge \ Q \ \rhd_p C'\} \\
& \cup \{\langle p, \mathcal{L}[\![C''C_1 \ldots C_n C' C]\!]\rangle \mid p \neq r \ \wedge \ R \ \rhd_p C'' \ \wedge \ R \ \rhd_r C_i \ \wedge \ Q \ \rhd_r C'\}
\end{aligned}$$

$=$ (cf. the remark on $(*)$ for the previous case)
$\{\langle p,\bot\rangle \mid (p \neq r \,\wedge\, Q \blacktriangleright p) \,\vee\, (P \blacktriangleright p \,\wedge\, Q \triangleright_r)\}$
$\cup\{\langle p, \mathcal{L}[\![C'C]\!]\rangle \mid p \neq r \,\wedge\, Q \triangleright_p C'\}$
$\cup\{\langle p, \mathcal{L}[\![C''C'C]\!]\rangle \mid P \triangleright_p C'' \,\wedge\, Q \triangleright_r C'\}$
$=$ (by Prop. 3.22 5. and 3.22 3.)
$\{\langle p,\bot\rangle \mid Q[P/r] \blacktriangleright p\} \cup \{\langle p, \mathcal{L}[\![C'C]\!]\rangle \mid Q[P/r] \triangleright_p C'\}$
$=$ (by Prop. 3.24 2.)
$\{\langle p,\bot\rangle \mid \hat{Q} \blacktriangleright p\} \cup \{\langle p, \mathcal{L}[\![C']\!]\rangle \mid \hat{Q} \triangleright_p C'\} = \mathbf{E}(\hat{Q})$. Theorem 3.26 □

3.5 Finitely representable subsets

In this section we state sufficient syntactic conditions for terms to be finitely representable. Recall that by Theorem 2.11 there exists no algorithm which for a given term outputs a consistent finite transition system if and only if it exists and otherwise states its non-existence.

A first very simple approach is to syntactically disallow the intertwining of recursion and parallelism, and to disallow functions without finite renaming. It is taken in the next theorem. We will use the following lemma.

Lemma 3.28 Let $P \in$ *terms*, and $\mathcal{F}[\![P]\!] = \langle S, D, E, z\rangle$ be defined. Then

$$\{p \in \mathit{Idf} \mid E(p) \neq \emptyset\} \subseteq \mathit{FI}(P).$$

Proof This fact is easily checked, using an induction on the structure of P. □
But note that in general equality does not hold. E.g. for $P \equiv (ap)\text{–}a$, $\mathit{FI}(P) = \{p\}$ but $\mathcal{F}[\![P]\!] = \mathcal{F}[\![\mathit{nil}]\!]$, i.e. $\{p \mid E(p) \neq \emptyset\} = \emptyset$.

Theorem 3.29 For $P \in$ *terms* such that

for every subterm of the form $Q_1 \nmid Q_2$ $\mathit{FI}(Q_1) = \mathit{FI}(Q_2) = \emptyset$ and
for every subterm of the form Qf f has finite renaming (cf. Def. 3.9)

$\mathcal{F}[\![P]\!]$ is defined and finite.

Proof We perform an induction on the structure of P to prove the stronger claim: If P is as stated in the theorem, then

a) $\mathcal{F}[\![P]\!] = \langle S, D, E, z\rangle$ is defined and finite,

b) $\forall p \in \mathit{Idf} :\ f \in E(p) \;\Rightarrow\; f \neq \bot \,\wedge\, f$ has finite renaming.

The cases $\underline{P \equiv \mathit{nil}}$, $\underline{P \equiv p}$, $\underline{P \equiv aP'}$, $\underline{P \equiv P_1 + P_2}$, are trivial.

$\underline{P \equiv P'f}$ Then by assumption f has finite renaming, and as by ind. hyp. $\mathcal{F}[\![P']\!] = \langle S', D', E', z'\rangle$ is defined and finite, clearly $\mathcal{F}[\![P]\!] = \langle S, D, E, z\rangle$ is defined and finite. Now to prove b) let for $p \in \mathit{Idf}$, $h \in E(p)$. Then $\exists s \in S' : \langle s, p, g\rangle \in E'$ and $(g = \bot = h \ \vee\ h = g \cdot f \ \wedge\ g \neq \bot)$, by ind. hyp. b) $g \neq \bot$ and g has finite renaming. Hence $h \neq \bot$, and as the composition of functions with finite renaming again has finite renaming we conclude that h has finite renaming.

$\underline{P \equiv P_1 \nmid P_2}$ Trivially a) holds. By assumption $FI(P_1) = FI(P_2) = \emptyset$. Hence $FI(P) = \emptyset$. By Lemma 3.28 for all $p \in \mathit{Idf} : E(p) = \emptyset$, hence b) follows trivially.

$\underline{P \equiv rec\, r.R}$ for some $r \in \mathit{Idf}$. By ind. hyp. a) $\mathcal{F}[\![R]\!] = \langle S_R, E_R, D_R, z_R\rangle$ is defined and finite. By ind. hyp. b) $\bot \notin E_R(r)$ and $\forall f \in E_R(r) : f$ has finite renaming. Hence $\mathcal{F}[\![P]\!]$ is defined, and by Theorem 3.10 $\mathcal{F}[\![P]\!]$ is finite, i.e. a) follows.
b) Follows from the ind. hyp. b), the fact that the finite composition of functions with finite renaming again has finite renaming and considerations similar to that of the case "$P \equiv P'f$". □

This theorem shows that the limitation to action manipulation functions with finite renaming and the disallowance of the intertwining of recursion and parallelism makes terms finitely representable as transition systems. But this restriction also disallows any intertwining of recursion and sequential composition as the latter is based on the parallel composition (cf. Definition 1.17).

In the next theorem we weaken the restriction with respect to the second component of sequential composition. Recall example 4. on page 48 to see that recursion through the first component of sequential composition already leads to a context-free (and non-regular) set of traces, which cannot be finitely represented by a transition system.

Lemma 3.30 Let $P \in \mathit{terms}_{\surd}$ and $\mathcal{F}[\![P]\!] = \langle S, D, E, z\rangle$ be defined. Then for all $\langle s_1, a, s_2\rangle \in D$

$$a \notin \mathit{Ticks} \ \vee\ a = \surd \ \wedge\ D(s_2) = E(s_2) = \emptyset.$$

Proof Let $\langle s_1, a, s_2\rangle \in D$. By Property 3.11 $\exists w \in \mathit{Act}^* : z \xrightarrow{w}_D s_1$. By Theorem 3.26 exists a bisimulation B for $\mathcal{F}[\![P]\!]$ and $\mathcal{E}[\![P]\!]$. Hence $\exists Q : P \xrightarrow{wa} Q$ such that $\langle s_2, Q\rangle \in B$. By Theorem 1.47 $a \notin \mathit{Ticks} \vee a = \surd \wedge Q \not\rightarrow \wedge FI(Q) = \emptyset$. As $\langle s_2, Q\rangle \in B$, $D(s_2) = \emptyset$, and as $FI(Q) = \emptyset$ by Prop. 3.22 1. and 2. $Q \not\triangleright \wedge Q \not\triangleright$, hence $E(s_2) = \emptyset$. □

Theorem 3.31 Let $P \in terms_{\surd}$ such that for every subterm Q of P

if $Q \equiv Q_1; Q_2$ then $FI(Q_1) = \emptyset$
else if $Q \equiv Q_1 \mid_{\surd} Q_2$ or $Q \equiv Q_1 \parallel_A Q_2$ then $FI(Q_1) = FI(Q_2) = \emptyset$
else if $Q \equiv Q'f$ then f has finite renaming.

Then $\mathcal{F}[\![P]\!]$ is defined and finite.

Proof We perform an induction on the structure of P to prove the stronger claim: If P is as stated in the theorem, then

a) $\mathcal{F}[\![P]\!]$ is defined and finite,

b) $\forall p \in Idf: \; f \in E(p) \;\Rightarrow\; f \neq \bot \;\wedge\; f$ has finite renaming.

The cases $\underline{P \equiv nil}$, $\underline{P \equiv skip}$, $\underline{P \equiv p}$, $\underline{P \equiv aP'}$, $\underline{P \equiv P_1 + P_2}$, are trivial. $\underline{P \equiv P'f}$, $\underline{P \equiv rec\, r.R}$ are as in 3.29.

$\underline{P \equiv P_1 \,;\, P_2}$ Then $P \equiv (P_1 g_1 \nmid \bar{\surd}_1 P_2)g\text{–}\{\surd_1, \bar{\surd}_1\}$ for some $P_1, P_2 \in terms_{\surd}, g_1 = \{\surd \mapsto \surd_1, \bar{\surd} \mapsto \bar{\surd}_1\}$ and g as in Definition 1.12. By assumption $FI(P_1) = \emptyset$. By induction hypothesis clearly follows that

$$\langle S_1, D_1, E_1, z_1\rangle := \mathcal{F}[\![P_1 g_1]\!] \text{ and } \langle S_2, D_2, E_2, z_2\rangle := \mathcal{F}[\![\bar{\surd}_1 P_2]\!] \text{ satisfy a) and b).} \qquad (*1)$$

And then clearly $\langle S, D, E, z\rangle := \mathcal{F}[\![P]\!]$ is defined and finite and $\forall p \in Idf:$ $f \in E(p) \;\wedge\; f \neq \bot \;\Rightarrow\; f$ has finite renaming. (Note that g has finite renaming.)
Let for some $s \in S, p \in Idf$ $\langle s, p, f\rangle \in E$. We have to show $f \neq \bot$. Clearly $s = \langle s_1, s_2\rangle$ for some $s_1 \in S_1, s_2 \in S_2$, and it suffices to show

$$\bot \notin E_1(s_1) \;\wedge\; \bot \notin E_2(s_2) \wedge \Big(E_1(s_1, p) = \emptyset \;\vee\; E_2(s_2) \cup D_2(s_2) = \emptyset\Big)$$
$$\wedge \Big(E_2(s_2, p) = \emptyset \;\vee\; E_1(s_1) \cup D_1(s_1) = \emptyset\Big).$$

By (*1) $\bot \notin E_1(s_1) \cup E_2(s_2)$ follows. And as $FI(P_1) = \emptyset = FI(P_1 g_1)$ Lemma 3.28 implies $E_1(s_1, p) = \emptyset$.
If $s_2 = z_2$ clearly $E_2(s_2, p) = \emptyset$, otherwise $s_2 \neq z_2$. Then as $\langle s_1, s_2\rangle$ is reachable in $\mathcal{F}[\![P]\!]$, and as $\langle z_2, a, s'\rangle \in D_2$ implies $a = \bar{\surd}_1$, and as $\surd_1, \bar{\surd}_1$ are restricted in $\mathcal{F}[\![P]\!]$ we conclude that for some $s'' \in S_1: \langle s'', \surd_1, s_1\rangle \in D_1$. And hence for $\langle S_1', D_1', E_1', z_1'\rangle := \mathcal{F}[\![P_1]\!]$ we have $\langle s'', \surd, s_1\rangle \in D_1'$ by Lemma 3.30 (note that $P_1 \in terms_{\surd}$). And then by the same lemma $D_1'(s_1) = E_1'(s_1) = \emptyset$. This implies $E_1(s_1) = D_1(s_1) = \emptyset$.

$\underline{P \equiv P_1 \,|_{\surd}\, P_2}$ or $\underline{P \equiv P_1 \parallel_A P_2}$ One easily checks a). By assumption $FI(P_1) = FI(P_2) = \emptyset = FI(P)$. Let $\mathcal{F}[\![P]\!] = \langle S, D, E, z\rangle$. By Lemma 3.28 for all $p \in Idf$: $E(p) = \emptyset$, hence b) holds trivially (even though g_A as in Definition 1.12 does not have finite renaming). □

Let us conclude this section with the remark that every program of COSY (as presented in [Best 87]) satisfies the conditions of the above theorem and hence is finitely representable as a transition system. Recall that a COSY program consists of a fixed finite number of parallel processes, but each single process is sequential.

As far as the control flow of CSP (or Occam) can be modelled with COSY (see [Best 87]), it can due to the above result also be modelled as a finite transition system. For the latter point see also [Bergstra, Klop 84]. They demonstrate how the flow of control of CSP is modelled by regular ACP processes. The latter also satisfy the conditions of the above theorem.

Conclusion to Chapter 3

This chapter owes very much to Milner's work. His paper [Milner 84] was the starting point for the construction of finite extended transition systems. Nevertheless the emphasis in [Milner 84] is laid upon a complete inference system for proving strong bisimularity[1] there is no consistency statement with respect to the transition system given in [Milner 85]. Although one intuitively tends to take this consistency for granted, its proof is not completely trivial.

We have added to Milner's construction the parallel composition and the action manipulation. With respect to the transitions this was straightforward from well-known constructions for automata. On the other hand with respect to the extensions we have not found anything comparable in the literature. In particular we had to refine the extensions to carry information about the action manipulation function which is to be applied on the recursive substitute.

[1] See also [Bergstra, Klop 88] and [Milner 86] for complete inference systems for proving weak bisimularity.

Chapter 4

Representation by finite and safe Petri nets

In this chapter we transfer the syntax-driven construction elaborated in the previous chapter to safe (= 1-safe) Petri nets.

Finite and safe Petri nets and finite transition systems are closely related insofar as the reachability graph of a finite and safe net is a finite transition system. Hence it is not surprising that the above mentioned transfer is possible. Our motivation for the constructions of this chapter is twofold.

Firstly, as we aim at representations of abstract programs which are easy to comprehend by humans, it is desirable to have not only finite, but small representations, carrying all the relevant information. Moreover it is desirable that the structuring into subprocesses is reflected by the representation. Let us illustrate this point with a simple example.

Example Let $P \equiv (a\,nil \mid b\,nil) \mid c\,nil$. The transition system $\mathcal{F}[\![P]\!]$ is given below on the left, whereas the safe net representation $\mathcal{N}[\![P]\!]$ developed in this chapter is given on the right.

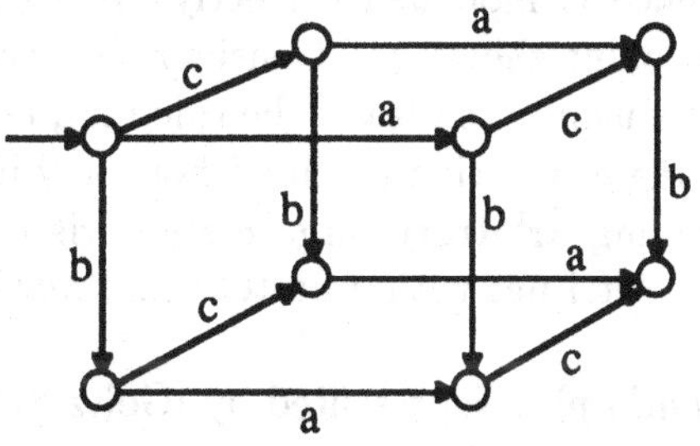

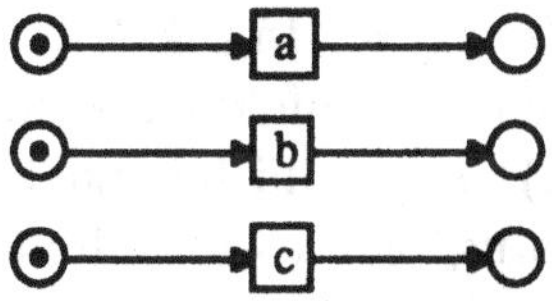

The net representation is smaller (as a graph), and we feel that the subprocesses are more directly visible. □

The second aim is to provide a representation which formally allows to distinguish between parallelism and arbitrary choice. The catchword "true concurrency" is often used with semantics (or representations) allowing this distinction. As explained in section 1.3 we prefer to call such a semantics or representation *distributed.*

A trivial approach to transfer the constructions of the previous chapter to nets would be to consider the transition systems constructed there as safe Petri nets (where every transition has just one place in its preset and one place in its postset, and every reachable marking consists of a single token). Although such a representation would satisfy our notion of consistency, it is not what we want.

We aim at representing the parallelism which is intuitively contained in an abstract program correctly. We claim that the constructions below have this property although we will prove no formal statement about it. A consistency result with respect to a distributed semantics will be given for the representation with predicate/transition nets in chapter 6. For a remark on the relation of both representations see the conclusion to chapter 6.

In this chapter we concentrate our attention to the subset *qterms* of *terms* for the following reasons. Net representations of the sum operator are known to cause trouble if the alternatives contain initial parallelism [Degano et al. 87], [Degano et al. 88], [Olderog 87], [Goltz 87]. We prefer to keep the constructions clear and straightforward in order to keep the essential points visible. Moreover in concrete parallel programming languages (such as Ada, Occam, Chill) the choice constructs always offer choices only between alternatives which start sequentially. Therefore in qterms the choice is restricted syntactically to such choices.

The second difference of qterms and (general) terms is that the former demand every body of a recursion to start with the invisible action τ. We have already argued in section 1.7 that then divergence is modelled correctly. If distributed representations are looked for, a second point shows up. Consider the term $P \equiv rec\, p.(a\, nil \mid p)$. In a distributed semantics using the idea of the rule rec), i.e. doing the recursive unfolding without performing any action (even without any invisible action), P should be capable of performing arbitrary large a-steps right at the beginning. Even with a finite (non-safe) Petri net with a finite initial marking, P could not be represented.

On the other hand $\sigma(P) \equiv rec\, p.\tau(a\, nil \mid p)$ is represented by [Goltz 87] as the (non-safe) net

intuitively capturing the parallelism correctly.

Another approach would be, to demand any (other) form of well-guardedness. But we think a τ for the recursive unfolding is very useful and harmless.

4.1 Definitions and terminology of net theory

This section collects the necessary definitions, notations and terminology of net theory. We try to keep it as short as possible. For a broader introduction to net theory the reader is referred to the literature.

Definition 4.1 1. A *Petri net* N over *Act* is a triple $\langle S, D, Z\rangle$, where

S	is the set of *places*,
$D \subseteq \mathcal{P}(S) \times Act \times \mathcal{P}(S)$	is the set of *transitions*,
$Z : S \rightarrow \mathbb{N}$	is the *initial marking*.

N is called a *net* for short.

2. N is *finite* if S and D are finite. All nets under consideration here will be countable, i.e. S and D are countable.

3. For $t = \langle S_1, a, S_2\rangle \in D$ we write $\bullet t := S_1$ ($t\bullet := S_2$) for the preset (postset) of t and $l(t) := a$ for the labelling of t. □

Analogous to the interpretation of transition systems as directed multi-graphs, Petri nets as above can be interpreted as directed multi-hypergraphs: The places are the vertices of the hypergraph, and a transition is a hyperedge connecting all vertices in its pre- and postsets. It is directed in the sense that the set of incident vertices is partitioned into two parts.

The above notation of a Petri net first appeared in [Greibach 78, p. 320]. It deviates from the typical notation used in the literature, but is has turned out to be very convenient for the definition of operators on nets corresponding to those of abstract programming languages, see e.g. [Goltz 87], [Olderog 87]. It also clearly discloses the similarities and differences to labelled transition systems.

Nevertheless the conventional notation is easily derived as follows.

Definition 4.2 (translation to conventional notation)

Let $N = \langle S, D, Z\rangle$ be as above, then it denotes a place/transition system $\Sigma = \langle S, T; F, K, W, M_0\rangle$ in the sense of [Best, Fernández 86, p. 19], where

$$
\begin{array}{lcl}
T & := & D \\
F & := & \{(s,t) \mid s \in S, t \in T, s \in \bullet t\} \;\cup\; \{(t,s) \mid s \in S, t \in T, s \in t\bullet\} \\
K(s) & := & \infty \quad \text{for all } s \in S \\
W(f) & := & 1 \quad \text{for all } f \in F \\
M_0 & := & Z.
\end{array}
$$

Furthermore l is a labelling of the transitions. □

We will only work with the notation given in Definition 4.1, but we will use the above translation to derive further useful notions and results of net theory. In particular we will use the usual graphical representation of nets.

Let us finally remark that in the above place/transition system the underlying net [Best, Fernández 86, p. 5] is a pre-net, since in 4.1 we make no assumptions about the emptiness of any set nor about the presence of isolated elements. Note on the other hand that not every transition labelled place/transition system can be denoted as in 4.1, even if all capacities are infinite and all weights are 1. E.g. the net

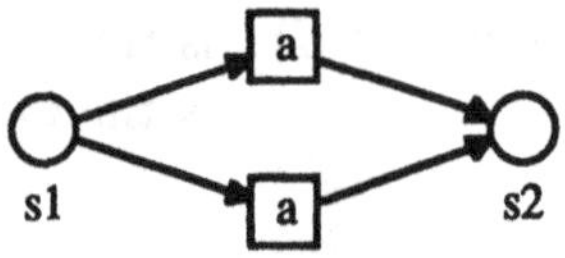

cannot be denoted as in 4.1, both transitions would be identified. A generalization of 4.1 to handle arc weights has been used in [Greibach 78] and [Goltz 87].

Definition 4.3 Let $N = \langle S, D, Z \rangle$ be a Petri net.

1. A *marking* of N is a function $S \to I\!N$.
   We will identify a subset S' of places with its characteristic function, i.e. for $s \in S$
   $$S'(s) = \begin{cases} 0 & \text{if } s \notin S', \\ 1 & \text{if } s \in S'. \end{cases}$$
   And for those functions addition (+), subtraction (−) and comparison (e.g. $\leq$) are understood to be componentwise.
2. A transition $\langle S_1, a, S_2 \rangle \in D$ is *enabled* at a marking M if $S_1 \leq M$.
3. If a transition $d \in D$ is enabled at a marking M_1, then it may *occur*, yielding a new marking $M_2 := (M_1 - S_1) + S_2$. We denote this fact by $M_1[d\rangle M_2$. And this notation is extended to arbitrary sequences $u \in D^*$ as usual:
   $$\forall M : \; M[\varepsilon\rangle M, \text{ and}$$
   $$M_1[ud\rangle M_3 \text{ iff } \exists M_2 : \; M_1[u\rangle M_2 \;\wedge\; M_2[d\rangle M_3.$$
4. The set of *reachable markings* of N is defined as
   $$[Z\rangle_D \;:=\; \{M \mid \exists u \in D^* : \; Z[u\rangle M\}.$$
   Notation: For the net $N_i = \langle S_i, D_i, Z_i \rangle$ we write $[Z_i\rangle_i$ etc.
5. N is *safe* if $\forall M \in [Z\rangle_D : \; M(S) \subseteq \{0, 1\}$. I.e. if every reachable marking is a set. We can and will use set notation for such markings. □

The terminology used in [Best, Fernández 86] for "safe" as above is "1-safe" and that for $[Z\rangle_D$ is "set of forward reachable markings".

Definition 4.4 (reachable subnet) Let $N = \langle S, D, Z \rangle$ be a safe net. Then

$$Reach(N) := \left\langle \bigcup [Z\rangle_D,\ \{d \in D \mid \exists M \in [Z\rangle_D : \bullet d \subseteq M\},\ Z \right\rangle. \qquad \square$$

Definition 4.5 (the transition system associated with a net)

Let $N = \langle S, D, Z \rangle$ be a net. Then we associate with N the transition system $Transys(N) := \left\langle [Z\rangle_D, D', Z \right\rangle$, where

$$D' = \{\langle M_1, l(d), M_2 \rangle \mid M_1 \in [Z\rangle_D \ \wedge\ d \in D \ \wedge\ M_1[d\rangle M_2\}. \qquad \square$$

Transys(N) corresponds to what is known as "reachability graph" in net theory, but the arcs of the former are labelled with transition labels (= actions) instead of transitions.

The transition system associated with a net reflects the interleaving behaviour of the net with respect to actions, and with the help of the transition systems of nets we can immediately carry over all equivalence notions on transition systems to nets. See also [Pomello 86]. For the non-interleaving behaviour the reader is referred to the rich literature on the subject, confer e.g. [Goltz, Reisig 83], [Best, Devillers 87], [Kiehn 88], [Vogler 87].

We define a representation of an abstract program as a net to be consistent, if the interleaving behaviour of the net is strongly bisimular to the interleaving operational semantics of the program.

Definition 4.6 (consistency)

Let $P \in terms$, and N be a net. We say that N is a *consistent representation* of P if $\mathcal{T}[\![P]\!] \ \sim\ Transys(N)$. $\square$

Of course, if we consider the transition systems constructed in the previous chapter as nets we already have a consistent safe net representation, but this is not what we want as explained in the introduction to this chapter.

Analogous to the previous chapter our constructions corresponding to the operators of **A** are not given for safe nets directly, but for so-called extended safe nets. Such an extended safe net additionally carries information on the free identifiers of the term which it is representing.

Definition 4.7 (extended safe net)

1. $N = \langle S, D, E, Z \rangle$ is an *extended safe net*, if

   $\langle S, D, Z \rangle$ is a safe net, and
   $E \subseteq \mathcal{P}(S) \times Idf \times Fun_\perp$ is the set of *extensions.*

   An extension can be seen as a special transition with empty postset and an identifier/function pair as label. In contrast to elements of D we do not consider the occurrence of an extension, but we use the usual graphical representation for transitions. We write for $t = \langle M, p, f\rangle \in E$

$$\begin{array}{rcl} \bullet t & := & M, \\ t\bullet & := & \emptyset, \end{array} \quad \text{and} \quad \begin{array}{rcl} l(t) & := & \langle p, f\rangle, \\ l_1(t) & := & p, \\ l_2(t) & := & f. \end{array}$$

Furthermore we use the following notations.

$$\begin{array}{rcll} E(M,p) & := & \{f \in Fun_\perp & \mid \langle M,p,f\rangle \in E\} \\ E(M) & := & \{\langle p,f\rangle & \mid \langle M,p,f\rangle \in E\} \\ E(p) & := & \{f \in Fun_\perp & \mid \langle M,p,f\rangle \in E\} \end{array}$$

2. For $u \in D^*$ let $M_1[u\rangle M_2$, and $[Z\rangle_D$ be as in Definition 4.3, i.e. these notations refer to the underlying safe net.
3. N is *finite* if S, D, and E are finite. □

In this section we will not distinguish isomorphic extended safe nets, i.e. nets where the only difference is that the places are named differently.

Definition 4.8 (isomorphic extended safe nets)
Two extended safe nets $\langle S_1, D_1, E_1, Z_1\rangle$ and $\langle S_2, D_2, E_2, Z_2\rangle$ are called *isomorphic*, if there exists a bijection $\varphi : S_1 \rightarrow S_2$ such that $Z_2 = \varphi(Z_1)$, $\langle M_1, a, M_2\rangle \in D_1$ iff $\langle \varphi(M_1), a, \varphi(M_2)\rangle \in D_2$, and $\langle M, p, f\rangle \in E_1$ iff $\langle \varphi(M), p, f\rangle \in E_2$. We write $N_1 \cong N_2$ if N_1 and N_2 are isomorphic. □

The next two definitions transfer the respective notions from nets to extended safe nets.

Definition 4.9 (the extended transition system associated with an extended net)
Let $N = \langle S, D, E, Z\rangle$ be an extended safe net. Then

$$Transys(N) := \Big\langle [Z\rangle_D, D', E', Z\Big\rangle, \text{ where}$$

$$\begin{array}{rcll} D' & = & \Big\{\langle M_1, l(t), M_2\rangle & \mid M_1 \in [Z\rangle_D \wedge t \in D \wedge M_1[t\rangle M_2\Big\}, \\ E' & = & \Big\{\langle M, l_1(t), l_2(t)\rangle & \mid M \in [Z\rangle_D \wedge t \in E \wedge \bullet t \subseteq M\Big\}. \end{array}$$ □

Definition 4.10 (reachable extended subnet)
Let N be as above. Then $Reach(N) := \Big\langle \bigcup [Z\rangle_D, D', E', Z\Big\rangle$, where

$$\begin{array}{rcll} D' & = & \{t \in D & \mid \exists M \in [Z\rangle_D : \bullet t \subseteq M\}, \\ E' & = & \{t \in E & \mid \exists M \in [Z\rangle_D : \bullet t \subseteq M\}. \end{array}$$ □

We conclude this section with a couple of facts needed later.

Lemma 4.11 Let $N = \langle S, D, E, Z\rangle$ be an extended safe net, and $Reach(N) = \langle \hat{S}, \hat{D}, \hat{E}, \hat{Z}\rangle$, then

1. $[Z\rangle_D = [\hat{Z}\rangle_{\hat{D}}$
2. $Transys(N) = Transys(Reach(N))$
3. $Reach(N) = Reach(Reach(N))$
4. If $Transys(N)$ is finite, $Reach(N) = N$ and for all $M \in [Z\rangle_D$: M is finite, then N is finite.

Proof 1. "$\supseteq$" is obvious, and "$\subseteq$" follows by an induction on $u \in D^*$.
2. and 3. follow by 1.
4. $\langle S, D, E, Z\rangle = Reach(N) = \langle \bigcup[Z\rangle_D, D', E', Z\rangle$, where D' and E' are as in Definition 4.10. And $Transys(N) = \langle [Z\rangle_D, D'', E'', Z\rangle$, where

$$\begin{array}{lll} D'' &=& \{\langle M_1, l(t), M_2\rangle \mid M_1 \in [Z\rangle_D \;\wedge\; t \in D \;\wedge\; M_1[t\rangle M_2\} \\ E'' &=& \{\langle M, l_1(t), l_2(t)\rangle \mid M \in [Z\rangle_D \;\wedge\; t \in E \;\wedge\; \bullet t \subseteq M\}. \end{array}$$

As $Transys(N)$ is finite, $[Z\rangle_D$, D'', and E'' are finite. And as $\forall M \in [Z\rangle_D : M$ is finite, we conclude that $S = \bigcup[Z\rangle_D$ is finite. Clearly $|D'| \leq |D''|$ and $|E'| \leq |E''|$, hence the claim follows. □

4.2 Syntax-driven construction

We are now ready to give the operators on extended safe nets, which correspond to the operators of **A**. Their definition is inspired by the operators on extended transition systems and by similar constructions found in the literature. Special care has been needed for the sensible definition of the extensions, especially of those of the parallel composition.

As in the previous chapter we use the same operator symbols as in **A** for operators on nets. They are not always defined (see the sum and the recursion operator). When a term $P \in terms$ is interpreted as an extended safe net this is denoted by $\mathcal{N}[\![P]\!]$.

Definition 4.12 $nil := \big\langle \{z\}, \emptyset, \emptyset, \{z\} \big\rangle$ 

For $p \in Idf$ define $p := \big\langle \{z\}, \emptyset, \{\, \langle \{z\}, p, id\rangle \,\}, \{z\} \big\rangle$ 

Let $N = \langle S, D, E, Z\rangle$ be an extended safe net.
For $a \in Vis \cup \{\tau\}$ define $aN := \big\langle S \cup \{s\}, D \cup \{\, \langle \{s\}, a, Z\rangle \,\}, E, \{s\} \big\rangle$ where $s \notin S$.

$aN =$ 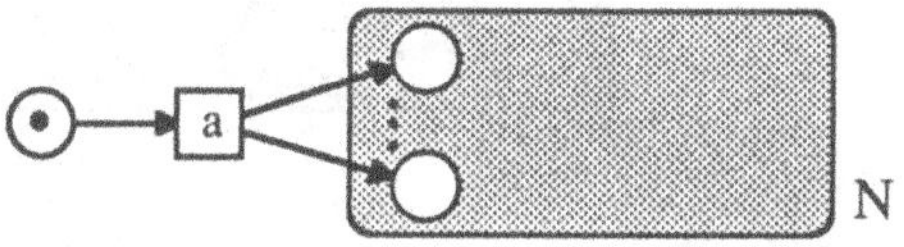

For $f \in \mathit{Fun}$ define $Nf := \mathit{Reach}(\langle S, D', E', Z\rangle)$, where

$$\begin{array}{rcll} D' & = & \{\langle M_1, af, M_2\rangle & \mid \langle M_1, a, M_2\rangle \in D \ \wedge\ af \neq \bot\} \\ E' & = & \{\langle M, p, g\cdot f\rangle & \mid \langle M, p, g\rangle \in E \ \wedge\ g \neq \bot\} \\ & \cup & \{\langle M, p, \bot\rangle & \mid \langle M, p, \bot\rangle \in E\}. \end{array}$$

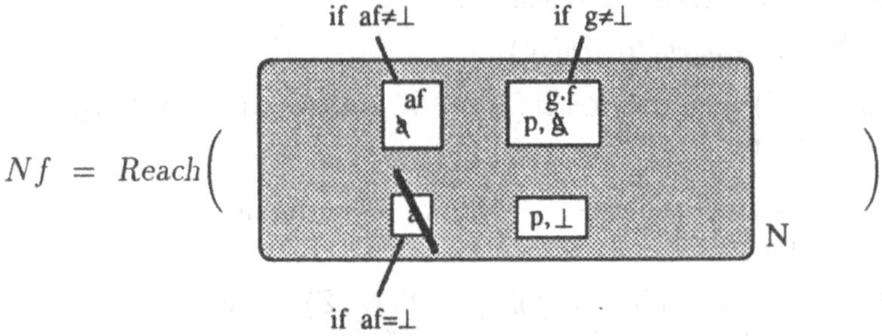

The sum is only defined, if both alternatives have just one initial place each. Hence no alternative allows any parallelism initially. See the discussion at the beginning of this chapter.

Definition 4.13 (sum) Let $N_i = \langle S_i, D_i, E_i, \{z_i\}\rangle$ for $i \in \{1,2\}$ be extended safe nets, where $S_1 \cap S_2 = \emptyset$.

$$N_1 + N_2 := \mathit{Reach}(\langle S_1 \cup S_2 \cup \{z\},\ D_1 \cup D_2 \cup D_+,\ E_1 \cup E_2 \cup E_+,\ \{z\}\rangle)$$

where $z \notin S_1 \cup S_2$ and

$$\begin{array}{rcll} D_+ & = & \{\langle\{z\}, a, M\rangle & \mid \langle\{z_1\}, a, M\rangle \in D_1 \ \vee\ \langle\{z_2\}, a, M\rangle \in D_2\} \\ E_+ & = & \{\langle\{z\}, p, f\rangle & \mid \langle\{z_1\}, p, f\rangle \in E_1 \ \vee\ \langle\{z_2\}, p, f\rangle \in E_2\}. \end{array}$$

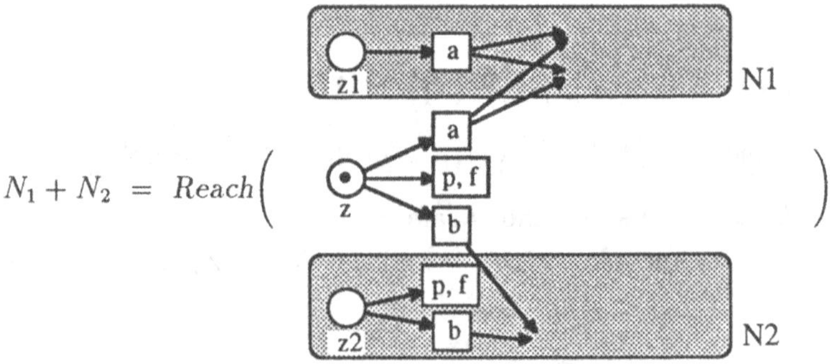

Definition 4.14 (parallel composition)
Let N_1, N_2 be extended safe nets where $S_1 \cap S_2 = \emptyset$.

$$
\begin{aligned}
N_1 \nmid N_2 &:= \langle S_1 \cup S_2,\ D_1 \cup D_2 \cup D_+,\ E,\ Z_1 \cup Z_2 \rangle, \text{ where} \\
D_+ &:= \Big\{ \langle M_1 \cup M_2, [a_1, a_2], M_1' \cup M_2' \rangle \ \Big| \\
&\qquad\qquad \forall i \in \{1,2\} :\ a_i \in \mathit{Vis} \ \wedge\ \langle M_i, a_i, M_i' \rangle \in D_i \Big\} \\
E &:= \Big\{ \langle M_1 \cup M_2, p, f \rangle \ | \\
&\qquad\qquad\qquad \langle M_1, p, g \rangle \in E_1 \ \wedge\ M_2 \in [Z_2\rangle_2 \\
&\qquad\qquad\qquad\quad \wedge\ (f = g \ \vee\ f = \bot \ \wedge\ \exists t \in D_2 \cup E_2 : \bullet t \subseteq M_2) \\
&\qquad\qquad\quad \vee\ \ \langle M_2, p, g \rangle \in E_2 \ \wedge\ M_1 \in [Z_1\rangle_1 \\
&\qquad\qquad\qquad\quad \wedge\ (f = g \ \vee\ f = \bot \ \wedge\ \exists t \in D_1 \cup E_1 : \bullet t \subseteq M_1) \Big\}.
\end{aligned}
$$
□

The motivation for a hot extension $\langle M, p, \bot \rangle$ is analogous to that given for the construction of extended transition systems, see page 66.

Example Let $P :\equiv a\,\mathit{nil} + b\,\mathit{nil}$, $Q :\equiv cp$.

$\mathcal{N}[\![P]\!]$ is 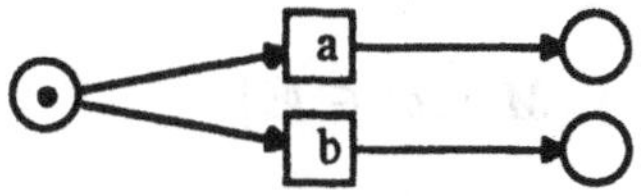

$\mathcal{N}[\![Q]\!]$ is 

Then $\mathcal{N}[\![P \nmid Q]\!]$ is

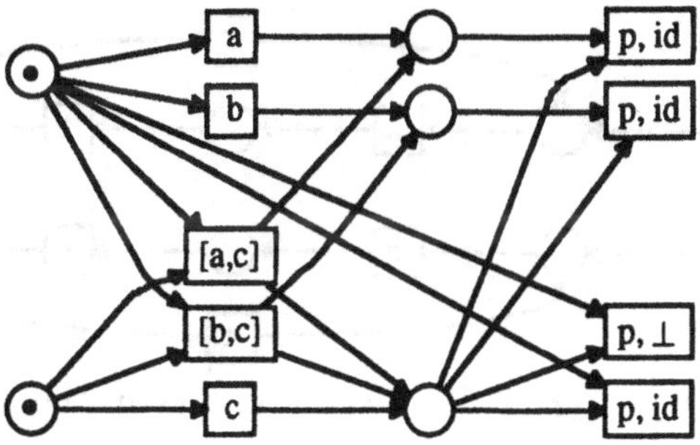

If synchronization is enforced, e.g. by restricting a, b, and c, then $\mathcal{N}[\![\,(P \nmid Q)\text{–}\{a,b,c\}\,]\!]$ is as follows (where $f = \{a \mapsto \bot, b \mapsto \bot, c \mapsto \bot\}$)

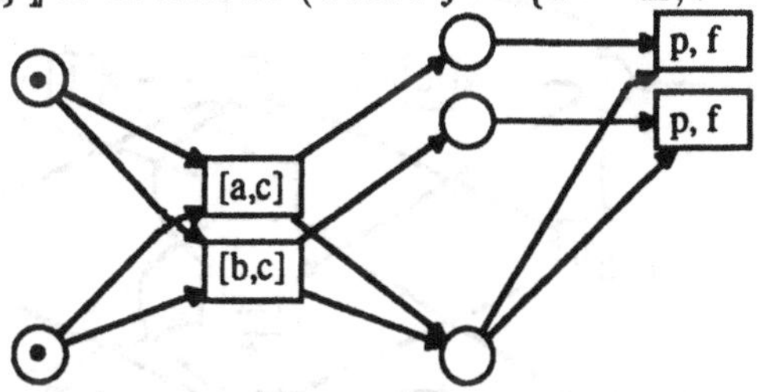

□

The definition of the recursion operator for safe nets is considerably less complex than that for transition systems, namely the set "SF" and the extra set of extensions "E_+" are not needed, and "D_+" is much simpler.

This simplification is possible because of the assumption that the recursive body starts with a τ. A similar simplification would be possible for the recursion operator on transition systems with this assumption.

Definition 4.15 (recursion operator for extended safe nets)
Let $r \in Idf$, and $N = \langle S, D, E, Z \rangle$ be some extended safe net, where $\bot \notin E(r)$.
Define $F := \{id \cdot f_1 \cdot \ldots \cdot f_n \mid n \geq 0, f_1, \ldots, f_n \in E(r)\}$.
For $f \in F$ let $\langle S_f, D_f, E_f, Z_f \rangle := Nf$, where for $f \neq g \quad S_f \cap S_g = \emptyset$.
Define $\quad rec\, r.\tau N \; :=$

$$Reach\Big(\Big\langle\, \boldsymbol{S} \cup \{z\},\ \mathbb{D} \cup D_+ \cup \{\langle \{z\}, \tau, Z_{id} \rangle\},\ \mathbb{E} - (\mathcal{P}(\boldsymbol{S}) \times \{r\} \times Fun),\ \{z\} \Big\rangle \Big)$$

where $\qquad \boldsymbol{S} = \bigcup_{f \in F} S_f, \quad \mathbb{D} = \bigcup_{f \in F} D_f, \quad \mathbb{E} = \bigcup_{f \in F} E_f,$

$z \notin \boldsymbol{S}$ is a new place, and $\quad D_+ = \{\, \langle M, \tau, Z_g \rangle \mid \langle M, r, g \rangle \in \mathbb{E} \}$. □

Examples 1. (reworking the example on page 68 with nets)
Let $P :\equiv rec\, p.\tau abp$, and $Q :\equiv P\{b \mapsto c\}$.

$\mathcal{N}[\![P]\!]$ is 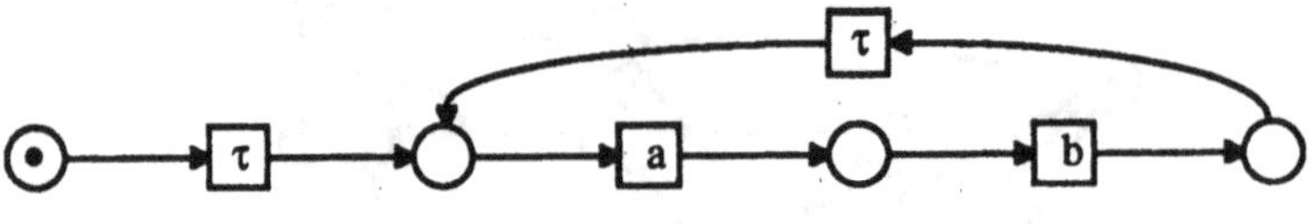

$\mathcal{N}[\![Q]\!]$ is 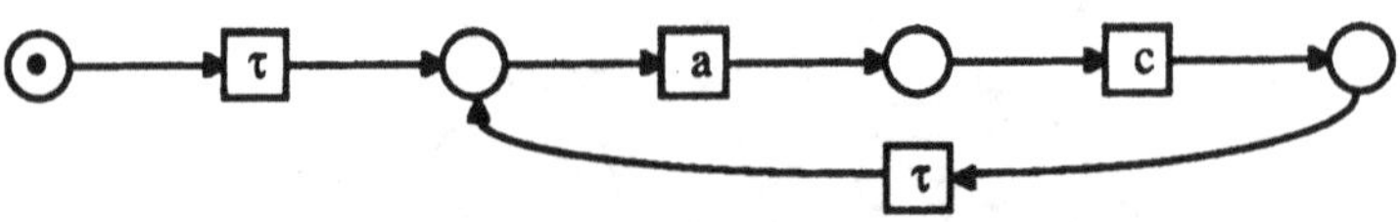

Now consider $P \parallel_a Q \equiv (P \nparallel Q)g$, where g is as in the example starting on page 68. $\quad \mathcal{N}[\![P \nparallel Q]\!]$ is

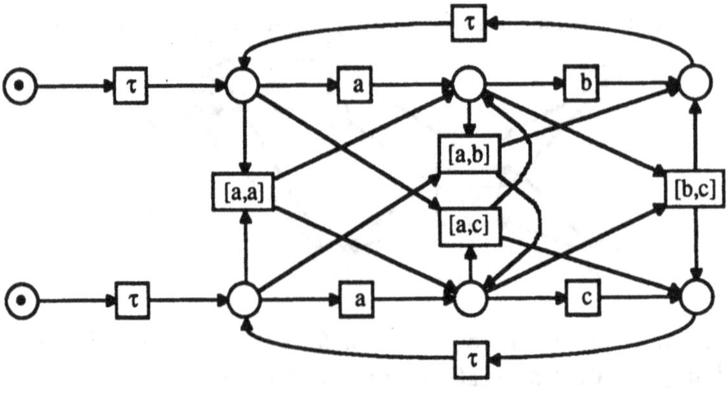

Finally $\mathcal{N}[\![P \parallel_a Q]\!]$ is

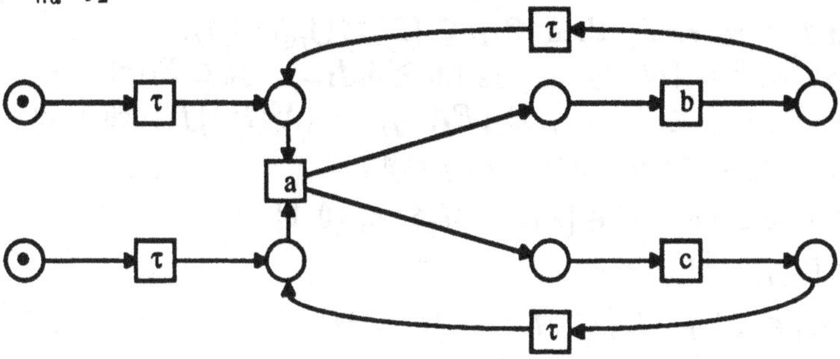

2. (continuing the example on page 103) Let $P :\equiv a\,nil + b\,nil$, $Q :\equiv cp$. Then $\mathcal{N}[\![rec\,p.\tau(\,(P \nparallel Q)\text{–}\{a,b,c\}\,)]\!]$ is

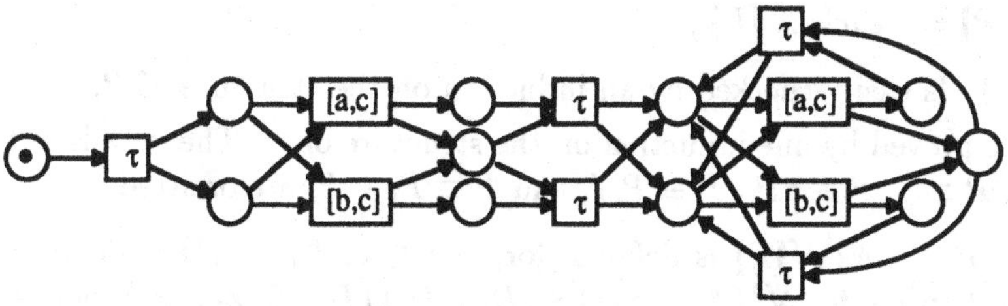

3. $\mathcal{N}[\![rec\,p.\tau\Big(((ac\,nil \parallel_c bc\,nil) \parallel_c cdp) \setminus c\Big)]\!]$ is

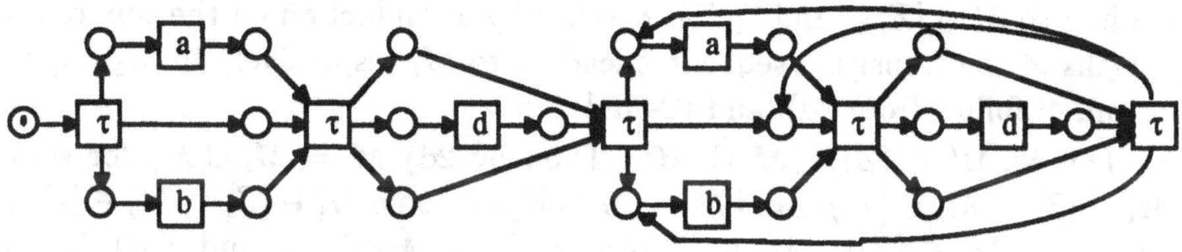

□

The following proposition collects a number of properties of the nets constructed for terms. In particular it is shown that they are safe (3). Most important for the proof of the consistency theorem (4.17) is 6.

Proposition 4.16 Let $P \in terms$. If $\mathcal{N}[\![P]\!] = \langle S, D, E, Z\rangle$ is defined, then

1. $Z \neq \emptyset$, $\quad \forall t \in D:\ \bullet t \neq \emptyset \neq t\bullet$, $\quad \forall t \in E:\ \bullet t \neq \emptyset$.
2. Assume for $i \in \{1,2\}$ that $\mathcal{N}[\![P_i]\!] = \langle S_i, D_i, E_i, Z_i\rangle$ and $S_1 \cap S_2 = \emptyset$,
   (a) if $P \equiv aP_1$ for $a \in \{\tau\} \cup Vis$, then $[Z\rangle_D = \{Z\} \cup [Z_1\rangle_1$
   (b) if $P \equiv P_1 f$ for $f \in Fun$, then $[Z\rangle_D \subseteq [Z_1\rangle_1$
   (c) if $P \equiv P_1 + P_2$, then $[Z\rangle_D \subseteq \{Z\} \cup [Z_1\rangle_1 \cup [Z_2\rangle_2$

(d) if $P \equiv P_1 \nmid P_2$, then $[Z\rangle_D = \{M_1 \cup M_2 \mid M_1 \in [Z_1\rangle_1 \wedge M_2 \in [Z_2\rangle_2\}$

(e) if $P \equiv rec\, r.\tau P_1$, then $[Z\rangle_D \subseteq \{Z\} \cup \bigcup_{f \in F}[Z_f\rangle_f$, where $F = \{id \cdot f_1 \cdot \ldots \cdot f_n \mid n \geq 0, f_1, \ldots, f_n \in E_1(r)\}$, and for $f \in F$ $\langle S_f, D_f, E_f, Z_f\rangle = \big(\mathcal{N}[P_1]\big)f$ such that for $f \neq g$ $S_f \cap S_g = \emptyset$ and $Z \cap \bigcup_{f \in F} S_f = \emptyset$.

3. $\mathcal{N}[P]$ is safe, i.e. $\forall M \in [Z\rangle_D : M(S) \subseteq \{0,1\}$
4. $\forall M \in [Z\rangle_D : M \neq \emptyset$
5. $\forall M_1, M_2 \in [Z\rangle_D : M_1 \subseteq M_2 \Rightarrow M_1 = M_2$
6. $\forall t \in E : \forall M \in [Z\rangle_D : \bullet t \subseteq M \Rightarrow M = \bullet t$
7. $\forall M \in [Z\rangle_D :$ M is finite
8. $\mathcal{N}[P] = Reach(\mathcal{N}[\![P]\!])$

Proof 1. Is easily checked by an induction on the structure of P.

2. - 6. are proved by one induction on the structure of P. The details of the cases $P \equiv nil$, $P \equiv p$, $P \equiv aP_1$, $P \equiv P_1 f$, and $P \equiv P_1 + P_2$ are omitted.

<u>$P \equiv P_1 \nmid P_2$</u> As $\mathcal{N}[P]$ is defined, for all $i \in \{1,2\}$ $\mathcal{N}[P_i]$ is defined and (by ind. hyp.) safe. $\mathcal{N}[\![P]\!] = \langle S_1 \cup S_2, D_1 \cup D_2 \cup D_+, E, Z_1 \cup Z_2\rangle$, where D_+ and E are as in Definition 4.14.

2d) "$\subseteq$" is checked by an induction on the length of the transition sequence leading to $M \in [Z\rangle_D$, and "$\supseteq$" is checked by an induction on the sum of the lengths of the transition sequences leading to M_1 respectively to M_2.
3. and 4. follow from 2d), and the ind. hyp.

5. Let $M, M' \in [Z\rangle_D$, $M \subseteq M'$. Then by 2d) $M = M_1 \cup M_2$ for some $M_1 \in [Z_1\rangle_1$, $M_2 \in [Z_2\rangle_2$, and $M' = M_1' \cup M_2'$ for some $M_1' \in [Z_1\rangle_1$, $M_2' \in [Z_2\rangle_2$. As for all $\bar{M}_1 \in [Z_1\rangle_1$, $\bar{M}_2 \in [Z_2\rangle_2 : \bar{M}_1 \subseteq S_1$, $\bar{M}_2 \subseteq S_2$, and $S_1 \cap S_2 = \emptyset$ we know that $\bar{M}_1 \cap \bar{M}_2 = \emptyset$. Hence $M_1 \subseteq M_1'$ and $M_2 \subseteq M_2'$. By ind. hyp. $M_1 = M_1'$ and $M_2 = M_2'$, hence $M = M'$.

6. Let $t \in E$, $M \in [Z\rangle_D$, $\bullet t \subseteq M$. Then by 2d) $M = M_1 \cup M_2$ for some $M_1 \in [Z_1\rangle_1$, $M_2 \in [Z_2\rangle_2$. W.l.o.g. $t = \langle M_1' \cup M_2', p, f\rangle$ such that $\langle M_1', p, g\rangle \in E_1$ and $M_2' \in [Z_2\rangle_2$. And as $\bullet t \subseteq M$ we conclude $M_1' \subseteq M_1 \wedge M_2' \subseteq M_2$. By ind. hyp. $M_1' = M_1$, and by 5. $M_2' = M_2$, hence $\bullet t = M$.

<u>$P \equiv rec\, r.\tau P_1$</u> for $r \in Idf$. As $\mathcal{N}[\![P]\!]$ is defined, $\mathcal{N}[P_1]$ is defined and $\perp \notin E_1(r)$. Let F and $\langle S_f, D_f, E_f, Z_f\rangle$ be as in the claim of 2e).
By the case "$P \equiv P_1 f$" follows

$$\text{for all } f \in F \quad 2.\text{ - }6. \text{ holds for } (\mathcal{N}[\![P_1]\!])f. \qquad (*)$$

$\mathcal{N}[P] = Reach(\langle \mathbf{S} \cup \{z\}, \mathbb{D} \cup D_+ \cup \{\langle \{z\}, \tau, Z_{id}\rangle\}, \mathbb{E} - (\mathcal{P}(\mathbf{S}) \times \{r\} \times Fun), \{z\}\rangle)$ where $z \notin \mathbf{S} = \bigcup_{f \in F} S_f$, $\mathbb{D} = \bigcup_{f \in F} D_f$, $\mathbb{E} = \bigcup_{f \in F} E_f$ and $D_+ = \{ \langle M, \tau, Z_g\rangle \mid \langle M, r, g\rangle \in \mathbb{E}\}$.

2e) By Lemma 4.11 1. $M \in [Z\rangle_D$ iff $\exists u \in (\mathbb{D} \cup D_+ \cup \{\langle\{z\}, \tau, Z_{id}\rangle\})^* :$ $Z[u\rangle M$. We perform an inner induction on u.

<u>$u = \varepsilon$</u> Then $M = Z$.

<u>$u = u't$</u> Then $Z[u'\rangle M'[t\rangle M$, for some M'. By inner ind. hyp. $M' \in \{Z\} \cup \bigcup_{f \in F}[Z_f\rangle_f$. If $t = \langle\{z\}, \tau, Z_{id}\rangle$, then $M' = \{z\}$, hence $M = Z_{id} \in [Z_{id}\rangle_{id}$. Else if $t \in D_f$ for some $f \in F$, then as $\emptyset \neq \bullet t \subseteq S_f$ and $\bullet t \subseteq M'$ by the disjointness conditions $M' \in [Z_f\rangle_f$, and then $M \in [Z_f\rangle_f$.
Else if $t \in D_+$, then $t = \langle \bar{M}, \tau, Z_g\rangle$ for some $g \in F$ and $\langle \bar{M}, r, g\rangle \in E_f$ for some $f \in F$. As $M'[t\rangle M$ we know that $\bullet t = \bar{M} \subseteq M'$. Furthermore $\bullet t \neq \emptyset$, hence $M' \in [Z_f\rangle_f$. By 6. for $(\mathcal{N}[\![P_1]\!])f$ (see $(*)$), $\bullet t = M'$. Thus $M = Z_g$, and clearly $Z_g \in [Z_g\rangle_g$. □ 2e)

3. and 4. follow from 2e) and $(*)$.

5. follows from 2e), 4., the disjointness conditions, and $(*)$.

6. follows from 1., 2e), the disjointness conditions, and $(*)$. □ 2. - 6.

7. and 8. Follow by an induction on the structure of P using 2. respectively Lemma 4.11 3. Proposition 4.16 □

4.3 Consistency, definedness, and finiteness

The main result of this section given in the next theorem shows that for any term, if its extended safe net as constructed in this chapter is defined, then its extended transition system as constructed in the previous chapter is defined and isomorphic to the transition system associated with the net.

With the help of this theorem the consistency immediately follows (Corollary 4.18). Furthermore the net is finite if and only if the transition system is finite. For $P \in$ *qterms* we show that if $\mathcal{F}[\![P]\!]$ is defined, then $\mathcal{N}[\![P]\!]$ is defined (Proposition 4.19). Hence as a corollary (4.20) we can carry over the results of Theorems 3.29 and 3.31 for qterms.

Theorem 4.17 For $P \in$ *terms*. If $\mathcal{N}[\![P]\!]$ is defined, then

$$\mathcal{F}[\![P]\!] \text{ is defined, and } \mathcal{F}[\![P]\!] \cong \mathit{Transys}\big(\mathcal{N}[\![P]\!]\big).$$

Proof Induction on the structure of P. The cases <u>$P \equiv nil$</u>, and <u>$P \equiv p$</u> for $p \in Idf$ are trivial. For the other cases we use the following denotations (for $i \in \{1, 2\}$ and $P_i \in$ *terms*). $\mathcal{F}[\![P_i]\!] = \langle \bar{S}_i, \bar{D}_i, \bar{E}_i, \bar{z}_i\rangle$, $\mathcal{N}[\![P_i]\!] = \langle S_i, D_i, E_i, Z_i\rangle$, and $\mathit{Transys}(\mathcal{N}[\![P_i]\!]) = \langle [Z_i\rangle_i, D_i', E_i', Z_i\rangle$, where

$$\begin{aligned} D_i' &= \{\langle M_1, l(t), M_2\rangle \mid M_1 \in [Z_i\rangle_i \wedge t \in D_i \wedge M_1[t\rangle M_2\} \\ E_i' &= \{\langle M, p, f\rangle \mid M \in [Z_i\rangle_i \wedge \langle M', p, f\rangle \in E_i \wedge M' \subseteq M\}. \end{aligned}$$

Furthermore we use φ_i to denote a bijection $\varphi_i : \bar{S}_i \to [Z_i\rangle_i$ such that

$$(\ast\mathbf{1})\quad \varphi_i(\bar{z}_i) = Z_i$$
$$(\ast\mathbf{2})\quad \forall s_1, s_2 \in \bar{S}_i, a \in Act: \quad \langle s_1, a, s_2\rangle \in \bar{D}_i \text{ iff } \langle \varphi_i(s_1), a, \varphi_i(s_2)\rangle \in D_i'$$
$$(\ast\mathbf{3})\quad \forall s \in \bar{S}_i, p \in Idf, f \in Fun_\perp: \quad \langle s, p, f\rangle \in \bar{E}_i \text{ iff } \langle \varphi_i(s), p, f\rangle \in E_i'.$$

<u>$P \equiv aP_1$</u> for $a \in Vis \cup \{\tau\}$. Let $\mathcal{N}[\![P]\!]$ be defined, then $\mathcal{N}[\![P_1]\!]$ is defined, and $\mathcal{N}[\![P]\!] = \langle S_1 \cup \{z\}, D, E_1, \{z\}\rangle$ where $z \notin S_1$, and $D = D_1 \cup \{\langle\{z\}, a, Z_1\rangle\}$. By ind. hyp. $\mathcal{F}[\![P_1]\!]$ is defined and there exists a bijection $\varphi_1 : \bar{S}_1 \to [Z_1\rangle_1$ such that $(\ast\mathbf{1})$-$(\ast\mathbf{3})$ hold. Let $\bar{z}$ be the starting state of $\mathcal{F}[\![P]\!]$.

Define $\varphi : \bar{S}_1 \cup \{\bar{z}\} \to [\{z\}\rangle_D$ such that $\varphi(s) := \begin{cases} \{z\} & \text{if } s = \bar{z} \\ \varphi_1(s) & \text{if } s \in \bar{S}_1. \end{cases}$

As $[\{z\}\rangle_D = \{\{z\}\} \cup [Z_1\rangle_1$ we conclude that φ is well-defined and bijective. And one easily checks that φ fulfills the isomorphism properties.

<u>$P \equiv P_1 f$</u> for $f \in Fun$. Let $\mathcal{N}[\![P]\!]$ be defined, then $\mathcal{N}[\![P_1]\!]$ is defined, and $\mathcal{N}[\![P]\!] = Reach(\langle S_1, D, E, Z_1\rangle)$ for some D and E. By Lemma 4.11 2. the set of states of $Transys(\mathcal{N}[\![P]\!])$ is $[Z_1\rangle_D$. By ind. hyp. $\mathcal{F}[\![P_1]\!]$ is defined and there exists a bijection $\varphi_1 : \bar{S}_1 \to [Z_1\rangle_1$ such that $(\ast\mathbf{1})$-$(\ast\mathbf{3})$ hold. Let $\hat{S}$ be the set of states of $\mathcal{F}[\![P]\!]$. Define $\varphi : \hat{S} \to [Z_1\rangle_D$ where $\varphi(s) := \varphi_1(s)$. One checks with inductions on the length of the transition sequences leading to the state s respectively to the marking M that

a) $\forall s \in \hat{S} : \varphi_1(s) \in [Z_1\rangle_D$ (this proves that φ is well-defined)

b) $\forall M \in [Z_1\rangle_D : M \in [Z_1\rangle_1 \wedge \exists s \in \hat{S} : \varphi(s) = M$ (this proves that φ is surjective).

Injectivity of φ follows from the injectivity of φ_1, hence φ is a bijection.

The three isomorphism properties for φ follow from $(\ast\mathbf{1})$-$(\ast\mathbf{3})$.

<u>$P \equiv P_1 + P_2$</u> Let $\mathcal{N}[\![P]\!]$ be defined. Then $\mathcal{N}[\![P_i]\!]$ is defined for $i \in \{1,2\}$, and $\mathcal{N}[\![P]\!] = Reach(\langle S_1 \cup S_2 \cup \{z\}, D, E, \{z\}\rangle)$ for some D and E. By Lemma 4.11 2. the set of states of $Transys(\mathcal{N}[\![P]\!])$ is $[\{z\}\rangle_D$. By ind. hyp. $\forall i \in \{1,2\}$: $\mathcal{F}[\![P_i]\!]$ is defined and there exists a bijection $\varphi_i : \bar{S}_i \to [Z_i\rangle_i$ such that $(\ast\mathbf{1})$-$(\ast\mathbf{3})$ hold. Let $\hat{S}$ be the set of states of $\mathcal{F}[\![P]\!]$, and $\bar{z}$ be its initial state.

Define $\varphi : \hat{S} \to [\{z\}\rangle_D$ where $\varphi(s) = \begin{cases} \{z\} & \text{if } s = \bar{z} \\ \varphi_1(s) & \text{if } s \in \bar{S}_1 \\ \varphi_2(s) & \text{if } s \in \bar{S}_2. \end{cases}$

Using Prop. 4.16 one easily checks that φ is the wanted isomorphism.

<u>$P \equiv P_1 \nmid P_2$</u> Let $\mathcal{N}[\![P]\!]$ be defined. Then $\mathcal{N}[\![P_1]\!], \mathcal{N}[\![P_2]\!]$ are defined, $S_1 \cap S_2 = \emptyset$, $\mathcal{N}[\![P]\!] = \langle S_1 \cup S_2,\ D,\ E,\ Z_1 \cup Z_2\rangle$, and the set of states of $Transys(\mathcal{N}[\![P]\!])$ is $[Z_1 \cup Z_2\rangle_D$. By ind. hyp. $\forall i \in \{1,2\}$: $\mathcal{F}[\![P_i]\!]$ is defined, $\bar{S}_1 \cap \bar{S}_2 = \emptyset$, and there exists a bijection $\varphi_i : \bar{S}_i \to [Z_i\rangle_i$ such that $(\ast\mathbf{1})$-$(\ast\mathbf{3})$ hold. Moreover $\mathcal{F}[\![P]\!]$ is defined and equals $\left\langle \bar{S}_1 \times \bar{S}_2, \bar{D}, \bar{E}, \langle \bar{z}_1, \bar{z}_2\rangle \right\rangle$.

Define $\varphi : \hat{S}_1 \times \hat{S}_2 \rightarrow [Z_1 \cup Z_2\rangle_D$ such that $\varphi(\langle s_1, s_2\rangle) := \varphi_1(s_1) \cup \varphi_2(s_2)$. By Proposition 4.16 $[Z_1 \cup Z_2\rangle_D = \{M_1 \cup M_2 \mid M_1 \in [Z_1\rangle_1 \wedge M_2 \in [Z_2\rangle_2\}$. Hence φ is a bijection.

The three isomorphism properties for φ are proved from (*1)-(*3) by tedious but straightforward calculations which are omitted here.

$\underline{P \equiv rec\, r.\tau P_1}$ for $r \in Idf$. The proof for this case is given in full detail. As $\mathcal{N}[\![P]\!]$ is defined, $\mathcal{N}[\![P_1]\!]$ is defined and $\perp \notin E_1(r)$.
Let $F = \{id \cdot f_1 \cdot \ldots \cdot f_n \mid n \geq 0, f_1, \ldots, f_n \in E_1(r)\}$, and for $f \in F$ let $\langle S_f, D_f, E_f, Z_f\rangle = \big(\mathcal{N}[\![P_1]\!]\big)f$, where for $f \neq g$ $S_f \cap S_g = \emptyset$.
Then $\mathcal{N}[\![P]\!] = Reach(\langle \mathbf{S} \cup \{z\},\ D,\ \mathbb{E} - (\mathcal{P}(\mathbf{S}) \times \{r\} \times Fun),\ \{z\}\rangle)$, where $D = \mathbb{D} \cup D_+ \cup \{\langle\{z\}, \tau, Z_{id}\rangle\}$, $\mathbf{S} = \bigcup_{f\in F} S_f$, $\mathbb{D} = \bigcup_{f\in F} D_f$, $\mathbb{E} = \bigcup_{f\in F} E_f$, and $z \notin \mathbf{S}$, and $D_+ = \{\, \langle M, \tau, Z_g\rangle \mid \langle M, r, g\rangle \in \mathbb{E}\}$.
By Lemma 4.11 2. $Transys(\mathcal{N}[\![P]\!]) = \big\langle [\{z\}\rangle_D, \hat{D}, \hat{E}, \{z\}\big\rangle$, where

$$\begin{aligned} \hat{D} &= \{\langle M_1, l(t), M_2\rangle \mid M_1 \in [\{z\}\rangle_D \wedge t \in D \wedge M_1[t\rangle M_2\} \\ \hat{E} &= \{\langle M, p, f\rangle \mid \langle M', p, f\rangle \in \mathbb{E} \wedge p \neq r \wedge M' \subseteq M \in [\{z\}\rangle_D\}. \end{aligned}$$

By ind. hyp. $\mathcal{F}[\![P_1]\!]$ is defined, and there exists a bijection $\varphi_1 : \bar{S}_1 \rightarrow [Z_1\rangle_1$ such that (*1)-(*3) hold. And then $\mathcal{F}[\![\tau P_1]\!] = \tau\mathcal{F}[\![P_1]\!] = \langle \bar{S}_1 \cup \{\bar{z}\}, \bar{D}_1 \cup \{\langle \bar{z}, \tau, \bar{z}_1\rangle\}, \bar{E}_1, \bar{z}\rangle$ for $\bar{z} \notin \bar{S}_1$. By (*3) $\bar{E}_1(r) = E_1(r) \not\ni \perp$, hence $\mathcal{F}[\![rec\, r.\tau P_1]\!]$ is defined. Note that $\bar{E}_1(\bar{z}) = \emptyset$, hence $\{id \cdot f_1 \cdot \ldots \cdot f_n \mid n \geq 0, f_1, \ldots, f_n \in \bar{E}_1(r)\} = F$ and $\{id \cdot f_1 \cdot \ldots \cdot f_n \mid n \geq 0, f_1, \ldots, f_n \in \bar{E}_1(\bar{z}, r)\} = \{id\}$.
Furthermore for $f \in F$ let $\langle \bar{S}_f, \bar{D}_f, \bar{E}_f, \bar{z}_f\rangle := (\mathcal{F}[\![P_1]\!])f$, and then $(\tau\mathcal{F}[\![P_1]\!])f = \langle \bar{S}_f \cup \{\bar{\bar{z}}_f\}, \bar{D}_f \cup \{\langle \bar{\bar{z}}_f, \tau, \bar{z}_f\rangle\}, \bar{E}_f, \bar{\bar{z}}_f\rangle$ where $\bar{\bar{z}}_f \notin \bar{S}_f$ and $f \neq g \Rightarrow (\bar{S}_f \cup \{\bar{\bar{z}}_f\}) \cap (\bar{S}_g \cup \{\bar{\bar{z}}_g\}) = \emptyset$.
By definition $\mathcal{F}[\![rec\, r.\tau P_1]\!] = Reach(\langle \bar{\mathbf{S}}, \bar{\mathbb{D}} \cup \bar{D}_+, \bar{\mathbb{E}} - (\bar{\mathbf{S}} \times \{r\} \times Fun), \bar{\bar{z}}_{id}\rangle)$, where $\bar{\mathbf{S}} = \bigcup_{f\in F}(\bar{S}_f \cup \{\bar{\bar{z}}_f\})$, $\bar{\mathbb{D}} = \bigcup_{f\in F}(\bar{D}_f \cup \{\langle \bar{\bar{z}}_f, \tau, \bar{z}_f\rangle\})$, $\bar{\mathbb{E}} = \bigcup_{f\in F} \bar{E}_f$, and $\bar{D}_+ = \{\langle s, \tau, \bar{z}_g\rangle \mid \langle s, r, g\rangle \in \bar{\mathbb{E}}\}$. Note for $\bar{D}_+$ that "$SF = \{id\}$", and then $\langle \bar{\bar{z}}_g, a, s'\rangle \in \bar{\mathbb{D}}$ implies $a = \tau$ and $s' = \bar{z}_g$. Furthermore note that "E_+" as in the Definition 3.8 is empty, as for all $g \in F : \bar{\mathbb{E}}(\bar{\bar{z}}_g) = \emptyset$.
And then we conclude $\mathcal{F}[\![rec\, r.\tau P_1]\!] =$
$\big\langle \hat{S}, (\bar{\mathbb{D}} \cup \bar{D}_+) \cap (\hat{S} \times Act \times \hat{S}), (\bar{\mathbb{E}} - (\bar{\mathbf{S}} \times \{r\} \times Fun)) \cap (\hat{S} \times Idf \times Fun_\perp), \bar{\bar{z}}_{id}\big\rangle$, where $\hat{S} = \{s \in \bar{\mathbf{S}} \mid \exists w \in Act^* : \bar{\bar{z}}_{id} \xrightarrow{\;w\;}_{\bar{\mathbb{D}} \cup \bar{D}_+} s\}$.

For all $f \in F$: $Transys(\mathcal{N}[\![P_1]\!]f) = \big\langle [Z_f\rangle_f, D'_f, E'_f, Z_f\big\rangle$ where

$$\begin{aligned} D'_f &= \{\langle M_1, l(t), M_2\rangle \mid M_1 \in [Z_f\rangle_f \wedge t \in D_f \wedge M_1[t\rangle M_2\} \\ E'_f &= \{\langle M, p, g\rangle \mid \langle M', p, g\rangle \in E_f \wedge M' \subseteq M \in [Z_f\rangle_f\}. \end{aligned}$$

And by the case "$P \equiv P_1 f$" we know that there exists $\varphi_f : \bar{S}_f \rightarrow [Z_f\rangle_f$ such that

(†1) $\varphi_f(\bar{z}_f) = Z_f$
(†2) $\forall s_1, s_2 \in \bar{S}_f, a \in Act :\quad \langle s_1, a, s_2\rangle \in \bar{D}_f$ iff $\langle \varphi_f(s_1), a, \varphi_f(s_2)\rangle \in D'_f$
(†3) $\forall s \in \bar{S}_f, p \in Idf, g \in Fun_\perp :\ \langle s, p, g\rangle \in \bar{E}_f$ iff $\langle \varphi_f(s), p, g\rangle \in E'_f$.

Define $\varphi : \hat{S} \to [\{z\}\rangle_D$ where $\varphi(s) := \begin{cases} \varphi_f(s) & \text{if } s \in \bar{S}_f \text{ for some } f \in F \\ \{z\} & \text{if } s = \bar{\bar{z}}_{id}. \end{cases}$

We will prove that

a) $\forall s \in \hat{S} : s = \bar{\bar{z}}_{id} \vee \exists f \in F : s \in \bar{S}_f \wedge \varphi_f(s) \in [\{z\}\rangle_D$ (showing that φ is totally defined)

b) $\forall M \in [\{z\}\rangle_D : \exists s \in \hat{S} : \varphi(s) = M$ (showing that φ is surjective)

And then the injectivity follows from the injectivity of φ_f (for all $f \in F$) and the disjointness conditions. Hence φ is a bijection.

Proof of a) Let $s \in \hat{S}$, then for some $w \in Act^* : \bar{\bar{z}}_{id} -w\to_{\bar{\mathbb{D}} \cup \bar{D}_+} s$. We perform an induction on w.

<u>$w = \varepsilon$</u> Then $s = \bar{\bar{z}}_{id}$.

<u>$w = w'a$</u> Then for some $s' \in \hat{S} : \bar{\bar{z}}_{id} -w'\to_{\bar{\mathbb{D}} \cup \bar{D}_+} s' -a\to_{\bar{\mathbb{D}} \cup \bar{D}_+} s$. By ind. hyp. $s' = \bar{\bar{z}}_{id} \vee \exists f \in F : s' \in \bar{S}_f \wedge \varphi_f(s') \in [\{z\}\rangle_D$.
If $s' = \bar{\bar{z}}_{id}$, then $a = \tau$ and $s = \bar{z}_{id} \in \bar{S}_{id}$. Moreover $\varphi_{id}(\bar{z}_{id}) = Z_{id}$ by (†**1**). Clearly $Z_{id} \in [\{z\}\rangle_D$.
Else let for $f \in F : s' \in \bar{S}_f \wedge \varphi_f(s') \in [\{z\}\rangle_D$. If $\langle s', a, s\rangle \in \bar{\mathbb{D}}$, then $\langle s', a, s\rangle \in \bar{D}_f$. By (†**2**) $\langle \varphi_f(s'), a, \varphi_f(s)\rangle \in D'_f$. And then $\varphi_f(s) \in [\{z\}\rangle_D$. Else $\langle s', a, s\rangle \in \bar{D}_+$, then $\langle s', r, g\rangle \in \bar{E}_f$ for some $g \in F$ and $\langle s', a, s\rangle = \langle s', \tau, \bar{z}_g\rangle$. Then clearly $\bar{z}_g \in \bar{S}_g$ and $\varphi_g(s) = Z_g$. We want to show $Z_g \in [\{z\}\rangle_D$. By (†**3**) $\langle \varphi_f(s'), r, g\rangle \in E'_f$, hence $\exists M' \subseteq \varphi_f(s') : \langle M', r, g\rangle \in E_f$. As $\varphi_f(s') \in [Z_f\rangle_f$, by Proposition 4.16 6. $M' = \varphi_f(s')$. And then $\langle \varphi_f(s'), \tau, Z_g\rangle \in D_+$, hence as $\varphi_f(s') \in [\{z\}\rangle_D$ we conclude $Z_g \in [\{z\}\rangle_D$. □ a)

Proof of b) Let $M \in [\{z\}\rangle_D$, then $\exists u \in D^* : \{z\}[u\rangle M$. Induction on u:

<u>$u = \varepsilon$</u> Then $M = \{z\}$, and $\bar{\bar{z}}_{id} \in \hat{S}$, and $\varphi(\bar{\bar{z}}_{id}) = \{z\}$.

<u>$u = u't$</u> Then for some $M' \in [\{z\}\rangle_D : \{z\}[u'\rangle M'[t\rangle M$. By ind. hyp. $\exists s' \in \hat{S} : \varphi(s') = M'$. By a) $s' \in \{\bar{\bar{z}}_{id}\} \cup \bigcup_{f \in F} \bar{S}_f$.
If $s' = \bar{\bar{z}}_{id}$, then $M' = \{z\}$. And the only transition $t \in D$ such that $\{z\}[t\rangle M$ is $t = \langle \{z\}, \tau, Z_{id}\rangle$, hence $M = Z_{id}$. By (†**1**) $\varphi_{id}(\bar{z}_{id}) = Z_{id}$, and clearly $\bar{z}_{id} \in \hat{S}$. Hence $\varphi(\bar{z}_{id}) = Z_{id}$.
Else $s' \in \bar{S}_f$ for some $f \in F$. Then $\varphi_f(s') = M' \in [Z_f\rangle_f$. $t \in D$, but $\{z\} \not\subseteq M' \subseteq S_f$, and for all $g \in F : g \neq f \Rightarrow \forall t' \in D_g : \bullet t' \not\subseteq M'$, as $S_g \cap S_f = \emptyset$. Hence $t \in D_f$ or $t \in D_+$.
If $t \in D_f$, then $M \in [Z_f\rangle_f$. And as φ_f is surjective $\exists s \in \bar{S}_f : \varphi_f(s) = M$. Furthermore $\langle \varphi_f(s'), l(t), \varphi_f(s)\rangle \in D'_f$, hence by (†**2**) $\langle s', l(t), s\rangle \in \bar{D}_f$, this implies $s \in \hat{S}$ and $\varphi(s) = M$.
Otherwise $t \in D_+$, i.e. $t = \langle M'', \tau, Z_g\rangle$ for some $\langle M'', r, g\rangle \in E_{\bar{f}}$ for some $\bar{f} \in F$. As by Proposition 4.16 1. $M'' \neq \emptyset$ and $M'' \subseteq M' \subseteq S_f$ we conclude that $\bar{f} = f$. As $M' \in [Z_f\rangle_f$ by Proposition 4.16 6. $M'' = M'$. Thus $M'[t\rangle M$

implies $M = Z_g$, and clearly $g \in F$. And then $\varphi_g(\bar{z}_g) = Z_g$. We have to show that $\bar{z}_g \in \hat{S}$. Clearly $\langle \varphi_f(s'), r, g\rangle \in E'_f$, hence by (†3) $\langle s', r, g\rangle \in \bar{E}_f$. Hence $\langle s', \tau, \bar{z}_g\rangle \in D_+$, this implies $\bar{z}_g \in \hat{S}$. □ b)

We are now ready to prove the three isomorphism properties.

1) Clearly $\varphi(\bar{\bar{z}}_{id}) = \{z\}$.

2) Let $s_1, s_2 \in \hat{S}$, $a \in Act$. "⇒" Let $\langle s_1, a, s_2\rangle \in \bar{\bar{D}} \cup \bar{D}_+$. If $\langle s_1, a, s_2\rangle \in \bar{\bar{D}}$, then by a) either $\langle s_1, a, s_2\rangle = \langle \bar{\bar{z}}_{id}, \tau, \bar{z}_{id}\rangle$ and then $\varphi(s_1) = \{z\}$, $\varphi(s_2) = Z_{id}$ and $\langle\{z\}, \tau, Z_{id}\rangle \in \hat{D}$; or $\langle s_1, a, s_2\rangle \in \bar{D}_f$ for some $f \in Fun$. Then $\langle \varphi(s_1), a, \varphi(s_2)\rangle \in D'_f$ (by (†2)) and then $\exists t \in D_f \subseteq D : \varphi(s_1)[t\rangle\varphi(s_2) \wedge l(t) = a$.
Hence $\langle \varphi(s_1), a, \varphi(s_2)\rangle \in \hat{D}$.
Else if $\langle s_1, a, s_2\rangle \in \bar{D}_+$, then $\langle s_1, a, s_2\rangle = \langle s_1, \tau, \bar{z}_g\rangle$ for $\langle s_1, r, g\rangle \in \bar{E}_f$ for some $f, g \in Fun$ and $s_1 \in \bar{S}_f$. Clearly $\varphi(s_2) = Z_g$. By (†3) $\langle \varphi(s_1), r, g\rangle \in E'_f$ and then $\exists M' \subseteq \varphi(s_1) : \langle M', r, g\rangle \in E_f$. By Proposition 4.16 $M' = \varphi(s_1)$. Hence $t' := \langle \varphi(s_1), \tau, Z_g\rangle \in D_+$. And as $\varphi(s_1)[t'\rangle Z_g$ we conclude $\langle \varphi(s_1), \tau, \varphi(s_2)\rangle \in \hat{D}$.
"⇐" Let $\langle \varphi(s_1), a, \varphi(s_2)\rangle \in \hat{D}$. Then $\exists t \in D : l(t) = a \wedge \varphi(s_1)[t\rangle\varphi(s_2)$.
If $t = \langle\{z\}, \tau, Z_{id}\rangle$, then $\varphi(s_1) = \{z\}$, $\varphi(s_2) = Z_{id}$ and $s_1 = \bar{\bar{z}}_{id}$, $s_2 = \bar{z}_{id}$, and clearly $\langle \bar{\bar{z}}_{id}, \tau, \bar{z}_{id}\rangle \in \bar{\bar{D}}$.
Else if $t \in D_f$ for some $f \in F$, then by (†2) $\langle s_1, a, s_2\rangle \in \bar{D}_f \subseteq \bar{\bar{D}}$.
Finally if $t \in D_+$, then $t = \langle M', \tau, Z_g\rangle$ and $\langle M', r, g\rangle \in E_f$ for some $g, f \in F$. Moreover $M' \subseteq \varphi(s_1)$. By Proposition 4.16 1. $M' \neq \emptyset$, hence $\varphi(s_1) \cap S_f \neq \emptyset$, and by the disjointness conditions $\varphi(s_1) \in [Z_f\rangle_f$, and $s_1 \in \bar{S}_f$ and thus by 4.16 6. $M' = \varphi(s_1)$. And $\varphi(s_1) = \varphi_f(s_1)$. Furthermore $\varphi(s_2) = Z_g$, hence $s_2 = \bar{z}_g$. Then $\langle \varphi_f(s_1), r, g\rangle \in E'_f$, by (†3) $\langle s_1, r, g\rangle \in \bar{E}_f$. Hence $\langle s_1, \tau, \bar{z}_g\rangle \in \bar{D}_+$.

3) Let $s \in \hat{S}$, $p \in Idf$, $h \in Fun_\perp$. "⇒" Let $\langle s, p, h\rangle \in \bar{\bar{E}}$ and $p \neq r$. Then for some $f \in F : \langle s, p, h\rangle \in \bar{E}_f$, by (†3) $\langle \varphi_f(s), p, h\rangle \in E'_f$ and then for some $M' \subseteq \varphi_f(s)$: $\langle M', p, h\rangle \in E_f$. By Proposition 4.16 $M' = \varphi_f(s) = \varphi(s)$. Hence $\langle \varphi(s), p, h\rangle \in \mathbb{E} - (\mathcal{P}(\mathbf{S}) \times \{r\} \times Fun)$.
"⇐" Let $\langle \varphi(s), p, h\rangle \in \mathbb{E}$ and $p \neq r$. Then for some $f \in F : \langle \varphi(s), p, h\rangle \in E_f$. By Proposition 4.16 1. $\varphi(s) \neq \emptyset$, furthermore $\varphi(s) \subseteq S_f$, hence $\varphi(s) \in [Z_f\rangle_f$, and thus $s \in \bar{S}_f$ and $\varphi(s) = \varphi_f(s)$. And then $\langle \varphi_f(s), p, h\rangle \in E'_f$ and by (†3) $\langle s, p, h\rangle \in \bar{E}_f$. And hence $\langle s, p, h\rangle \in \bar{\bar{E}} - (\bar{\bar{\mathbf{S}}} \times \{r\} \times Fun)$. Theorem 4.17 □

Corollary 4.18 Let $P \in$ *terms*. If $\mathcal{N}[P] = \langle S, D, E, Z\rangle$ is defined, then $\mathcal{F}[P]$ is defined and

1. $\mathcal{F}[P] \sim Transys(\mathcal{N}[P])$
2. $\mathcal{E}[P] \sim Transys(\mathcal{N}[P])$
3. $\mathcal{T}[P] \sim Transys(\langle S, D, Z\rangle)$
4. $\mathcal{N}[P]$ is finite if and only if $\mathcal{F}[P]$ is finite.

Proof Let $\mathcal{N}[\![P]\!]$ be defined, then by Theorem 4.17 $\mathcal{F}[\![P]\!]$ is defined.
1. Follows by Theorem 4.17 and the generalization of 1.33 for extended transition systems (namely $\cong \subseteq \sim$).
2. Follows by 1. and Theorem 3.26.
3. Let $\mathcal{E}[\![P]\!] = \langle \bar{S}, \bar{D}, \bar{E}, \bar{z} \rangle$ and *Transys*$(\mathcal{N}[\![P]\!]) = \langle S', D', E', z' \rangle$. By 2. clearly $\langle \bar{S}, \bar{D}, \bar{z} \rangle \sim \langle S', D', z' \rangle$. And as $\mathcal{T}[\![P]\!] = \langle \bar{S}, \bar{D}, \bar{z} \rangle$ and *Transys*$(\langle S, D, Z \rangle) = \langle S', D', z' \rangle$, the claim follows.
4. "$\Rightarrow$" If $\mathcal{N}[\![P]\!]$ is finite, *Transys*$(\mathcal{N}[\![P]\!])$ is finite. By Theorem 4.17 $\mathcal{F}[\![P]\!]$ is finite. "$\Leftarrow$" If $\mathcal{F}[\![P]\!]$ is finite, then by 4.17 *Transys*$(\mathcal{N}[\![P]\!])$ is finite. By Proposition 4.16 7. and 8. we can apply Lemma 4.11 4., hence it follows that $\mathcal{N}[\![P]\!]$ is finite.

□

Proposition 4.19 Let $Q \in$ *qterms*. Then

$$\mathcal{F}[\![Q]\!] \text{ is defined if and only if } \mathcal{N}[\![Q]\!] \text{ is defined.}$$

Proof "$\Leftarrow$" Follows from Theorem 4.17. For "$\Rightarrow$" we perform an induction on $Q \in$ *qterms*. The cases $\underline{Q \equiv Q_1 f}$ for $f \in$ *Fun*, and $\underline{Q \equiv Q_1 \nmid Q_2}$ are trivial.
$\underline{Q \equiv P}$ for $P \in$ *singterms*.
We perform an inner induction on $P \in$ *singterms* to prove the stronger claim:
$(*)$ $\mathcal{F}[\![P]\!]$ defined $\Rightarrow \mathcal{N}[\![P]\!] =: \langle S, D, E, Z \rangle$ is defined $\wedge\, \exists z \in S : \ Z = \{z\}$.
The cases $\underline{P \equiv nil}$, $\underline{P \equiv p}$ for $p \in$ *Idf* are trivial.

$\underline{P \equiv aR}$ for $a \in \{\tau\} \cup$ *Vis*, $R \in$ *qterms*. If $\mathcal{F}[\![P]\!]$ is defined, then $\mathcal{F}[\![R]\!]$ is defined and by outer ind. hyp. $\mathcal{N}[\![R]\!]$ is defined. Clearly $\mathcal{N}[\![P]\!]$ is defined and $\exists z \in S : Z = \{z\}$.

$\underline{P \equiv P_1 + P_2}$ for P_1, $P_2 \in$ *singterms*. If $\mathcal{F}[\![P]\!]$ is defined, for both $i \in \{1,2\}$: $\mathcal{F}[\![P_i]\!]$ is defined. By inner ind. hyp. $\forall i \in \{1,2\}$: $\mathcal{N}[\![P_i]\!]$ is defined and $\exists z_i \in S_i : Z_i = \{z_i\}$. Hence $\mathcal{N}[\![P]\!]$ is defined. Clearly $\exists z \in S : Z = \{z\}$.

$\underline{P \equiv rec\, r.\tau R}$ for $r \in$ *Idf*, $R \in$ *qterms*. If $\mathcal{F}[\![P]\!]$ is defined, then $\mathcal{F}[\![\tau R]\!] = \langle \bar{S}, \bar{D}, \bar{E}, \bar{z} \rangle$ is defined and $\bot \notin \bar{E}(r)$. And then $\mathcal{F}[\![R]\!] = \langle \bar{\bar{S}}, \bar{\bar{D}}, \bar{\bar{E}}, \bar{\bar{z}} \rangle$ is defined and $\bar{E} = \bar{\bar{E}}$. By outer ind. hyp. $\mathcal{N}[\![R]\!] =: \langle S_R, D_R, E_R, Z_R \rangle$ is defined. With the help of Prop. 4.16 8. and Theorem 4.17 we conclude $E_R(r) = \bar{E}(r)$. Hence $\mathcal{N}[\![P]\!]$ is defined. Clearly $\exists z \in S : Z = \{z\}$. □

Corollary 4.20 1. Let $P \in$ *qterms*. If for every subterm Q of P
if $Q \equiv Q_1 \nmid Q_2$ then $FI(Q_1) = FI(Q_2) = \emptyset$,
and if $Q \equiv Qf$ then f has finite renaming; then

$$\mathcal{N}[\![P]\!] \text{ is defined and finite.}$$

2. Let $P \in terms_{\surd} \cap qterms$ such that for every subterm Q of P

if	$Q \equiv Q_1 \,;\, Q_2$	then $FI(Q_1) = \emptyset$
else if	$Q \equiv Q_1 \,|_{\surd}\, Q_2 \;\vee\; Q \equiv Q_1 \parallel_A Q_2$	then $FI(Q_1) = FI(Q_2) = \emptyset$
else if	$Q \equiv Q'f$	then f has finite renaming.

Then

$$\mathcal{N}[\![P]\!] \text{ is defined and finite.}$$

Proof 1. By Theorem 3.29 $\mathcal{F}[\![P]\!]$ is defined and finite. As $P \in qterms$ by Proposition 4.19 $\mathcal{N}[\![P]\!]$ is defined. And then by Corollary 4.18 $\mathcal{N}[\![P]\!]$ is finite.
2. By Theorem 3.31 $\mathcal{F}[\![P]\!]$ is defined and finite, and as in the proof of 1. $\mathcal{N}[\![P]\!]$ is defined and finite. □

4.4 Further properties of the constructed nets

In this section we show that if for some term its extended safe net is defined and finite, then the underlying safe net is state machine decomposable.

A general result shows that for finite and safe nets state machine decomposability implies that the net is covered by place invariants. Hence as a corollary we have that in the above case the net is also covered by place invariants.

Definition 4.21 Let $N = \langle S, D, Z \rangle$ be a finite and safe net.

1. The *subnet induced by* $S' \subseteq S$ is defined to be $N' = \langle S', D', Z \cap S' \rangle$, where

$$D' = \{\langle M_1 \cap S', a, M_2 \cap S' \rangle \mid \langle M_1, a, M_2 \rangle \in D \;\wedge\; S' \cap (M_1 \cup M_2) \neq \emptyset\}.$$

2. N is a *state machine* if $|Z| = 1 \;\wedge\; \forall t \in D : |\bullet t| = |t \bullet| = 1$.
3. N is *state machine decomposable* if there exists $\mathcal{S} \subseteq \mathcal{P}(S)$ such that $S = \bigcup \mathcal{S}$, and for every $S' \in \mathcal{S}$ the subnet of N induced by S' is a state machine. $\mathcal{S}$ is then called a *state machine decomposition*. □

State machine decomposability is extensively studied in [Geissler 85]. Note that S-net decomposability as in [Best, Fernández 86, p. 8] differs from the above notion as there the sets of places have to be disjoint. A superposed automata scheme as in [De Cindio et al. 82] is a special case of a state machine decomposable net.

Fact 4.22 Let $N = \langle S, D, Z \rangle$ be a finite and safe net, and $\mathcal{S}$ a state machine decomposition for N. Then $\forall M \in [Z\rangle_D : \; \forall S' \in \mathcal{S} : \; |M \cap S'| = 1$.

Proof By induction on the length of the transition sequence leading to M. □

Theorem 4.23 Let $P \in terms$. If $\mathcal{N}[Q]$ is defined and finite for every subterm Q of P, then for $\mathcal{N}[\![P]\!] = \langle S, D, E, Z\rangle$

$$\langle S, D, Z\rangle \text{ is state machine decomposable.}$$

Proof We perform an induction on P.

$\underline{P \equiv nil,}$ $\underline{P \equiv p}$ for $p \in Idf$. Then $\mathcal{S} = \{S\}$ is a state machine decomposition for $\langle S, D, Z\rangle$.

$\underline{P \equiv aP_1}$ for $a \in \{\tau\} \cup Vis$. If $\mathcal{N}[Q]$ is defined and finite for every subterm Q of P, clearly $\mathcal{N}[\![Q]\!]$ is defined and finite for every subterm Q of P_1. Let $\mathcal{N}[\![P_1]\!] = \langle S_1, D_1, E_1, Z_1\rangle$. By ind. hyp. there exists a state machine decomposition $\mathcal{S}_1$ for $\langle S_1, D_1, Z_1\rangle$.
$\langle S, D, E, Z\rangle = \langle S_1 \cup \{z\}, D_1 \cup \{\langle\{z\}, a, Z_1\rangle\}, E_1, \{z\}\rangle$.
Define $\mathcal{S} := \{S' \cup \{z\} \mid S' \in \mathcal{S}_1\}$. One easily checks that $\mathcal{S}$ is a state machine decomposition for $\langle S, D, Z\rangle$.

$\underline{P \equiv P_1 f}$ for $f \in Fun$. Then as above for $\mathcal{N}[\![P_1]\!] = \langle S_1, D_1, E_1, Z_1\rangle$ there exists $\mathcal{S}_1$ for $\langle S_1, D_1, Z_1\rangle$. Let $\mathcal{S} := \{S' \cap S \mid S' \in \mathcal{S}_1\}$. It is not hard to see that $\mathcal{S}$ is a state machine decomposition for $\langle S, D, Z\rangle$.

$\underline{P \equiv P_1 + P_2}$ As above for both $\mathcal{N}[P_i] = \langle S_i, D_i, E_i, Z_i\rangle$ $(i \in \{1,2\}, S_1 \cap S_2 = \emptyset)$ by ind. hyp. there exists a state machine decomposition $\mathcal{S}_i$ for $\langle S_i, D_i, Z_i\rangle$.
$\langle S, D, E, Z\rangle = Reach(\langle S_1 \cup S_2 \cup \{z\}, D_1 \cup D_2 \cup D_+, E_1 \cup E_2 \cup E_+, \{z\}\rangle)$ where $z \notin S_1 \cup S_2$, and D_+, E_+ are as in Definition 4.13.
Define $\mathcal{S} := \{(S' \cup S'' \cup \{z\}) \cap S \mid S' \in \mathcal{S}_1 \ \wedge \ S'' \in \mathcal{S}_2\}$. And again $\mathcal{S}$ is the wanted state machine decomposition.

$\underline{P \equiv P_1 \nmid P_2}$ For $\mathcal{N}[P_i]$ and $\mathcal{S}_i$ as above the wanted state machine decomposition is $\mathcal{S} := \mathcal{S}_1 \cup \mathcal{S}_2$.

$\underline{P \equiv rec\, r.\tau P_1}$ for $r \in Idf$. As above for $\mathcal{N}[P_1] = \langle S_1, D_1, E_1, Z_1\rangle$ by ind. hyp. there exists a state machine decomposition $\mathcal{S}_1$ for $\langle S_1, D_1, Z_1\rangle$. Moreover $\perp \notin E_1(r)$. Let $F = \{id \cdot f_1 \cdot \ldots \cdot f_n | n \geq 0, f_i \in E_1(r)\}$, and $\langle S_f, D_f, E_f, Z_f\rangle := (\mathcal{N}[P_1])f$ such that $f \neq g \Rightarrow S_f \cap S_g = \emptyset$. By the above case "$P \equiv P_1 f$" for all $f \in F$

$$\text{there exists a state machine decomposition } \mathcal{S}_f \text{ for } \langle S_f, D_f, Z_f\rangle. \qquad (*)$$

Let $\mathbf{S} = \bigcup_{f \in F} S_f$, $\mathbb{D} = \bigcup_{f \in F} D_f$, $\mathbb{E} = \bigcup_{f \in F} E_f$, and $z \notin \mathbf{S}$. Let $D_+ = \{\langle M, \tau, Z_g\rangle | \langle M, r, g\rangle \in \mathbb{E}\}$, $\bar{D} := \mathbb{D} \cup D_+ \cup \{\langle\{z\}, \tau, Z_{id}\rangle\}$. By definition $S = \bigcup[\{z\}\rangle_{\bar{D}}$, $Z = \{z\}$, and $D = \{t \in \bar{D} \mid \exists M \in [\{z\}\rangle_{\bar{D}} : \bullet t \subseteq M\}$.
Define $\mathcal{S} := \left\{\{z\} \cup \bigcup_{f \in F} S'_f \cap S \ \mid \ S'_f \in \mathcal{S}_f\right\}$. In words an element of $\mathcal{S}$ is built from $\{z\}$ and for every $f \in F$ some element of $\mathcal{S}_f$ is chosen (and intersected with S).

We will show that $\mathcal{S}$ is a state machine decomposition of $\langle S, D, Z\rangle$. Clearly $S = \bigcup \mathcal{S}$. Now let $S' \in \mathcal{S}$, then $S' = \{z\} \cup \bigcup_{f \in F} S'_f \cap S$ for some $S'_f \in \mathcal{S}_f$. The subnet induced by S' is $\langle S', D', \{z\}\rangle$, where
$D' = \{\langle M_1 \cap S', a, M_2 \cap S'\rangle \mid \langle M_1, a, M_2\rangle \in D \ \wedge \ S' \cap (M_1 \cup M_2) \neq \emptyset\}$.
Obviously $|\{z\}| = 1$. Now let $t' \in D'$. Then $t' = \langle M_1 \cap S', a, M_2 \cap S'\rangle$ for some $t := \langle M_1, a, M_2\rangle \in D \wedge S' \cap (M_1 \cup M_2) \neq \emptyset$.
If $t \in \mathbb{D}$, then for some $f \in F : t \in D_f$. By the disjointness conditions $M_i \cap S' = M_i \cap S'_f$ for all $i \in \{1,2\}$. By $(*)$ $|\bullet t'| = |t' \bullet| = 1$ follows.
If $t = \langle \{z\}, \tau, Z_{id}\rangle$. Clearly $\{z\} \cap S' = \{z\} = \bullet t'$. By the disjointness conditions $Z_{id} \cap S' = Z_{id} \cap S'_{id}$. Hence by $(*)$ $|Z_{id} \cap S'_{id}| = 1$, i.e. $|t' \bullet| = 1$.
If $t \in D_+$, then $t = \langle M, \tau, Z_g\rangle$ where $\langle M, r, g\rangle \in E_f$ for some $f, g \in F$. By Proposition 4.16 6. and 8. we conclude that $M \in [Z_f\rangle_f$. Clearly $M \cap S' = M \cap S'_f$, and by Fact 4.22 and $(*)$ $|M \cap S'_f| = 1$, hence $|\bullet t'| = 1$. And similar to the previous case $Z_g \cap S' = Z_g \cap S'_g$, hence $|Z_g \cap S'_g| = |t' \bullet| = 1$. □

Place invariants

Definition 4.24 Let $N = \langle S, D, Z\rangle$ be a finite and safe net.
Let $\mathbb{Z} = \{\ldots, -1, 0, 1, \ldots\}$ be the set of integers.

1. $I : S \to \mathbb{Z}$ is called a *place invariant* of N if $\forall t \in T : \ 0 = \sum_{s \in S} \underline{t}(s) \cdot I(s)$, where $\underline{t}(s) = |\{s\} \cap t \bullet| - |\{s\} \cap \bullet t|$.
2. N is *covered by place invariants* if for each place $s \in S$ there exists a positive place invariant I of N with $I(s) > 0$ and $\forall s' \in S : I(s') \geq 0$.
(cf. [Reisig 85, p. 81]). □

Proposition 4.25 A finite and safe net which is state machine decomposable is covered by place invariants.

Proof Let $\mathcal{S}$ be a state machine decomposition of N. Let $I : S \to \mathbb{Z}$ be given as $I(s) := |\{S' \in \mathcal{S} \mid s \in S'\}|$, then since $\bigcup \mathcal{S} = S$ we have $\forall s \in S : I(s) > 0$, i.e. I covers the whole net. Furthermore for $t \in T$: $\sum_{s \in S} \underline{t}(s) \cdot I(s)$
$= \sum_{s \in t\bullet} |\{S' \in \mathcal{S} \mid s \in S'\}| - \sum_{s \in \bullet t} |\{S' \in \mathcal{S} \mid s \in S'\}|$
$= \sum_{S' \in \mathcal{S}} |t \bullet \cap S'| - \sum_{S' \in \mathcal{S}} |\bullet t \cap S'| = 0$ as $\mathcal{S}$ is a state machine decomposition. □

Corollary 4.26 Let P be as in 4.23 and $\mathcal{N}[\![P]\!] = \langle S, D, E, Z\rangle$, then

$\langle S, D, Z\rangle$ is covered by place invariants. □

Conclusion to Chapter 4

In recent years a lot of research has been devoted to the development of operators for the composition of Petri nets. In the following we give a brief overview on the papers which have influenced the constructions of this chapter or which are related.

Early constructions motivated by operators on formal languages are given in [Peterson 81, Section 6.5].

[Lauer, Campbell 75], [Kotov 78], [De Cindio et al. 83], and [Müller 85, Section 5] construct finite nets for restricted forms of recursion. No proof of consistency with respect to an abstract programming language is given. The restrictions of the recursion limit the number of parallel processes which may be created within one program to a fixed upper bound. The conditions in Corollary 4.20 have the same effect, nevertheless they allow larger classes of terms, yet they are very simply defined.

[Goltz, Mycroft 84] construct certain acyclic, safe, and in general infinite nets for CCS programs; for a remark on the consistency see [Degano et al. 87, pp. 163f.]. A similar construction of so-called event structures is given in [Loogen, Goltz 87]. [Winskel 87, pp. 163f.] gives categorical constructions on nets.

[van Glabbeck, Vaandrager 87] construct finite and safe nets for ACP without recursion. [Nielsen 87] informally gives nets for some CCS programs which are close to those constructed in this chapter. [Best 87, pp. 423ff.] systematically constructs finite safe nets for COSY and proofs consistency with respect to vector firing sequences.

Closest related to the construction here is [Goltz 87]. Goltz was the first who generalized the idea concerning the construction for the recursion of [Milner 84] to Petri nets. Goltz does not treat action manipulation functions (see the next chapter for a discussion of that point) but allows, different to the present chapter, arbitrary intertwining of recursion and CCS parallel composition.

But even for the common subset of CCS covered by Goltz as well as by this chapter, the constructions differ, as we take a different approach to generalize the extensions of Milner's charts. While Goltz labels certain places with the free identifier they represent, we generalized the extensions to special transitions, labelled by the corresponding identifier. As the preset of such a transition may contain more than one place this approach is more than just the 'transition dual' of the solution of Goltz. Let us look at the following example.

The net constructed for *rec p.τa(nil | bp)* according to [Goltz 87] is

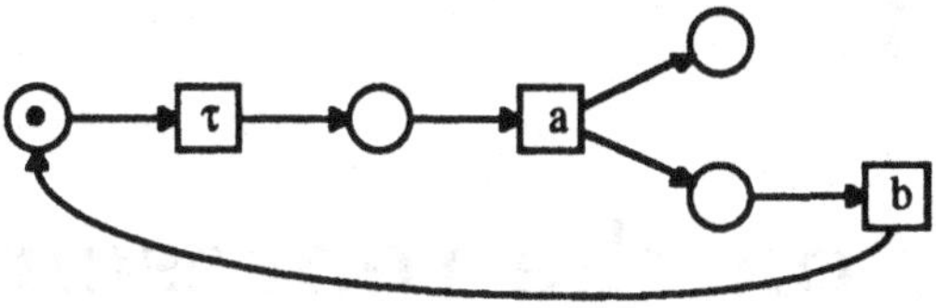

vhereas the net $\mathcal{N}[\![rec\, p.\tau a(nil \nmid bp)]\!]$ according to this chapter is[1]

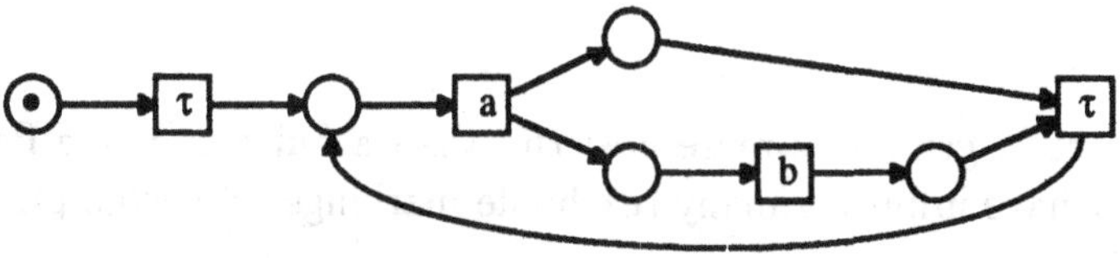

Vhile the latter net is safe, the former is not, and moreover the former is not :overed by place invariants, as an arbitrary number of tokens can pile up on the dead end' place (cf. also [Goltz 87, Beispiel 5.3]). In particular the first component of sequential composition would cause such dead end places, cf. also example 3 on age 105.

Another approach to avoid this problem would be to model *nil* as the empty 1et [Goltz 87, p. 73]. But then for example the net for *a nil* would be , and in contrast to $\mathcal{N}[\![a\, nil]\!]$ this net is not covered by place invariants. To get a esult which is similar to Theorem 4.23 and Corollary 4.26 it would be necessary o introduce some auxiliary place(s).

Apart from the above mentioned technical matters the constructions by Goltz ind those presented in this chapter are closely related for the common subset of CCS.

The main contribution of this work so far is the generalization of Milner's :onstruction of finite transition systems and the proof of its consistency. The construction of safe nets given in this chapter is just a more or less straightforward ransference from the previous chapter using well-known ideas for the combination of nets from the literature. Particularly useful is the smooth and tight interrelaionship given in Theorem 4.17.

[1] We deliberately choose the parallel composition $\nmid$ instead of | here, as the function *g* occuring in the abbreviated term (cf. Definition 1.12) causes an unwinding in the construction for ecursion. This would take the attention from the point we want to discuss here.

Chapter 5

A remark on the representation by finite Petri nets

A finite Petri net in general is more powerful than a finite and safe Petri net, as the former may have infinitely many reachable markings. For example the net

has infinitely many reachable markings. Moreover its transition system is strongly bisimular with $\mathcal{T}[\![rec\,p.(a\,nil \mid bp)]\!]$. But there exists no finite automaton which is strongly bisimular with it, as for arbitrary $n \in I\!N$ there exists a reachable marking M, such that from M exactly n-times an a-transition can occur, and then without occurrence of a b-transition no further a-transition can occur.

On the other hand it is well-known that finite Petri nets are not "Turing-powerful". Hence with the results of chapter 2 one cannot expect that every abstract program in **A** (or in CCS or in TCSP) can be represented by a finite Petri net.

For a subset of CCS Goltz has shown how abstract programs can be represented by finite nets [Goltz 87] (a short version written in English is [Goltz 88]). In this chapter we will prove that this subset cannot be extended significantly. The subset used by Goltz (it is called RCCS in [Goltz 87, Def. 5.1]) is stated in the next definition.

Definition 5.1 (Goltz's subset of CCS)

1. A term $P \in$ *terms* is *well-formed*, if in every subterm of the form $rec\,q.Q$ every free occurrence of an identifier lies within the scope of a prefixing operator.

2. Let $terms_G$ be the set of terms which are produced by the following syntax <u>and</u> which are well-formed.

$$P ::= nil \mid p \mid aP \mid aP + bP \mid P \mid P \mid rec\, p.P$$

where $p \in Idf, a, b \in \{\tau\} \cup Vis$. □

The main difference of the above subset and $terms_{CCS}$ is, that the renaming and restriction operators are missing (cf. Definition 1.15). Minor differences are the limitations with respect to the sum and recursion, which are not far from the limitations of qterms. Finally in [Goltz 87] α-congruent terms are not identified syntactically, nevertheless in the above definition we continue to do so.

Note that for the modelling of parallel processes with CCS the renaming operator is not so important, but the restriction operator is indispensible, as only with this operator synchronization can be enforced.

Definition 5.2 (extensions of Goltz's subset of CCS)

1. Let $terms_{G+\text{Res}}$ be as $terms_G$ but additionally allowing the clause $P{-}A$ in the grammar producing it, where A is as in Definition 1.15.
2. Let $terms_{G+\text{Ren}}$ be as $terms_G$ but additionally allowing the clause Pf in the grammar producing it, where f is as in Definition 1.15. □

Fact 5.3 $terms_{G+\text{Res}} \subset terms_{CCS}$ and $terms_{G+\text{Ren}} \subset terms_{CCS}$. □

We will show that both extensions contain terms which are not representable by finite Petri nets. We use the following definitions and properties of nets.

Definition 5.4 Let N be a Petri net, then

$$traces(N) := traces(Transys(N)).$$ □

Fact 5.5 Let $N = \langle S, D, Z \rangle$ be a net, then

$$traces(N) = \{l(u) \setminus \tau \mid u \in D^* \wedge \exists M :\ Z[u\rangle M\},$$

where $l(u)$ is the canonical generalization of l to sequences of transitions. $w \setminus \tau$ cancels all τ's in w, see Definition 1.21. □

Definition 5.6 Let $X \subseteq (Act - \{\tau\})^*$ and $i, d, z \in Alph$.
We say that X *contains a counter* if

$$\forall n, m \in I\!N :\ (n = m \Rightarrow i^n d^m z \in X) \wedge (n \neq m \Rightarrow i^n d^m z \notin X).$$ □

The next theorem is due to [Agerwala 75], for an easier accessible reference see [Valk 81, p. 143].

Theorem 5.7 (Agerwala) There exists no finite Petri net N such that

$$traces(N) \text{ contains a counter.}$$

Proof Assume for the finite net $N = \langle S, D, Z \rangle$ that $traces(N)$ contains a counter. Then for all $n \in \mathbb{N}$ there exist $u_n, v_n \in D^*$ and $M_n, M_n' \in \mathbb{N}^S$ such that $Z[u_n\rangle M_n[v_n\rangle M_n' \ \wedge\ l(u_n) \setminus \tau = i^n \ \wedge\ l(v_n) \setminus \tau = d^n z$.
As S is finite by Dickson's Lemma there exists $n, m \in \mathbb{N}$ such that $n < m$ and $M_n \leq M_m$ (recall the notation $\leq$ for markings in Definition 4.3).
And then $Z[u_m\rangle M_m[v_n\rangle M'$ for some $M' \in \mathbb{N}^S$. Hence $i^m d^n z \in traces(N)$ for $n \neq m$ contradicting the assumption that $traces(N)$ contains a counter. □

We are now ready to prove the result of this chapter, namely that both extensions of Goltz's subset of CCS given in Definition 5.2 contain a term which is not consistently representable as a finite Petri net, i.e. both extensions contain a term P such that for all finite nets N

$$\mathcal{T}[\![P]\!] \not\approx Transys(N).$$

Actually the result proven is stronger (cf. Proposition 1.33) as it refers to trace equivalence.

Theorem 5.8

1. There exists $C \in terms_{\mathbf{G+Res}}$ such that for all finite nets N

$$\mathcal{T}[\![C]\!] \neq_{\mathrm{tr}} Transys(N).$$

2. There exists $C \in terms_{\mathbf{G+Ren}}$ such that for all finite nets N

$$\mathcal{T}[\![C]\!] \neq_{\mathrm{tr}} Transys(N).$$

Proof 1. Let C be as in Proposition 2.5. Clearly $C \in terms_{\mathbf{G+Res}}$ and $traces(\mathcal{T}[\![C]\!])$ contains a counter. Hence by Theorem 5.7 the claim follows.

2. We will use the following actions: $a, b, i, d, z, u \in Alph$. a and b are used for internal synchronization, i, d, and z are used as for counters, and u stands for 'unused', it is used to rename actions, such that no further synchronization via this action can occur. Let $p, q, x \in Idf$. Define

$$\begin{array}{rcll} C & :\equiv & rec\,p.\ zp & +i(C_1 \mid ap) \\ \text{where } C_1 & \equiv & rec\,q.\ d\bar{a}\,nil & +i\big((qf \mid bq)h\big), \end{array}$$

and where $f = \{a \mapsto b, \bar{a} \mapsto \bar{b}\}$, $h = \{b \mapsto u, \bar{b} \mapsto \bar{u}\}$.
Clearly $C \in terms_{\mathbf{G+Ren}}$. Before proving that C contains a counter, let us picture

a portion of $Reach(\mathcal{T}[\![C]\!]/\sim_\$)$. In this picture with a node every outgoing arc is indicated.

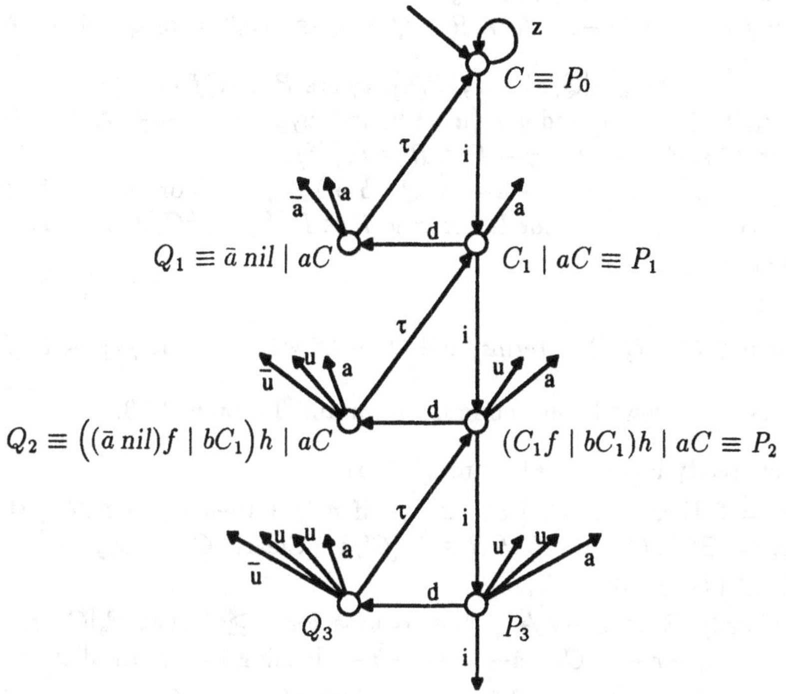

where $Q_3 \equiv \big(((\bar{a}\,nil)f \mid bC_1)hf \mid bC_1\big)h \mid aC$, $P_3 \equiv \big((C_1 f \mid bC_1)hf \mid bC_1\big)h \mid aC$.

Define $\tilde{P}_1 :\equiv x \mid aC$ and $\tilde{P}_{n+1} :\equiv \tilde{P}_n[(xf \mid bC_1)h/x]$ for $n \geq 1$.
Let $P_0 :\equiv C$ and for $n \geq 1$ $P_n :\equiv \tilde{P}_n[C_1/x]$
$Q_n :\equiv \tilde{P}_n[\bar{a}\,nil/x]$.

To show that C contains a counter it suffices to show the following facts for all $n \in \mathbb{N}$, $R \in terms$:

(∗1) $P_n -i\rightarrow R \;\Rightarrow\; R \equiv P_{n+1}$
(∗2) $P_n -\tau\not\rightarrow$.
And for $n \geq 1$ (∗3) $P_n -z\not\rightarrow$
(∗4) $P_n -d\rightarrow R \;\Rightarrow\; R \equiv Q_n$
(∗5) $Q_n -\tau\rightarrow R \;\Rightarrow\; R \sim_\$ P_{n-1}$
(∗6) $Q_n -d\not\rightarrow \;\wedge\; Q_n -z\not\rightarrow$.

We will use the following two facts.

(∗) For $n \in \mathbb{N}_1$, $Q \in terms$, $\tilde{P}_n[Q/x] -y\rightarrow R \wedge y \notin \{a, u\}$ we have

$\exists Q' :\; Q -y\rightarrow Q' \;\wedge\; R \equiv \tilde{P}_n[Q'/x] \;\vee\; y = \tau \;\wedge\; (Q -\bar{a}\rightarrow \;\vee\; Q -\bar{b}\rightarrow\,)$.

Proof of $(*)$. Induction on n.

<u>$n=1$</u> Then $\tilde{P}_1[Q/x] \equiv Q \mid aC -y\rightarrow R$.
As $y \neq a$ either $Q -y\rightarrow Q' \wedge R \equiv Q' \mid aC \equiv \tilde{P}_1[Q'/x]$ or $Q -\bar{a}\rightarrow \quad \wedge\, y = \tau$.

<u>$n \mapsto n+1$</u> Then $\tilde{P}_{n+1}[Q/x] \equiv \tilde{P}_n[P/x]$, where $P \equiv (Qf \mid bC_1)h$.
As $\tilde{P}_n[P/x] -y\rightarrow R$ and $y \notin \{a, u\}$ by ind. hyp. (as $P -\bar{a}\not\rightarrow \wedge P -\bar{b}\not\rightarrow$) there exists P' such that $P -y\rightarrow P' \wedge R \equiv \tilde{P}_n[P'/x]$.
As $y \neq u$ we have $(Q -\bar{a}\rightarrow \vee\, Q -\bar{b}\rightarrow) \wedge y = \tau$ or $\exists Q' : Q -y\rightarrow Q' \wedge P' \equiv (Q'f \mid bC_1)h$. In the latter case $R \equiv \tilde{P}_n[(Q'f \mid bC_1)h/x] \equiv \tilde{P}_{n+1}[Q'/x]$.
$\square$ $(*)$

$(**)$ For $n \in \mathbb{N}_1$, $Q, Q' \in$ *terms*, and $Q \sim_\$ Q'$ we have $\tilde{P}_n[Q/x] \sim_\$ \tilde{P}_n[Q'/x]$.

Proof of $(**)$ Follows by an induction on n and Theorem 1.29. $\square$ $(**)$

We are now ready to prove $(*1)$ through $(*6)$.
$(*1)$ If $n = 0$ then $R \equiv C_1 \mid aC \equiv P_1$. If $n \geq 1$ then $P_n \equiv \tilde{P}_n[C_1/x] -i\rightarrow R$ implies by $(*)$ $\exists C' : C_1 -i\rightarrow C' \wedge R \equiv \tilde{P}_n[C'/x]$. Clearly $C' \equiv (C_1 f \mid bC_1)h$, hence $R \equiv \tilde{P}_n[(C_1 f \mid bC_1)h/x] \equiv P_{n+1}$.
$(*2)$ Obviously $P_0 \equiv C -\tau\not\rightarrow$. Now assume for $n \geq 1$ that $\tilde{P}_n[C_1/x] -\tau\rightarrow R$, then by $(*)$ $C_1 -\tau\rightarrow \vee\, C_1 -\bar{a}\rightarrow \vee\, C_1 -\bar{b}\rightarrow$, leading to a contradiction.
$(*3)$ Assume $\tilde{P}_n[C_1/x] -z\rightarrow R$ for $n \geq 1$. Then by $(*)$ $C_1 -z\rightarrow$, leading to a contradiction.
$(*4)$ For $n \geq 1$ let $\tilde{P}_n[C_1/x] -d\rightarrow R$, then by $(*)$ $\exists C' : C_1 -d\rightarrow C' \wedge R \equiv \tilde{P}_n[C'/x]$. Clearly $C' \equiv \bar{a}\, nil$, hence $R \equiv Q_n$.
$(*5)$ If $n = 1$, then $Q_n \equiv \bar{a}\, nil \mid aC$, and $Q_n -\tau\rightarrow R$ implies $R \equiv nil \mid C$. Clearly $nil \mid C \sim_\$ C \equiv P_{n-1}$. Else if $n \geq 2$, then $Q_n \equiv \tilde{P}_n[\bar{a}\, nil/x] \equiv \tilde{P}_{n-1}[P/x]$, where $P \equiv ((\bar{a}\, nil)f \mid bC_1)h$. And then as $P -\bar{a}\not\rightarrow \wedge\, P -\bar{b}\not\rightarrow$ by $(*)$ $Q_n -\tau\rightarrow R$ implies $R \equiv \tilde{P}_{n-1}[(\, nilf \mid C_1)h/x]$. We have $C_1 \sim_\$ (\, nilf \mid C_1)h$, hence by $(**)$ $R \sim_\$ \tilde{P}_{n-1}[C_1/x] \equiv P_{n-1}$.
$(*6)$ Assuming $Q_n -d\rightarrow \vee\, Q_n -z\rightarrow$ for $n \geq 1$ again leads via $(*)$ to a contradiction. $\square$

In conclusion we have shown that the representation of certain CCS programs given by Goltz cannot be generalized for programs with renaming and restriction operators. But note that if these operators are not used recursively (i.e. if for every subterm Pf or P–A it is guaranteed that $FI(P) = \emptyset$), then corresponding operators on nets are not difficult to define. Hence at least in the case, where no intertwining of parallel composition and recursion occurs, synchronization could be enforced.

Chapter 6

Representation by finite and strict predicate/transition nets

A predicate/transition net (PrT-net) is a high-level form of a Petri net. The difference from a Petri net as introduced in chapter 4 is that individual tokens are used, and that the occurrence of a transition not only depends on the fact that there are enough tokens in its preset, but also that there are the "right" tokens, i.e. tokens satisfying some condition.

A PrT-net is strict if every place can hold at most one token of every type (= "colour"), predicate/event nets [Reisig 85, p. 115] are similar. We require PrT-nets to be finite by definition.

The aim of this work is to give finite representations of abstract programs as automata or nets, and, if the latter are used, also to represent the inherent parallelism. As PrT-nets are more powerful than finite Petri nets one may expect that more terms of **A** are representable as a PrT-net. And indeed in this chapter we exhibit a syntax-driven construction of PrT-nets for a subset of terms, which contains $terms_{CCS} \cap qterms$.

We hit on the fundamental idea for this chapter while studying the properties (Proposition 3.25) of the interleaving operational semantics used for the consistency proof of the automata construction. This idea is based on the observation that, when deriving sequences of actions in $\mathcal{T}[\![P]\!]$ for some term P without parallel composition, then the reached states in $\mathcal{T}[\![P]\!]$ (i.e. elements of *terms*) have a "core" which does not change (or changes only finitely often) and a "context" in which this core occurs. Let us consider the example $P :\equiv rec\, p.\tau 0(pf)$, where $I\!N \subseteq Alph$ and

$$af := \begin{cases} a+1 & \text{if } a \in I\!N, \\ a & \text{otherwise.} \end{cases}$$

(Cf. example 1. on page 47). The following picture shows an initial portion of $\mathcal{T}[\![P]\!]$ and the cores and contexts corresponding to the states.

$$\mathcal{T}[P] \quad \rightarrow P \xrightarrow{\tau} 0(Pf) \xrightarrow{0} Pf \xrightarrow{\tau} (0(Pf))f \xrightarrow{1} Pff \xrightarrow{\tau} (0(Pf))ff \xrightarrow{2} \cdots$$

cores	P	$0(Pf)$	P	$0(Pf)$	P	$0(Pf)$
contexts	κ	κ	κf	κf	κff	κff

The idea now consists in taking the constant cores as places in the PrT-net, and the changing contexts as individual tokens. E.g. for P the PrT-net looks like

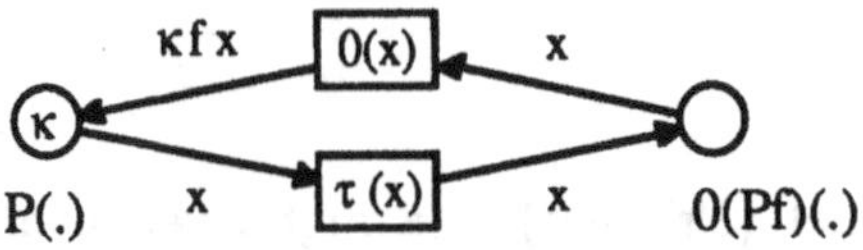

The initial part of the occurrence sequence of this net is (as alternating sequence of place/token-pairs and the action shown by the transition): $\langle P, \kappa\rangle$—τ→$\langle 0(Pf), \kappa\rangle$ —0→$\langle P, \kappa f\rangle$—$\tau$→$\langle 0(Pf), \kappa f\rangle$—1→$\langle P, \kappa ff\rangle$—$\tau$→$\langle 0(Pf), \kappa ff\rangle$—2→...
Note that P is neither representable as finite automaton, nor as finite Petri net.

The second fundamental point of our PrT-net construction is inspired by an idea of [Degano et al. 87], it concerns the indication which tokens may synchronize. Let us explain this with the following example. Let

$$P :\equiv \Big((b\,nil)f \nmid \bar{a}\,nil\Big)g,$$

where $f = \{b \mapsto a\}$ and $g = \{a \mapsto \bot, \bar{a} \mapsto \bot, [a, \bar{a}] \mapsto \tau\}$. The PrT-net representation of $(b\,nil)f$ is

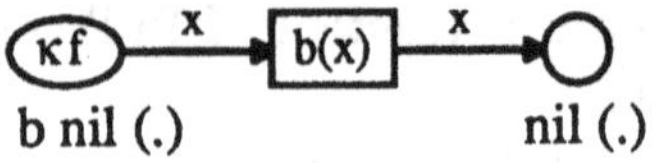

and that of $\bar{a}\,nil$ is

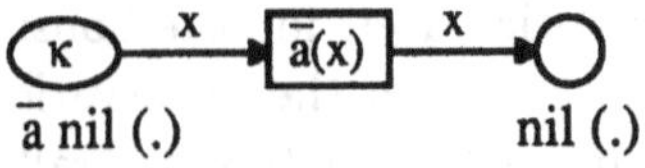

.

And then it is quite natural to have for P the net structure

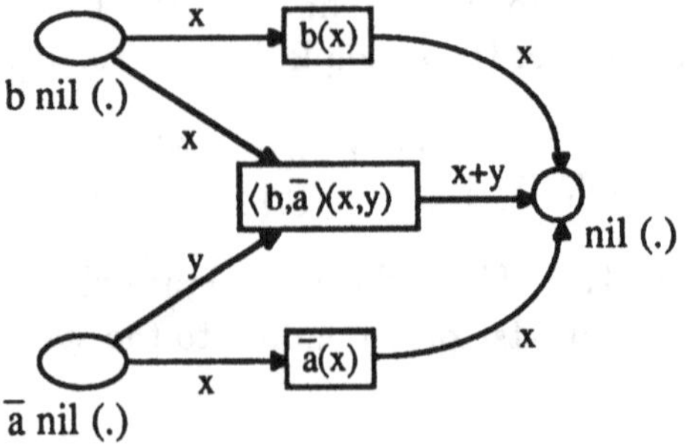

but which are the appropriate tokens? If we would choose κfg on the place $b\,nil(\cdot)$ and κg on the place $\bar{a}\,nil(\cdot)$, then the representation could not be distinguished from that of $Q :\equiv (b\,nil)fg \nmid (\bar{a}\,nil)g$, although P can perform an action, whereas Q cannot. The solution is to introduce a marker within the contexts to indicate which action manipulations are to be considered before synchronization and which after synchronization.

Hence the PrT-net for P has as initial marking $\kappa f \llcorner g$ on the place $b\,nil(\cdot)$ and $\kappa \lrcorner g$ on the place $\bar{a}\,nil(\cdot)$. Matching pairs of $\llcorner$ and $\lrcorner$ are used to indicate the possibility of a synchronization. We have already used them in Definition 3.13. [Degano et al. 87] gave the inspiration for this treatment, there e.g. $\kappa\llcorner$ is written $\kappa \mid id$ and $\kappa\lrcorner$ is written $id \mid \kappa$, but the difference is only of syntactic nature. Our postfix notation allows to omit parentheses unambiguously.

An additional effect of the markers $\llcorner$ and $\lrcorner$ is the distinction of different recursive instances in terms with recursively growing parallelism as for example in $rec\, p.\tau(a\,nil \mid p)$. That example is treated in detail on page 139. We can rephrase an earlier remark on terms without parallel composition for arbitrary terms now. Let $P \in terms$, then there exists a finite set of cores which suffices to build any reachable state (= term) of $\mathcal{T}[\![P]\!]$. For this composition of reachable terms from cores in general infinitely many contexts are needed. The finite set of cores will form the set of places in our PrT-net construction while the arbitrary increasing set of contexts is represented by the individual tokens.

As in chapter 4 we concentrate on qterms for the same reasons as stated there. Moreover we will require every action manipulation function f to satisfy

$$(EVis)f \cap Vis = \emptyset.$$

Loosely speaking this means that every action can at most synchronize once, the resulting action of a synchronization cannot synchronize another time. In particular the $\|_A$ construct is not treated by our PrT-net construction. At the end of this chapter we will discuss a term with an intertwining of $\|_A$ and recursion, which is not representable by a finite PrT-net.

Nevertheless every qterm, which is in CCS, can be represented by a PrT-net without any limitation of the intertwining of parallel composition and recursion. Recall that qterms are less general than terms with respect to two points. One point is the requirement that every recursive body starts with the invisible action τ. As we have shown (pp. 39ff.) this restriction is equivalent to taking the alternative rule for recursion. We have argued (p. 42) that the concurrency with respect to the visible actions is not affected by this restriction. Additionally let us remark that the analogue of Theorem 1.50 b) can be proved for the distributed operational semantics which will be presented in section 6.3 below.

Secondly in a qterm every sum is a choice between singular terms, i.e. terms without initial parallelism. We feel that both points are not severe. Note that concrete parallel programming languages such as Ada, Occam, and Chill also do not allow initial parallelism within the alternatives of their choice constructs. Furthermore note that the subset $qterms \cap terms_{CCS}$ of terms is Turing powerful, as we can apply σ (defined on page 41) to the term $P \in terms_{CCS}$ which has been constructed for Theorem 2.2, yielding an element of $qterms \cap terms_{CCS}$ while leaving the terminating traces unchanged, i.e. $\surd traces(\mathcal{T}[\![P]\!]) = \surd traces(\mathcal{T}[\![\sigma(P)]\!])$.

At the end of this introduction, we must warn the reader that the example PrT-nets presented here for terms are not exactly as they are constructed later on. We have omitted some details deliberately to keep the attention on the important aspects. Nevertheless the semantics of the PrT-nets shown in this introduction is the same as that of the nets constructed below.

6.1 Predicate/transition nets

PrT-nets are rather complex structures, but we only need a special class which is much simpler to define and explain. We start out from [Genrich 87] but give the definitions tailored for our special case. Our representation here is self-contained and comments indicate at which points the general case differs, but for a general exhibition of PrT-nets the reader is referred to [Genrich 87].

In PrT-nets places, transitions, and arcs are annotated, and this annotation determines the behaviour of the net. For this annotation a "first order language" **L** is used as the syntax, and a "structure" $\mathcal{R}$ for **L** is used as semantics. For all PrT-nets in this chapter we have the same first order language and structure.

Definition 6.1 (first order language **L**)

For every $C \in contexts$ there is a nullary operator denoted by C, and a unary operator denoted by $C(\cdot)$.

For every $a \in \{\tau\} \cup Vis$ there is a unary static predicate denoted by $a(\cdot)$, and for every ordered pair $\langle a, b\rangle \in Vis^2$ there is a binary static predicate denoted by $\langle a, b\rangle(\cdot,\cdot)$.

For every $P \in singterms$ there is a unary dynamic predicate $P(\cdot)$.

There are *variables* x and y. (Note that $x, y \notin Idf$.)

Terms of **L** are defined as follows: x , y , and C for $C \in contexts$ are terms.
If t is a term, then $C(t)$ is a term.

As *formulae* of **L** we only need:
For every $a \in \{\tau\} \cup Vis$ $\quad a(x)$ is a formula.
For every $\langle a, b\rangle \in Vis^2$ $\quad \langle a, b\rangle(x, y)$ is a formula. □

Definition 6.2 (the structure $\mathcal{R}$ for **L**) The *domain* of the structure $\mathcal{R}$ is *contexts*. The operators are interpreted as follows.

Every nullary operator $C \in contexts$ in **L** denotes itself.

Every unary operator $C(\cdot)$ for $C \in contexts$ in **L** denotes the function

$$\cdot[C/\kappa] : contexts \rightarrow contexts$$

(where $\cdot[\cdot/\cdot]$ denotes syntactic substitution, see also Definition 3.15). For example $\kappa f(\kappa g) \equiv \kappa g[\kappa f/\kappa] \equiv \kappa f g$. We will sometimes unambiguously omit parentheses, e.g. for the above example we will write $\kappa f \kappa g$.

The static predicates of **L** are interpreted as follows.

Let $a \in \{\tau\} \cup Vis, C \in contexts$, then

$$a(C) \text{ is true iff } a\mathcal{L}[\![C]\!] \neq \bot \quad \text{(for the definition of } \mathcal{L}[\![\cdot]\!] \text{ see 3.14).}$$

Let $\langle a, b\rangle \in Vis^2$, $C_1, C_2 \in contexts$, then

$$\begin{aligned} \langle a,b\rangle(C_1,C_2) \text{ is true iff } & \exists C_1', C_2', C \in contexts, c \in EVis : \\ & C_1 \equiv C_1' \llcorner C \wedge C_2 \equiv C_2' \lrcorner C \\ & \wedge \left[a\mathcal{L}[\![C_1']\!], b\mathcal{L}[\![C_2']\!]\right] = c \wedge c\mathcal{L}[\![C]\!] \neq \bot. \end{aligned}$$ □

The use of the set *contexts* at so many places might be confusing on first sight, but it turns out to be very useful and natural.

As we need only very simple PrT-nets, and in order to keep the constructions manageable, we introduce a shorthand notation for the PrT-nets we use. The compact notation for transitions and arcs is inspired by the notation of [Greibach 78] for Petri nets, which we have already used in Definition 4.1.

A second point is that in our notation only one type of transitions appears. These transitions are so-called *singular transitions*, they have a singleton preset. The second type of transitions, the so-called *synchronization transitions*, do not appear in the shorthand notation, but can be derived from the singular transitions.

Definition 6.3 (shorthand for predicate/transiton nets)
$G = \langle S, D, Z\rangle$ is a *predicate/transiton net (PrT-net) in shorthand notation* if

$$\begin{aligned} S &\subseteq singterms \\ D &\subseteq S \times (\{\tau\} \cup Vis) \times \mathcal{P}(S \times contexts) \\ Z &\subseteq S \times contexts, \end{aligned}$$

such that S, D, and Z are finite, S and Z are non-empty, and for all $\langle P, a, M\rangle \in D$: M is finite and non-empty. □

We choose the letter G for PrT-nets as our presentation is based on [Genrich 87]. The shorthand graphical representation of $G = \langle S, D, Z \rangle$ is as follows: An element $P \in S$ (called a *place*, or a *dynamic predicate*) is represented as 

i.e. as a circle with label P. An element $\langle P, a, M \rangle \in D$ (called a *singular transition*) is represented and connected with places as follows.

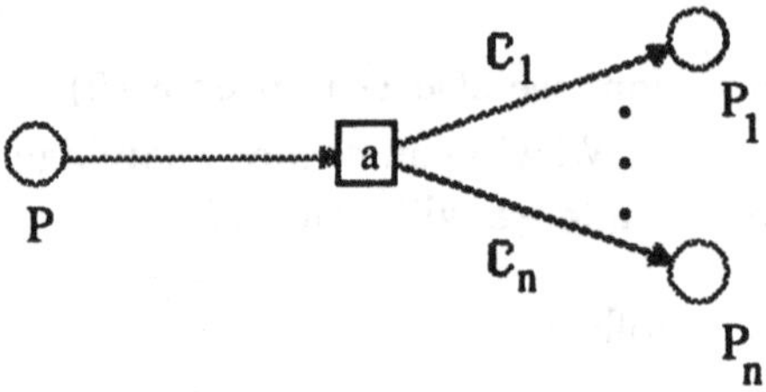

if for $i \in \{1, \ldots, n\}$:
$\emptyset \neq \mathcal{C}_i := \{C \mid \langle P_i, C \rangle \in M\}$.

In words P is the single place in the preset and the postset is determined by the places occurring in pairs in M. All contexts occurring in a pair in M with P_i are collected in a set, and this set labels the arc from the transition to P_i, for these sets we drop the braces. The transition is labelled with a. The *initial marking* Z is represented by labelling every $P \in S$ with $\mathcal{C} := \{C \mid \langle P, C \rangle \in Z\}$, if $\mathcal{C} \neq \emptyset$.

Pictorially this looks like 

. Again we drop the braces.

As a complete example the shorthand graphical representation of the PrT-net for $P :\equiv ((b\,nil)f \nmid \bar{a}\,nil)g$ is

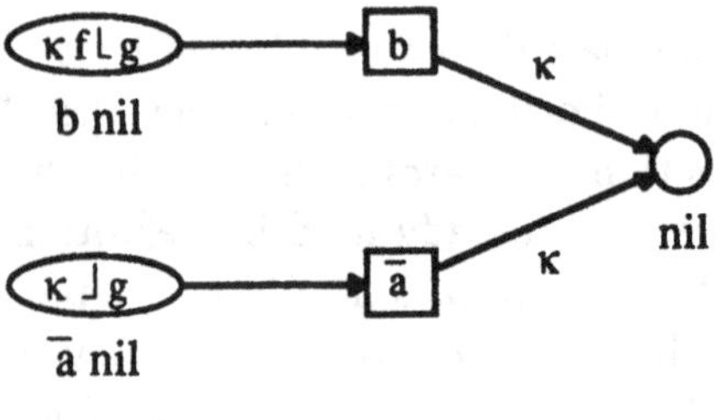

and the shorthand notation is

$$\begin{aligned}\Big\langle\ & \{b\,nil, \bar{a}\,nil,\ nil\}, \\ & \Big\{ \langle b\,nil, b, \{\langle\ nil, \kappa\rangle\}\rangle,\ \langle \bar{a}\,nil, \bar{a}, \{\langle\ nil, \kappa\rangle\}\rangle \Big\}, \\ & \Big\{ \langle b\,nil, \kappa f \lfloor g\rangle,\ \langle \bar{a}\,nil, \kappa \rfloor g\rangle \Big\}\Big\rangle.\end{aligned}$$

Definition 6.4 (symbolic sums of one-tuples for **L**)

The set *Sysums* of symbolic sums of one-tuples of the language **L** is defined inductively as follows.

0 and every term of **L** is in *Sysums*.

If l_1, l_2 are in *Sysums*, then $l_1 + l_2$ is in *Sysums*. □

As we only need symbolic sums of one-tuples, we omit the tuple brackets and write for example $\langle\kappa\rangle + \langle\kappa f\rangle$ as $\kappa + \kappa f$. Moreover we are not as strict as [Genrich 87, p. 214-216] in distinguishing symbolic sums (= syntax) and the linear combinations (= semantics) they denote. We will deliberately write e.g. for $C_1x + (C_2x + (\ldots C_nx)\ldots)$ the sum $\sum_{C\in\mathcal{C}} Cx$, where $\mathcal{C} = \{C_1, \ldots, C_n\}$, although this is syntactically not unique (as different orderings of $C_1, \ldots, C_n$ could be chosen), semantically it is unique.

We will now state how our shorthand notation for a PrT-net can be translated to a predicate/transition net in the notation of [Genrich 87, p. 216]. We have used this translation to derive the Petri-net-semantics (Definition 6.7 below) and the symbolic transition rule (Definition 6.8 below) of a PrT-net in shorthand notation from the corresponding definitions in [Genrich 87].

Later on we will formally work only with the shorthand notation, so the reader is invited to glance quickly over the next definition. Nevertheless there is one important point. Note how elements of D *directly* determine the singular transitions; and how they *indirectly*, as ordered pairs, determine the synchronization transitions. We will sometimes use the graphical representation of [Genrich 87] to make the latter visible in figures. We also hope that while seeing the translation to the conventional notation the reader appreciates our compact shorthand notation.

Definition 6.5 (translation to conventional notation)

Let $G = \langle S, D, Z\rangle$ be a PrT-net in shorthand notation, then it abbreviates a strict predicate/transition net MN in the notation used in [Genrich 87, p. 216] as follows.

$$MN = (N, A, M^0), \quad \text{where}$$

1. $N = (S, T; F)$, where S is as in G, the elements are considered to be unary dynamic predicates (cf. Definition 6.1),
   $T := D \cup \Big\{ \langle d_1, d_2\rangle \;\Big|\; d_1, d_2 \in D \wedge pr_2(d_1) \in Vis \wedge pr_2(d_2) \in Vis \Big\}$,
   $F \subseteq (S \times T) \cup (T \times S)$
   such that for $P \in S \;\wedge\; d \in D$
   $\langle P, d\rangle$ iff $P = pr_1(d)$
   $\langle d, P\rangle$ iff $\langle P, C\rangle \in pr_3(d)$ for some C,
   and such that for $P \in S \;\wedge\; t \in T \;\wedge\; t = \langle d_1, d_2\rangle \in D^2$
   $\langle P, t\rangle$ iff $P = pr_1(d_1) \;\vee\; P = pr_1(d_2)$
   $\langle t, P\rangle$ iff $\langle P, C\rangle \in pr_3(d_1) \;\vee\; \langle P, C\rangle \in pr_3(d_2)$ for some C.

2. $A = (A_N, A_S, A_T, A_F)$, where
   (a) $A_N = \mathcal{R}$, where $\mathcal{R}$ is as in Definition 6.2.
   (b) $A_S = id : S \to S$.
   (c) A_T is a mapping of the set T into the set of formulae of **L** (cf. Def. 6.1),

$$A_T(t) := \begin{cases} pr_2(t)(x) & \text{if } t \in D, \\ \langle pr_2(d_1), pr_2(d_2)\rangle(x,y) & \text{if } t = \langle d_1, d_2\rangle \in D^2. \end{cases}$$

   (d) $A_F : F \to Sysums$
   A_F is specified by defining for every transition $t \in T$ the annotations of the arcs incident to t:

   If $t = \langle P, a, M\rangle \in D$, then
   $\langle P, t\rangle$ is annotated by x
   $\langle t, Q\rangle$ is annotated by $\sum_{\langle Q,C\rangle \in M} Cx$.

   If $t = \langle d_1, d_2\rangle \in D^2$ for $d_i = \langle P_i, a_i, M_i\rangle$ $(i \in \{1,2\})$,
   then for its ingoing arcs
   if $P_1 \equiv P_2$ then $\langle P_1, t\rangle$ is annotated by $x + y$
   else $\langle P_1, t\rangle$ is annotated by x and $\langle P_2, t\rangle$ by y;
   and for its outgoing arcs
   if for Q there exist C_1, C_2 such that $\langle Q, C_1\rangle \in M_1 \land \langle Q, C_2\rangle \in M_2$,
   then $\langle t, Q\rangle$ is annotated by $\sum_{\langle Q,C\rangle \in M_1} Cx + \sum_{\langle Q,C\rangle \in M_2} Cy$
   else if there exists C_1 such that $\langle Q, C_1\rangle \in M_1$,
   then $\langle t, Q\rangle$ is annotated by $\sum_{\langle Q,C\rangle \in M_1} Cx$,
   else if there exists C_2 such that $\langle Q, C_2\rangle \in M_2$,
   then $\langle t, Q\rangle$ is annotated by $\sum_{\langle Q,C\rangle \in M_2} Cy$.

3. $M^0 : S \to Sysums$

$$M^0(P) := \sum_{\langle P,C\rangle \in Z} C.$$

Definition 6.5 □

A similar translation to coloured nets [Jensen 87] is also possible, but not carried out here.

Example As an example let us again consider the term

$$P :\equiv ((b\,nil)f \nmid \bar{a}\,nil)g,$$

its shorthand graphical representation as a PrT-net has been given on page 128. The (longhand) graphical representation of that net is

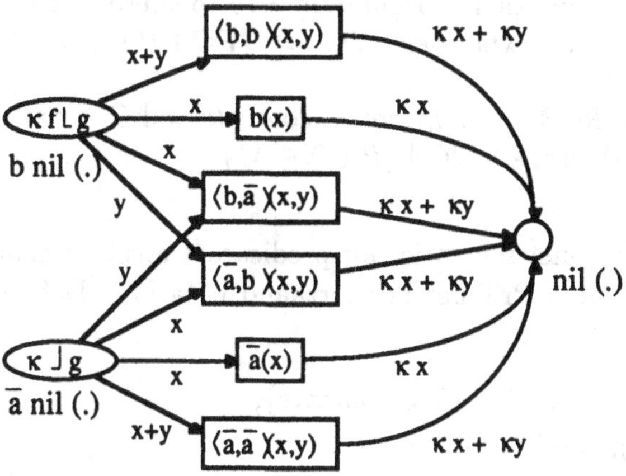

The main difference is that synchronization transitions and variables show up. For reasons of clarity we even indicate here for the dynamic predicates (= place annotation) where the argument goes. □

The behaviour (= semantics) of a high-level net, such as a PrT-net, is usually given in terms of lower level nets. In [Genrich 87, p. 217] this is done in terms of C/E-systems. But C/E-systems (for a definition see [Best, Fernández 86, p. 16]) have unnecessary and for our purposes impractical restrictions. In particular transitions on a loop (e.g. 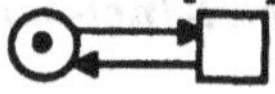) may not occur. Also E/N-systems [Thiagarajan 87] and Petri nets, where all places have capacity 1, [Best, Fernández 86, p. 19f.] do not allow transitions on a loop to occur. Therefore several authors have defined extensions, e.g. [Degano et al. 87] have defined "augmented C/E-systems".

In order to avoid introducing several additional definitions we choose the safe Petri nets of chapter 4 as semantics for PrT-nets. Our definition is guided by the C/E-semantics of PrT-nets given in [Genrich 87]. Most aspects carry over. The difference is that transitions on loops may occur, that transitions are labelled by elements of *Act*, and that the safe net may be non-simple and may contain dead transitions and isolated elements.

The safe-net-semantics of a PrT-net as given below is not always defined. But for all nets which we construct in the next section the safe-net-semantics will be defined. We will use the following notation.

Definition 6.6 1. Define $\gamma : (singterms \times contexts) \longrightarrow conterms$

$$\gamma(P, C) :\equiv PC.$$

For the definition of PC see 3.15. We extend γ to sets $M \subseteq singterms \times contexts$ as usual, i.e. $\gamma(M) := \{PC \mid \langle P, C\rangle \in M\}$.

2. We extend the notation of Definition 3.15 to subsets of *conterms*. Let $X \subseteq conterms$, $C \in contexts$, then $XC := \{PC \mid P \in X\}$. □

In particular below for $M \subseteq singterms \times contexts$ and $C \in contexts$ we will write $\gamma(M)C$ to denote the set $\{PC'C \mid \langle P, C'\rangle \in M\}$.

Definition 6.7 (safe-net-semantics for predicate/transition nets)
Let $G = \langle S, D, Z\rangle$ be a PrT-net in shorthand notation. Define $N := \langle \hat{S}, \hat{D}, \hat{Z}\rangle$, where

$$\begin{aligned}
\hat{S} :=\ & \{PC \mid P \in S \ \wedge\ C \in contexts\}, \\
\hat{Z} :=\ & \gamma(Z), \quad \text{and} \\
\hat{D} :=\ & \Big\{\big\langle \{QC\},\ b,\ \gamma(M)C \big\rangle \ \Big| \\
& \qquad \langle Q, a, M\rangle \in D \ \wedge\ C \in contexts \ \wedge\ a\mathcal{L}[\![C]\!] = b \neq \bot\Big\} \\
\cup\ & \Big\{\big\langle \{Q_1C_1, Q_2C_2\},\ b\mathcal{L}[\![C]\!],\ \gamma(M_1)C_1 \cup \gamma(M_2)C_2 \big\rangle \ \Big| \\
& \qquad \forall i \in \{1,2\} : \ \langle Q_i, a_i, M_i\rangle \in D \ \wedge\ C_i, C \in contexts \\
& \qquad \wedge\ C_1 \equiv C_1' \llcorner C \ \wedge\ C_2 \equiv C_2' \lrcorner C \\
& \qquad \wedge\ \Big[a_1\mathcal{L}[\![C_1']\!], a_2\mathcal{L}[\![C_2']\!]\Big] = b \in EVis \ \wedge\ b\mathcal{L}[\![C]\!] \neq \bot\Big\}.
\end{aligned}$$

If N is a safe Petri net, we define $Safenet(G) := N$, otherwise $Safenet(G)$ is undefined. $Safenet(G)$ is called the *safe-(Petri-)net-semantics of* G. If $Safenet(G)$ is defined we say that G is *safe*. □

As an example we give the safe-net-semantics of the PrT-net of the example on page 124, which in turn represents $P \equiv rec\, p.\tau 0(pf)$ where f is defined there. Of course even the reachable part of the safe-net-semantics is infinite. Below we draw the initial section of the reachable part.

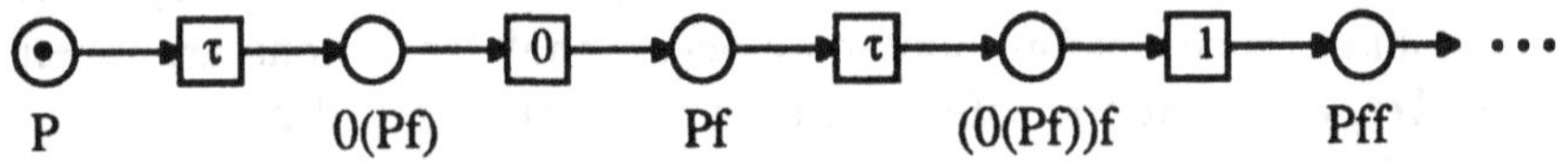

See example 5. on page 137 for an illustration of the fact that the order of the application of the action manipulation functions is chosen correctly.

Definition 6.8 (symbolic transition rule)

Let $G = \langle S, D, Z\rangle$ be a safe PrT-net in shorthand notation. M is a *marking* of G if it is a finite subset of $S \times$ *contexts*. A singular transition $\langle P, a, \bar{M}\rangle \in D$ is *enabled* at a marking M with $C \in$ *contexts* if $\langle P, C\rangle \in M \ \wedge\ a\mathcal{L}[\![C]\!] \neq \bot$.
If a singular transition $d = \langle P, a, \bar{M}\rangle \in D$ is enabled at M with C it may *occur* showing $b := a\mathcal{L}[\![C]\!]$ as *behaviour* and resulting in the *follower marking* $M' := \big(M - \{\langle P, C\rangle\}\big) \cup \{\langle Q, C'C\rangle \mid \langle Q, C'\rangle \in \bar{M}\}$. We write $M\left[\begin{smallmatrix} d \\ b \end{smallmatrix}\right\rangle M'$.

A synchronization transition $\langle d_1, d_2\rangle \in D^2$ where $d_i = \langle P_i, a_i, \bar{M}_i\rangle$ and $a_i \in Vis$ for $i \in \{1,2\}$ is *enabled* at a marking M with $C_1, C_2, C \in$ *contexts* if

$$\big\{\langle P_1, C_1 \llcorner C\rangle,\ \langle P_2, C_2 \lrcorner C\rangle\big\} \subseteq M \ \wedge\ \big[a_1\mathcal{L}[\![C_1]\!], a_2\mathcal{L}[\![C_2]\!]\big] = b \in EVis \ \wedge\ b\mathcal{L}[\![C]\!] \neq \bot.$$

In that case it may *occur* showing $c := \big([\,a_1\mathcal{L}[\![C_1]\!], a_2\mathcal{L}[\![C_2]\!]\,]\big)\mathcal{L}[\![C]\!]$ as *behaviour* and resulting in the *follower marking*

$$\begin{aligned} M' := \big(M - \{\langle P_1, C_1 \llcorner C\rangle,\ \langle P_2, C_2 \lrcorner C\rangle\}\big) \ &\cup \{\langle Q, C'C_1 \llcorner C\rangle \mid \langle Q, C'\rangle \in \bar{M}_1\} \\ &\cup \{\langle Q, C'C_2 \lrcorner C\rangle \mid \langle Q, C'\rangle \in \bar{M}_2\}. \end{aligned}$$

We then write $M\left[\begin{smallmatrix} \langle d_1, d_2\rangle \\ c \end{smallmatrix}\right\rangle M'$. □

6.2 Syntax-driven construction

In this section we give the syntax-driven constructions of PrT-nets (in shorthand notation) for qterms. The interpretation of a qterm P as PrT-net is indicated by $\mathcal{G}[\![P]\!]$. The construction is not defined for all qterms, but later we will show that the set of terms, where it is defined encloses $terms_{CCS} \cap qterms$. The definitions are very simple due to the shorthand notation. The rest of this section contains several examples.

Definition 6.9

$$\mathcal{G}[\![\,nil\,]\!] := \big\langle \{\,nil\}, \emptyset, \{\langle\, nil, \kappa\rangle\}\big\rangle$$

For $p \in Idf$

$$\mathcal{G}[\![p]\!] := \big\langle \{p\}, \emptyset, \{\langle p, \kappa\rangle\}\big\rangle.$$

Let $P \in qterms$ and $\mathcal{G}[\![P]\!] = \langle S, D, Z \rangle$ be defined.

For $a \in \{\tau\} \cup Vis$ $\quad \mathcal{G}[\![aP]\!] := \Big\langle S \cup \{aP\},\ D \cup \{\langle aP, a, Z\rangle\},\ \{\langle aP, \kappa\rangle\}\Big\rangle.$

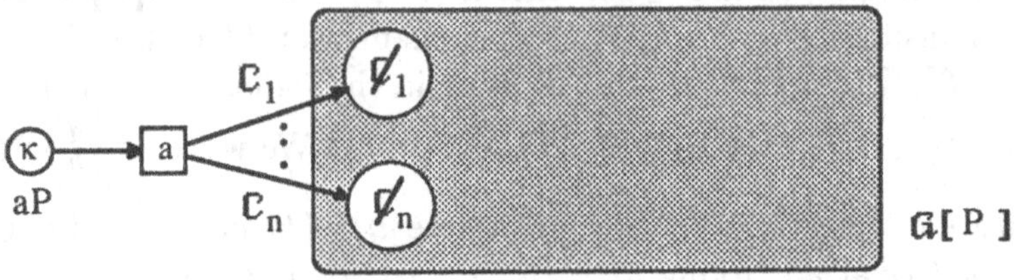

For $f \in Fun$, where $(EVis)f \cap Vis = \emptyset$,
$$\mathcal{G}[\![Pf]\!] := \Big\langle S,\ D,\ \{\langle Q, Cf\rangle \mid \langle Q, C\rangle \in Z\}\Big\rangle.$$

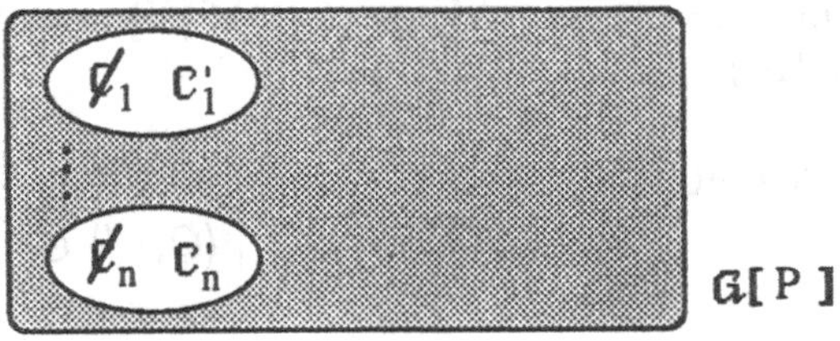

Let $P_1, P_2 \in qterms$, and $\mathcal{G}[\![P_i]\!] = \langle S_i, D_i, Z_i\rangle$ be defined for both $i \in \{1,2\}$.

If $P_1, P_2 \in singterms$, then $\mathcal{G}[\![P_1 + P_2]\!] :=$

$$\Big\langle \begin{array}{l} S_1 \cup S_2 \cup \{P_1 + P_2\}, \\ D_1 \cup D_2 \cup \{\, \langle P_1 + P_2, a, M\rangle \mid \exists i \in \{1,2\} :\ \langle P_i, a, M\rangle \in D_i \,\}, \\ \{\langle P_1 + P_2,\ \kappa\rangle\} \end{array} \Big\rangle.$$

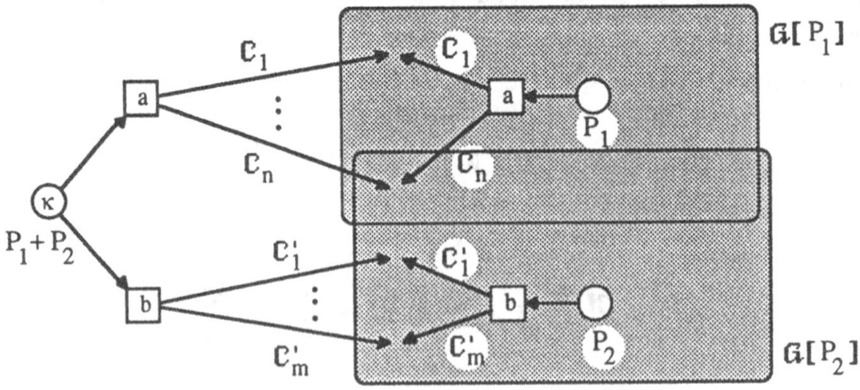

For $P_1, P_2 \in qterms$ define $\mathcal{G}[\![P_1 \ddagger P_2]\!] :=$

$$\Big\langle\ S_1 \cup S_2,\ D_1 \cup D_2,\ \{\, \langle Q,\, C\llcorner\rangle \mid \langle Q, C\rangle \in Z_1 \,\} \cup \{\, \langle Q,\, C\lrcorner\rangle \mid \langle Q, C\rangle \in Z_2 \,\}\ \Big\rangle.$$

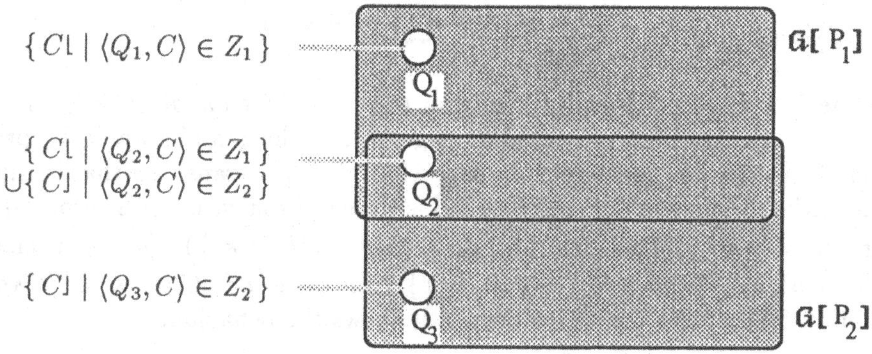

For $P, Q \in singterms$ define inductively the predicate 'summand of':

$$P \ smd\_of\ Q \ \text{ iff } \ P \equiv Q \ \vee\ Q \equiv Q_1 + Q_2 \wedge (P\ smd\_of\ Q_1 \ \vee\ P\ smd\_of\ Q_2).$$

Let $R \in qterms$, $r \in Idf$, and $\mathcal{G}[\![R]\!] = \langle S, D, Z\rangle$ be defined.
For $\bar{R} :\equiv rec\, r.\tau R$ let $\bar{S} := \{\bar{R}\} \cup \{\, P[\bar{R}/r] \mid P \in S \,\}$ and define $\mathcal{G}[\![\bar{R}]\!] :=$

$$\Big\langle\ \bar{S},\quad \Big\{\Big\langle P[\bar{R}/r], a, \{\langle Q[\bar{R}/r], C\rangle \mid \langle Q, C\rangle \in M\}\Big\rangle \ \mid \langle P, a, M\rangle \in D\Big\}$$
$$\cup\Big\{\qquad \Big\langle P, \tau, \{\langle Q[\bar{R}/r], C\rangle \mid \langle Q, C\rangle \in Z\}\Big\rangle \ \mid P \in \bar{S} \wedge \bar{R}\ smd\_of\ P\Big\},$$
$$\{\langle \bar{R}, \kappa\rangle\}\ \Big\rangle$$

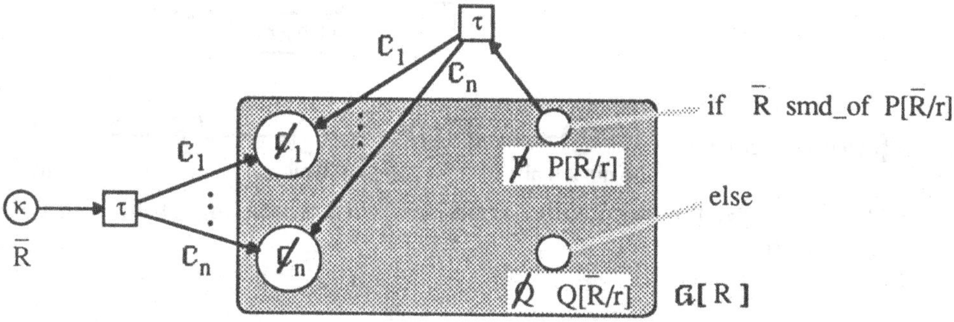

Definition 6.9 □

Examples

1. $\mathcal{G}[\![b\,nil]\!]$ is 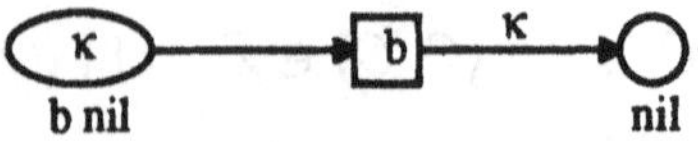

$\mathcal{G}[\![(b\,nil)f]\!]$ is 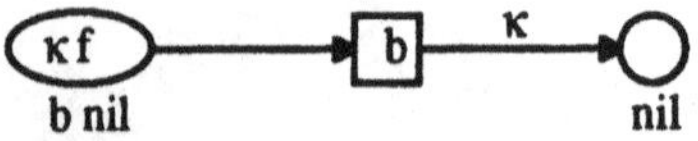

And the PrT-net for $\mathcal{G}[\![(b\,nil)f \mid \bar{a}\,nil]\!] = \mathcal{G}[\![\big((b\,nil)f \between \bar{a}\,nil\big)g]\!]$, where g is as in Definition 1.12, has been presented on page 128, the longhand graphical representation of this net has been given on page 131. The only transition that is enabled at the initial marking in $\mathcal{G}[\![(b\,nil)f \mid \bar{a}\,nil]\!]$ is the synchronization transition $\langle d_1, d_2\rangle$, where $d_1 = \big\langle b\,nil, b, \{\langle\, nil, \kappa\rangle\}\big\rangle$ and $d_2 = \big\langle \bar{a}\,nil, \bar{a}, \{\langle\, nil, \kappa\rangle\}\big\rangle$. $\langle d_1, d_2\rangle$ is enabled at the marking $\{\,\langle b\,nil, \kappa f \llcorner g\rangle\,,\,\langle \bar{a}\,nil, \kappa \lrcorner g\rangle\,\}$ with $C_1 \equiv \kappa f$, $C_2 \equiv \kappa$, $C \equiv \kappa g$ (cf. Definition 6.8). If this transition occurs, it shows the behaviour

$$\big([\,b\mathcal{L}[\![\kappa f]\!], \bar{a}\mathcal{L}[\![\kappa]\!]\,]\big)\mathcal{L}[\![\kappa g]\!] \;=\; \big([a,\bar{a}]\big)\mathcal{L}[\![\kappa g]\!] \;=\; \tau,$$

and the follower marking $\{\langle\, nil, \kappa f \llcorner g\rangle, \langle\, nil, \kappa \lrcorner g\rangle\}$ is reached. At that marking no further transition is enabled. We denote this occurrence sequence as

$$\begin{matrix}\langle b\,nil, \kappa f \llcorner g\rangle \\ \langle \bar{a}\,nil, \kappa \lrcorner g\rangle\end{matrix} \left[\begin{matrix}\langle d_1, d_2\rangle \\ \tau\end{matrix}\right\rangle \begin{matrix}\langle\, nil, \kappa f \llcorner g\rangle \\ \langle\, nil, \kappa \lrcorner g\rangle.\end{matrix}$$

2. $\mathcal{G}[\![b\,nil \between b\,nil]\!]$ is 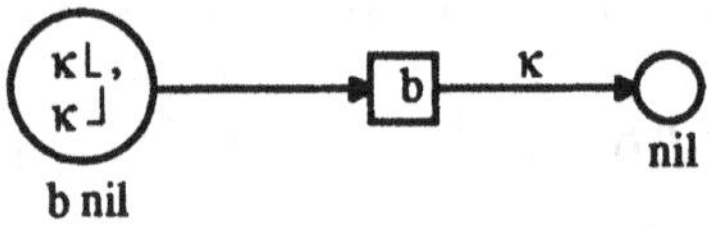

and the longhand graphical representation for this net is 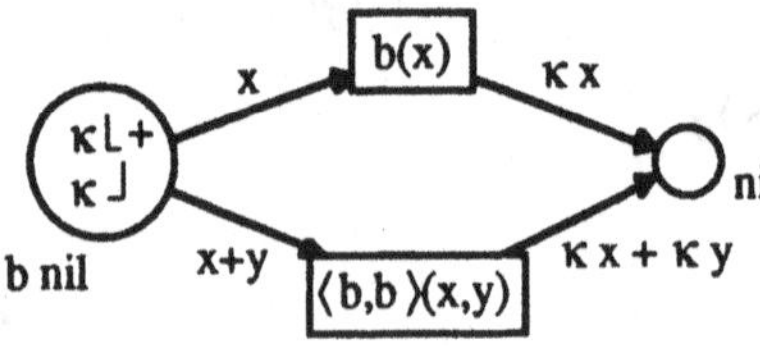

3. $\mathcal{G}[\![a(b\,nil \between b\,nil)]\!]$ is 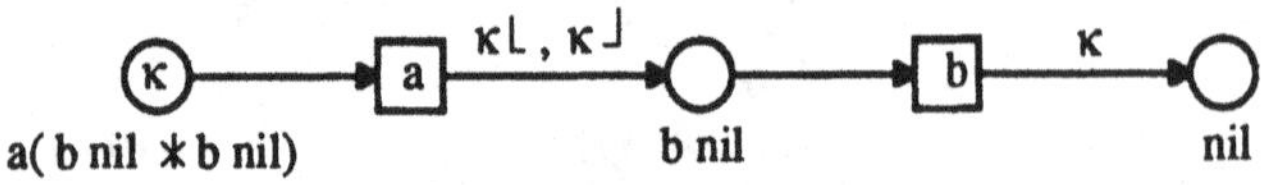

This example shows, how a singular transition with a non-singleton set on its outgoing arc arises.

4. $\mathcal{G}[\![(a\,nil \nmid b\,nil) \nmid c\,nil]\!]$ is

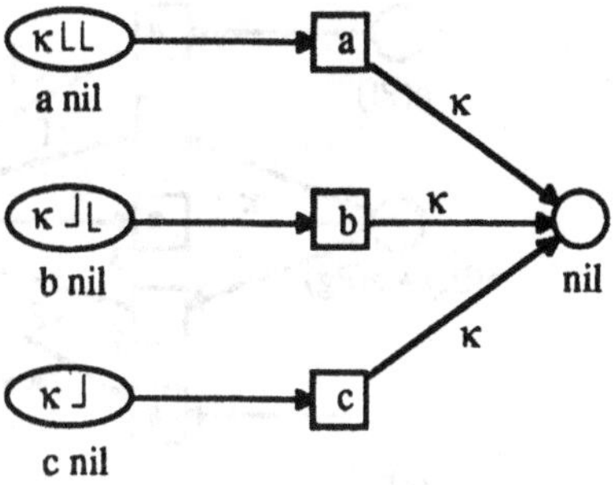

5. Let $f = \{a \mapsto b\}$, $g = \{b \mapsto c\}$, and $P \equiv \big(b((a\,nil)f)\big)g$. Then $\mathcal{G}[\![P]\!]$ is

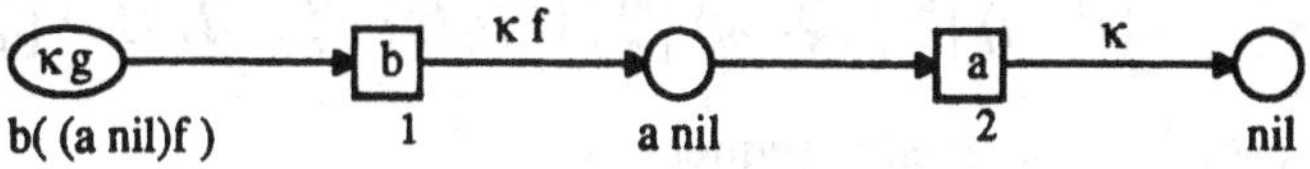

and the only maximal occurrence sequence (using transition names as indicated) is

$$\langle b((a\,nil)f), \kappa g\rangle \begin{bmatrix} d_1 \\ c \end{bmatrix}\!\Big\rangle \langle a\,nil, \kappa fg\rangle \begin{bmatrix} d_2 \\ c \end{bmatrix}\!\Big\rangle \langle\, nil, \kappa fg\rangle.$$

This example is meant to illustrate that the order of the application of the action manipulation functions is chosen correctly.

6. Let us consider $P \equiv rec\,p.\tau\big(a(pf) + a(pg)\big)$, where f and g are as above (cf. also example 2. on page 72).

$\mathcal{G}[\![pf]\!]$ is  , $\mathcal{G}[\![a(pf)]\!]$ is 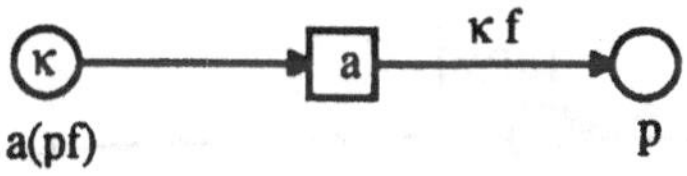 , and

$\mathcal{G}[\![a(pf) + a(pg)]\!]$ is

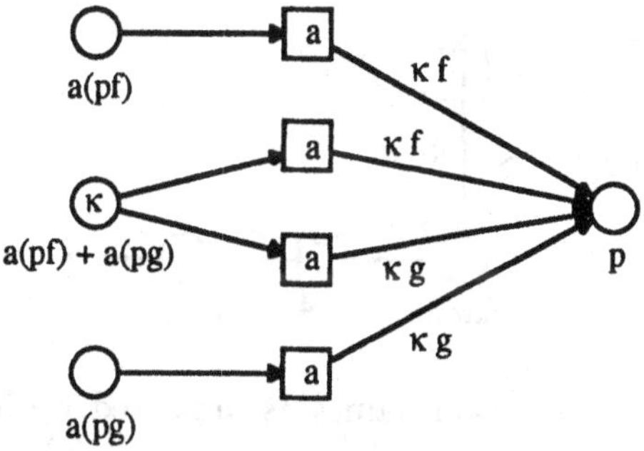

$\mathcal{G}[\![P]\!]$ is

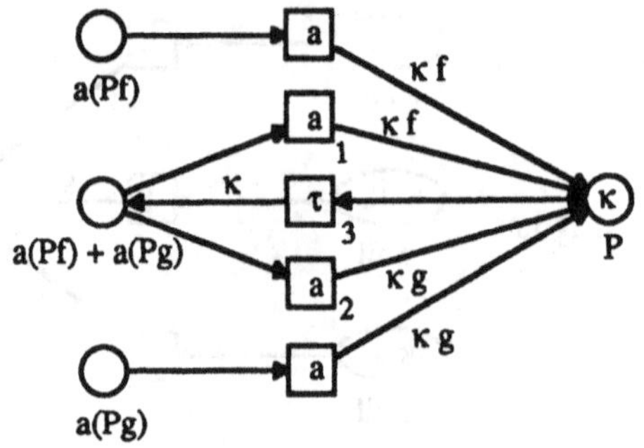

Let $Q :\equiv a(Pf) + a(Pg)$, then (using the transition names as indicated)

$$\langle P,\kappa\rangle \left[{}^{d_3}_{\tau}\right\rangle \langle Q,\kappa\rangle \left[{}^{d_2}_{a}\right\rangle \langle P,\kappa g\rangle \left[{}^{d_3}_{\tau}\right\rangle \langle Q,\kappa g\rangle \left[{}^{d_1}_{a}\right\rangle \langle P,\kappa fg\rangle \left[{}^{d_3}_{\tau}\right\rangle \langle Q,\kappa fg\rangle \left[{}^{d_1}_{c}\right\rangle \langle P,\kappa ffg\rangle$$

is one of many possible occurrence sequences.

7. Next we exhibit another term P where $traces(\mathcal{T}[\![P]\!])$ contains a counter (see Definition 5.6) and which is neither representable as a finite automaton nor as a finite Petri net, although all action manipulation functions occurring in it have finite renaming. Let

$$P :\equiv rec\, p.\tau\Big(z\, nil + i((pf \mid \bar{a}dz\, nil)\text{–}\{a,\bar{a}\})\Big),$$

where $f = \{z \mapsto a\}$. Let g be as in Definition 1.12, $h = \{a \mapsto \bot, \bar{a} \mapsto \bot\}$, $Q \equiv (pf \nmid \bar{a}dz\, nil)gh$, and $R \equiv z\, nil + iQ$. Then $P \equiv rec\, p.\tau R$, and $\mathcal{G}[\![P]\!]$ is

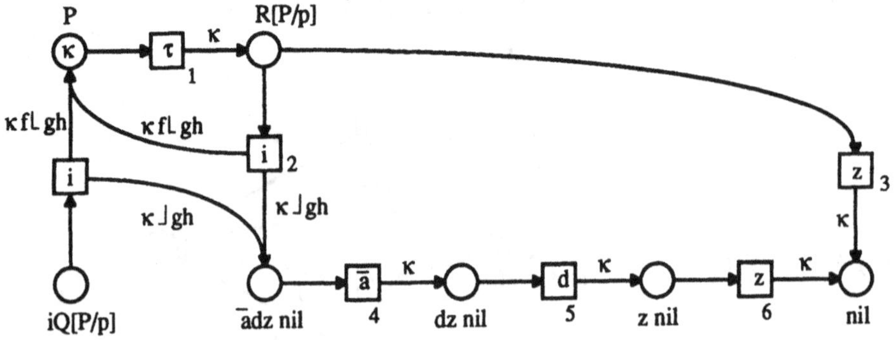

Then using the transition names as indicated we have for example the following occurrence sequence $\langle P,\kappa\rangle \begin{bmatrix} d_1 \\ \tau \end{bmatrix}\!\Big\rangle \langle R[P/p],\kappa\rangle \begin{bmatrix} d_2 \\ i \end{bmatrix}\!\Big\rangle \begin{matrix} \langle P,\kappa f\llcorner gh\rangle \\ \langle \bar{a}dz\, \text{nil}, \kappa\lrcorner gh\rangle \end{matrix} \begin{bmatrix} d_1 \\ \tau \end{bmatrix}\!\Big\rangle$

$$\begin{matrix} \langle R[P/p],\kappa f\llcorner gh\rangle \\ \langle \bar{a}dz\, \text{nil}, \kappa\lrcorner gh\rangle \end{matrix} \begin{bmatrix} \langle d_3, d_4\rangle \\ \tau \end{bmatrix}\!\Big\rangle \begin{matrix} \langle\, nil,\kappa f\llcorner gh\rangle \\ \langle dz\, \text{nil}, \kappa\lrcorner gh\rangle \end{matrix} \begin{bmatrix} d_5 \\ d \end{bmatrix}\!\Big\rangle \begin{matrix} \langle\, nil,\kappa f\llcorner gh\rangle \\ \langle z\, \text{nil}, \kappa\lrcorner gh\rangle \end{matrix} \begin{bmatrix} d_6 \\ z \end{bmatrix}\!\Big\rangle \begin{matrix} \langle\, nil,\kappa f\llcorner gh\rangle \\ \langle\, \text{nil}, \kappa\lrcorner gh\rangle \end{matrix}.$$

8. Let $P \equiv rec\, p.\tau(a\, nil + p)$.
$\mathcal{G}[a\, nil + p]$ is as given below on the left, and $\mathcal{G}[P]$ is as given on the right.

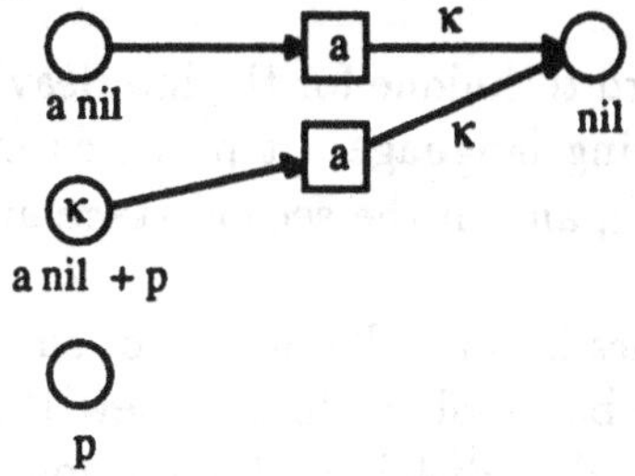

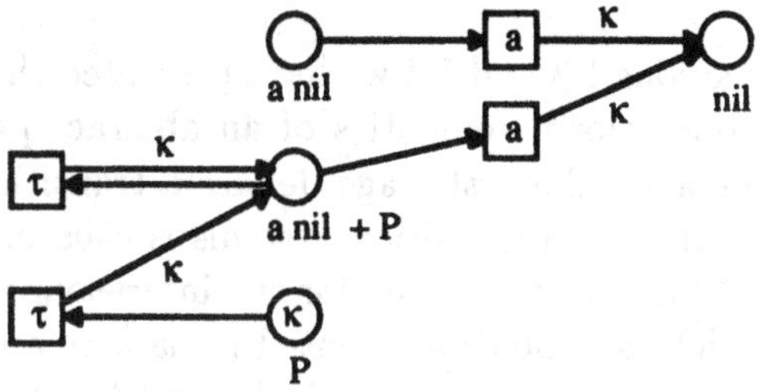

This example shows that for the construction for the recursion, it would not suffice to introduce just one τ-transition which starts from the place P. Instead a τ-transition has to start from every place Q with P *smd_of* Q.

9. $\mathcal{G}[\![rec\, p.\tau\, nil]\!]$ is 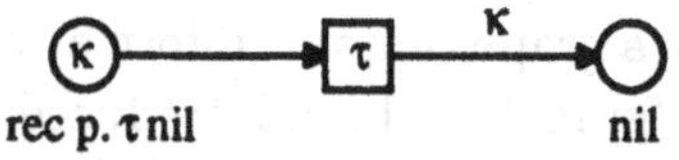 . If the body of the recursion does not contain the identifier, a new place is introduced.

10. Let $P \equiv rec\, p.\tau p$, $Q \equiv rec\, q.\tau aq$.

$\mathcal{G}[P]$ is 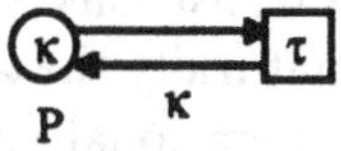 , $\mathcal{G}[\![Q]\!]$ is 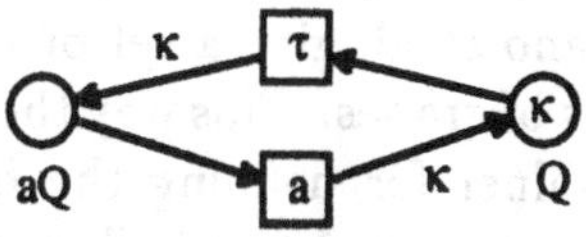 ,

and then $\mathcal{G}[P + Q]\!]$ is 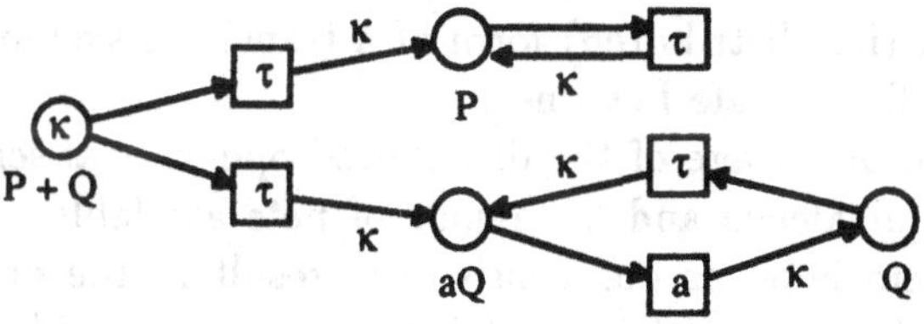 .

This example shows that for the sum a new place is necessary, the identification of both initial places would lead to an inconsistent representation.

11. Let $P \equiv rec\, p.\tau(a\, nil \mid p) \equiv rec\, p.\tau\big((a\, nil \nmid p)g\big)$, where g is as in 1.12.
$\mathcal{G}[P]$ is

Let $d = \big\langle P, \tau, \{\langle a\, nil, \kappa \lfloor g\rangle, \langle P, \kappa\rfloor g\rangle\}\big\rangle$, then e.g.

$$\langle P, \kappa\rangle \begin{bmatrix} d \\ \tau \end{bmatrix}\!\!\Big\rangle \begin{matrix}\langle a\, nil, \kappa\lfloor g\rangle \\ \langle P, \kappa\rfloor g\rangle\end{matrix} \begin{bmatrix} d \\ \tau \end{bmatrix}\!\!\Big\rangle \begin{matrix}\langle a\, nil, \kappa\lfloor g\rangle \\ \langle a\, nil, \kappa\lfloor g\rfloor g\rangle \\ \langle P, \kappa\rfloor g\rfloor g\rangle\end{matrix} \ldots$$

is a possible occurrence sequence.

6.3 Distributed operational semantics following Degano, De Nicola, Montanari, and Olderog

In sections 1.3 and 1.4 we have presented the standard technique for the interleaving operational semantics of an abstract programming language. It proceeds in two stages, the first stage defines a transition system, and in the second stage an equivalence on transition systems is chosen.

While this technique for the interleaving semantics is generally accepted, such a widely accepted distributed semantics appears to be missing. In our view the approach of Degano, De Nicola, and Montanari towards a distributed operational semantics is most promising.

The fundamental idea is contained in [Degano et al. 85]. It consists in decomposing a term P into a set of so-called *grapes*. Every grape of P represents a subprocess of P which is in parallel to the other grapes of P, but which initially starts sequentially. Additionally a grape contains information about the context in which it occurs in P. The name 'grape' has been introduced by Degano, De Nicola, and Montanari, and we will keep it here. It might help to keep in mind that a grape (Definition 6.10 1. below) is a singular term (Definition 1.13) which appears within some context (Definition 3.13).

Secondly Degano et al. give a set of rules to derive the transitions which can occur between sets of grapes. This way they generalize very naturally the technique of Plotkin and Milner for defining the first stage of the operational semantics. But in contrast to section 1.3 this does not lead to a transition system, but to a generalized (i.e. distributed) form of a transition system. As we will present it below this will be a safe Petri net.

For the second stage of the distributed operational semantics there are many notions of equivalence and behaviour of nets available. But we do not need to introduce them here, as our consistency result in the next section refers to the equality of safe nets and thus is the strongest conceivable consistency result.

Degano, De Nicola, and Montanari have refined their distributed operational semantics in a series of papers. For this section [Degano et al. 87] is the most appropriate reference. The semantics presented there has also been refined and made popular in [Olderog 87]. But that refinement is not so important for this section, as it concerns the initial parallelism in a sum and in a recursive body, which is excluded syntactically in qterms. Nevertheless similar to Olderog we prefer to work with safe nets and to avoid the introduction of yet another class of nets. Furthermore safe nets are almost the same as augmented C/E-systems, the class of nets used in [Degano et al. 87].

Definition 6.10 1. $grapes := \{ PC \mid P \in singterms \wedge C \in contexts \}$
For the definition of PC see 3.15, for that of *singterms* see 1.13, and for that of *contexts* 3.13.

2. The operators f, $\lfloor$, $\rfloor$ are extended for sets of grapes. Let $I \subseteq grapes$, we define (for $f \in Fun$)

$$If := \{Qf \mid Q \in I\},\ I\lfloor := \{Q\lfloor \mid Q \in I\}, \text{ and } I\rfloor := \{Q\rfloor \mid Q \in I\}.$$

3. $dec : qterms \to \mathcal{P}(grapes)$

$$dec(P) := \begin{cases} \{P\} & \text{if } P \in singterms \\ \big(dec(P')\big)f & \text{if } P \equiv P'f \\ \big(dec(P_1)\big)\lfloor \cup \big(dec(P_2)\big)\rfloor & \text{if } P \equiv P_1 \mid\!\!\!\ast\, P_2 \end{cases}$$

4. Let $I \subseteq grapes$, I is called *complete* if $\exists P \in qterms:\ dec(P) = I$. □

Fact 6.11 1. For all $P \in qterms:\quad dec(P)$ is finite and non-empty.

2. *dec* is injective.

3. $conterms \supset grapes \supset contexts$ (see also the overview on p. 165). □

In contrast to [Degano et al. 87], [Degano et al. 88] and [Olderog 87] we concentrate our attention to qterms, i.e. terms where every sum is a choice among processes which start with a single action which is not in the scope of an action manipulation function, and where every recursive body starts with a τ. For this set of terms the semantics of the above cited three papers agree for the common sublanguage. Furthermore we avoid (in our view) fruitless technical complications, and for the grapes we have a clear and natural dissection into a singular term and the context in which this singular term occurs.

Note that qterms are very general with respect to parallel composition and action manipulation. In particular the parallel composition operators of CCS (as used in [Degano et al. 87]) and of TCSP (as used in [Olderog 87]) can be modelled. Moreover sequential composition is treated (as a derived operator, cf. Definition 1.17). The latter is classified as a 'more subtle' topic in [Olderog 87, p. 220].

The decomposition function *dec* is in complete agreement with [Degano et al. 85], [Degano et al. 87] and [Olderog 87] for those qterms which are treated by the respective papers. The main difference concerns the parallel composition which is treated more general here. In particular Degano et al. have

$$dec(P_1 \mid P_2) = dec(P_1) \mid id\ \cup\ id \mid dec(P_2)$$

while we have $dec(P_1 \mid P_2) = dec(P_1)\lfloor g\ \cup\ dec(P_2)\rfloor g$, where g is as in Definition 1.12. Similarly Olderog has

$$dec(P_1 \parallel_A P_2) = dec(P_1) \parallel_A id\ \cup\ id \parallel_A dec(P_2)$$

while we have $dec(P_1 \parallel_A P_2) = dec(P_1)\lfloor g_A\ \cup\ dec(P_2)\rfloor g_A$, where g_A is as in Definition 1.12. A minor point is that we identify α-congruent terms syntactically (see section 1.1), while this point is not elaborated in the papers cited above. Finally Olderog has

$$dec(rec\,p.\tau P) = \{rec\,p.\tau P : \tau P\}$$

while we have $dec(rec\,p.\tau P) = \{rec\,p.\tau P\}$, but the binding information (τP :) is redundant for qterms.

The next definition gives the distributed operational semantics of a qterm following Degano, De Nicola, Montanari, and Olderog. It generalizes the interleaving operational semantics (Definitions 1.23 and 1.24): Instead of a transition system we get a safe Petri net. Instead of the global states of the transition system, namely the terms, we have distributed local states (= places), namely the grapes.

The transitions of the net are defined with the help of inference rules analogous to the definition of the transitions of the transiton system in Definition 1.24. But a transition of the net may depend on, and lead to more than just one local state.

Definition 6.12 (the safe net of a qterm) Let $P \in qterms$, then

$$\mathcal{D}[\![P]\!] := \big\langle \text{grapes}, \mathbf{D}_{\twoheadrightarrow}, dec(P)\big\rangle,$$

where $\mathbf{D}_{\twoheadrightarrow} \subseteq \mathcal{P}(grapes) \times Act \times \mathcal{P}(grapes)$ is the least relation satisfying the rules below. For $\langle I, a, J\rangle \in \mathbf{D}_{\twoheadrightarrow}$ we write $I -a\twoheadrightarrow J$. For every $b \in \{\tau\} \cup Vis$, $a, a_1, a_2 \in Act$, $f \in Fun$, $p \in Idf$, $P, Q \in qterms$, and $I, I_1, I_2, J, J_1, J_2 \subseteq$ grapes there exist rules:

act⟩	$\{bP\} -b\twoheadrightarrow dec(P)$
fun⟩	$\dfrac{I -a\twoheadrightarrow J \;\wedge\; af \neq \bot}{If -af\twoheadrightarrow Jf}$
sum⟩	$\dfrac{\{P\} -a\twoheadrightarrow J}{\{P+Q\} -a\twoheadrightarrow J \;\wedge\; \{Q+P\} -a\twoheadrightarrow J}$
asyn⟩	$\dfrac{I -a\twoheadrightarrow J}{I\llcorner -a\twoheadrightarrow J\llcorner \;\wedge\; I\lrcorner -a\twoheadrightarrow J\lrcorner}$
syn⟩	$\dfrac{a_1, a_2 \in Vis \;\wedge\; I_1 -a_1\twoheadrightarrow J_1 \;\wedge\; I_2 -a_2\twoheadrightarrow J_2}{I_1\llcorner \cup I_2\lrcorner -[a_1, a_2]\twoheadrightarrow J_1\llcorner \cup J_2\lrcorner}$
rec⟩	$\{rec\,p.\tau P\} -\tau\twoheadrightarrow dec\big(P[rec\,p.\tau P/p]\big)$

Let $M, M' \subseteq$ grapes, $d = \langle I, a, J\rangle \in \mathbf{D}_{\twoheadrightarrow}$, then for $M[d\rangle M'$ we write $M[I -a\twoheadrightarrow J\rangle M'$. □

Most important are the rules act⟩ and syn⟩. Rule act⟩ reflects the idea that a singular process after performing its initial action activates a set of parallel processes, namely the set of grapes of the prefixed term. Rule syn⟩ reflects the idea that matching pairs of sets of grapes combine to a synchronization transition. The other rules are rather straightforward generalizations of the rules in Definition 1.24. The rule rec⟩ is a combination of the generalizations of act) and of rec). This combination suffices here as we concentrate our attention to qterms.

Finally let us remark that [Degano et al. 87] use a so-called augmented C/E-system as the operational semantics of a term. The augmentation consists in allowing transitions on loops to occur, and to allow non-simple nets and isolated elements. An augmented C/E-system is almost the same as a safe Petri net. On the other hand Olderog uses safe Petri nets, but in a last step [Olderog 87, p. 208] he uses what he calls 'abstract nets' as semantics. The abstractness concerns the reachability and the naming of places [Olderog 87, p. 203].

Fact 6.13 If $I -a\twoheadrightarrow J$ then $I \neq \emptyset \neq J$. □

The next theorem transfers the results of [Degano et al. 87] to our case, which partially is a special case (with respect to sum and recursion, as they are starting sequentially) and which partially is a generalization (with respect to the parallel composition). 1. and 3. of the following theorem correspond to [Degano et al. 87, Prop. 4.2], 4. corresponds to [Degano et al. 87, Theorem 4.1]. 2. shows for every qterm P that $\mathcal{D}[\![P]\!]$ is a safe net, and 5. shows that it is a consistent net representation.

Theorem 6.14 Let $P \in$ *qterms*.

1. If $M \subseteq$ *grapes*, and $I -a\twoheadrightarrow J$ such that $dec(P)[I -a\twoheadrightarrow J\rangle M$, then

$$\exists Q \in qterms: \; M = dec(Q) \;\wedge\; P -a\rightarrow Q.$$

2. Every reachable marking of $\mathcal{D}[\![P]\!]$ is a complete set of grapes.
   In particular $\mathcal{D}[\![P]\!]$ is a safe net.
3. $P -a\rightarrow Q$ implies $Q \in qterms \wedge \exists I, J \subseteq grapes: \; dec(P)[I -a\twoheadrightarrow J\rangle dec(Q)$.
4. $Transys(\mathcal{D}[\![P]\!]) \cong Reach(\mathcal{T}[\![P]\!])$
5. $\mathcal{D}[\![P]\!]$ is a consistent net representation of P (cf. Definition 4.6).

Proof 1. $dec(P)[I -a\twoheadrightarrow J\rangle M$ implies $I \subseteq dec(P)$ and $M = dec(P) - I + J$ (the sets $dec(P)$, I, and J are considered as characteristic functions *grapes* $\rightarrow \{0,1\}$ here). We perform an induction on the length of the proof of $I -a\twoheadrightarrow J$. If the last rule applied is ... (the cases fun⟩, sum⟩, asyn⟩ are left to the reader) act⟩ Then $I = \{aQ\}$ and $J = dec(Q)$. As $\{aQ\} \subseteq dec(P)$, $P \equiv aQ$ follows. Hence $M = dec(Q)$. Clearly $P -a\rightarrow Q$.

syn⟩ Then $I = I_1\llcorner \cup I_2\lrcorner$, $J = J_1\llcorner \cup J_2\lrcorner$, and for $a_1, a_2 \in Vis:\ a = [a_1, a_2] \wedge I_1 -a_1\twoheadrightarrow J_1 \wedge I_2 -a_2\twoheadrightarrow J_2$. As $I \subseteq dec(P)$ we know that $P \equiv P_1 \nmid P_2$, and $I_1\llcorner \subseteq dec(P_1)\llcorner$ and $I_2\lrcorner \subseteq dec(P_2)\lrcorner$. Hence $\forall i \in \{1,2\}:\ I_i \subseteq dec(P_i)$. By ind. hyp. $\forall i \in \{1,2\}:\ \exists Q_i \in qterms:\ dec(Q_i) = dec(P_i) - I_i + J_i \wedge P_i -a_i\rightarrow Q_i$. By syn) $P -a\rightarrow Q_1 \nmid Q_2$. Furthermore
$M = \big(dec(P_1) - I_1 + J_1\big)\llcorner \cup \big(dec(P_2) - I_2 + J_2\big)\lrcorner = dec(Q_1 \nmid Q_2)$.

rec⟩ Then $I = \{rec\, r.\tau R\}$, $P \equiv rec\, r.\tau R$, and $J = dec(R[P/r])$. As $R, P \in qterms$ clearly $R[P/r] \in qterms$. Furthermore $(\tau R)[P/r] \equiv \tau(R[P/r])$. By act) $\tau(R[P/r]) -\tau\rightarrow R[P/r]$, hence by rec) $P -\tau\rightarrow R[P/r]$. □ 1.

2. An induction on the length of the transition sequence leading to the reachable marking using 1. shows the claim.
3. Induction on the length of the proof of $P -a\rightarrow Q$. If the last rule applied is ... (the cases fun), sum), asyn), and syn) are left to the reader)

act) Then $P \equiv aQ$ and $Q \in qterms$. By act⟩ $\{aQ\} -a\twoheadrightarrow dec(Q)$, and clearly $dec(P)[\{aQ\} -a\twoheadrightarrow dec(Q)\rangle dec(Q)$.

rec) Then $P \equiv rec\, r.R$, and as $P \in qterms$ we even know that $P \equiv rec\, r.\tau R'$, and $(\tau R')[P/r] -a\rightarrow Q$. Clearly $(\tau R')[P/r] \equiv \tau(R'[P/r])$, hence $a = \tau \wedge Q \equiv R'[P/r]$. As $R', P \in qterms$, clearly $Q \in qterms$. By rec⟩ $\{P\} -\tau\twoheadrightarrow dec(Q)$, and clearly $dec(P)[\{P\} -\tau\twoheadrightarrow dec(Q)\rangle dec(Q)$. □ 3.

4. Let $P \in qterms$. Let $S := [dec(P)\rangle_{\mathbf{D}_{\succ}}$, then $Transys(\mathcal{D}[\![P]\!]) = \langle S, D, dec(P)\rangle$, where $D = \{\, \langle M_1, a, M_2\rangle \mid M_1 \in S \wedge \exists I, J \subseteq grapes:\ M_1[I -a\twoheadrightarrow J\rangle M_2\}$.
Let $\hat{S} := \{Q \mid \exists w : P -w\rightarrow Q\}$, then $Reach(\mathcal{T}[\![P]\!]) = \langle \hat{S}, \mathbf{D} \cap (\hat{S} \times Act \times \hat{S}), P\rangle$. Due to 3. $\hat{S} \subseteq qterms$.

Now define $\varphi : \hat{S} \rightarrow S$ such that $\varphi(Q) := dec(Q)$. For $M \in S$ with $dec(P)[u\rangle M$ for $u \in \mathbf{D}_{\succ}^{*}$ an induction on the length of u using 1. proves that φ is surjective. Injectivity follows from 6.11.
Clearly $\varphi(P) = dec(P)$. Now for $Q, R \in \hat{S}$, $a \in Act$ we will show

$$Q -a\rightarrow R \quad \text{iff} \quad \langle dec(Q), a, dec(R)\rangle \in D.$$

"⇒" follows by 3. "⇐" Let $\langle dec(Q), a, dec(R)\rangle \in D$, then for some $I, J \subseteq grapes$ $dec(Q)[I -a\twoheadrightarrow J\rangle dec(R)$. By 1. $\exists R' \in qterms:\ dec(R) = dec(R') \wedge Q -a\rightarrow R'$. As dec is injective $Q -a\rightarrow R$ follows. □ 4.
5. By 4., 1.33, and 1.35 $Transys(\mathcal{D}[\![P]\!]) \sim \mathcal{T}[\![P]\!]$. □

6.4 Distributed consistency

This section is devoted to the proof of the consistency of the PrT-net construction which has been presented in section 6.2. In contrast to the consistency results for finite transition systems (Theorem 3.26) and for finite and safe Petri nets (Theorem 4.17) the consistency we will prove here (Theorem 6.21 below) refers to the distributed semantics. Of course by Theorem 6.14 5. we then also have consistency to the interleaving semantics.

A second difference to the previous consistency results is that Theorem 6.21 below does not just show equivalence with respect to bisimularity (which is already very strong) but even proves equality of the reachable part of the safe-net-semantics of our PrT-net construction and of the reachable part of the distributed semantics. This way we have consistency with respect to all equivalence notions (which are based on the reachable part), and in particular we also have consistency with respect to the concurrent behaviour.

The fundamental fact used for the proof of the consistency is that the set *grapes* and the set (*singterms* × *contexts*) are in a one-to-one correspondence. In the introduction to this chapter we have tried to motivate that the static core of a grape is represented as a place (i.e. as a singular term) in the PrT-net, while the context information appears as the dynamically changing individual token (i.e. as an element of *contexts*). This interrelation now formally shows up in our consistency result.

As we have seen in Definitions 6.6 and 6.7 for the safe-net-semantics of a PrT-net the function γ maps a pair of a singular term and a context to one contexted term. If the range of γ is restricted to the set *grapes*, then it even is a bijection, i.e. γ establishes the above mentioned one-to-one correspondence.

Fact 6.15 $\gamma : (\mathit{singterms} \times \mathit{contexts}) \rightarrow \mathit{grapes}$ is a bijection.

Proof For a given grape Q, there is exactly one dissection into a pair $P \in$ *singterms*, $C \in$ *contexts* such that $PC \equiv Q$. □

Throughout this section we understand the range of γ to be restricted to *grapes*, in particular we use γ^{-1} to denote the inverse of γ, i.e.

$$\gamma^{-1} : \mathit{grapes} \rightarrow (\mathit{singterms} \times \mathit{contexts}).$$

Due to the case for action manipulation functions of Definition 6.9 the PrT-net construction is not defined for all qterms. But if every action manipulation function f which appears in the qterm P fulfills $(EVis)f \cap Vis = \emptyset$, then the construction is defined. To this end let us define the following.

Definition 6.16 1. For $P \in conterms$

$$onesyn(P) \text{ iff for every subterm } Qf \text{ of } P: \quad (EVis)f \cap Vis = \emptyset.$$

2. For $X \subseteq conterms$ define $onesyn(X)$ iff $\forall P \in X : onesyn(P)$. □

The name for this predicate has been chosen as intuitively a term P with $onesyn(P)$ allows every action to take part in a synchronization at most once.[1] Formally this fact shows up in Lemma 6.20.

For the PrT-nets of our construction we have the following useful properties.

Property 6.17 Let $P \in qterms$.

1. $\mathcal{G}[\![P]\!]$ is defined if and only if $onesyn(P)$.
2. If $\mathcal{G}[\![P]\!] = \langle S, D, Z \rangle$ is defined, then

$$onesyn(\gamma(Z)) \wedge \forall Q \in S: onesyn(Q) \wedge \forall \langle Q, a, M \rangle \in D: onesyn(\gamma(M)).$$

Proof Induction on the structure of P, for 2. use 1. □

Due to the first fact we immediately have that our PrT-net construction is defined for all CCS-qterms.

Corollary 6.18 For all $P \in qterms \cap terms_{CCS}$

$$\mathcal{G}[\![P]\!] \text{ is defined.}$$ □

But the analogue for TCSP is not true, as the action manipulation function g_A used in the abbreviation $\|_A$ (see Definition 1.12) in general does not have the required property. For example for $a \in Alph$ we have $([a, a])g_a = a \in Vis$. See the end of this chapter for a discussion of this point.

The next proposition collects a number of facts which we use in the proof of the consistency. In particular the initial markings of the PrT-net construction and of the distributed semantics are related (1.). Furthermore it is shown that the singular transitions are in a one-to-one correspondence (2. and 3.).

Proposition 6.19 Let $P \in qterms$ such that $\mathcal{G}[\![P]\!] = \langle S, D, Z \rangle$ is defined. Then

1. $Z = \gamma^{-1}(dec(P))$,
2. $\langle Q, a, M \rangle \in D \Rightarrow \{Q\} \, {-a\twoheadrightarrow} \, \gamma(M)$,
3. $Q \in S \wedge \{Q\} \, {-a\twoheadrightarrow} \, J \Rightarrow \langle Q, a, \gamma^{-1}(J) \rangle \in D$.

---

[1] If all communications are binary in the sense of [Bergstra, Klop 85, p. 100] the predicate *onesyn* is true.

Proof We perform an induction on the structure of P, the cases $P \equiv P'f$ and $P \equiv P_1 \nparallel P_2$ are easily checked. For $P \in singterms$ we perform an inner induction, and additionally show that if $\mathcal{G}[\![P]\!] = \langle S, D, Z\rangle$ is defined, then

4. $P \in S$.

Again the cases $P \equiv nil$, $P \equiv p$, and $P \equiv aP'$ are immediate.

<u>$P \equiv P_1 + P_2$</u> where $P_1, P_2 \in singterms$. Let $\mathcal{G}[\![P_i]\!] = \langle S_i, D_i, Z_i\rangle$. Then $\mathcal{G}[\![P]\!] = \langle S_1 \cup S_2 \cup \{P\}, D_1 \cup D_2 \cup \{\langle P, a, M\rangle \mid \exists i \in \{1,2\} : \langle P_i, a, M\rangle \in D_i\}, \{\langle P, \kappa\rangle\}\rangle$.
1. $\gamma^{-1}(dec(P)) = \{\langle P, \kappa\rangle\}$, as $P \in singterms$.
2. For $d \in D_1 \cup D_2$ the claim follows by ind. hyp. for P_1 respectively P_2. Now let $d = \langle P, a, M\rangle$ for (w.l.o.g.) $\langle P_1, a, M\rangle \in D_1$. Then by ind. hyp. $\{P_1\} -a\twoheadrightarrow \gamma(M)$. By sum$\rangle$ $\{P\} -a\twoheadrightarrow \gamma(M)$ follows.
3. For $Q \in S_1 \cup S_2$ the claim follows by ind. hyp. for P_1 respectively P_2. Now if $Q \equiv P$ and $\{P\} -a\twoheadrightarrow J$, the last rule applied in the proof of $\{P\} -a\twoheadrightarrow J$ must have been sum$\rangle$. Hence w.l.o.g. $\{P_1\} -a\twoheadrightarrow J$. By ind. hyp. 4. for P_1 we know $P_1 \in S_1$, hence by ind. hyp. 3. for P_1 we know $\langle P_1, a, \gamma^{-1}(J)\rangle \in D_1$. The claim follows.
4. Trivial.

Before we prove the last case "$P \equiv rec\, r.\tau\bar{R}$", we show the following facts. Let $P \in singterms, Q \in qterms$, and $r \in Idf$. Then

(∗1) $dec(Q[P/r]) = \{R[P/r] \mid R \in dec(Q)\}$,

(∗2) $\forall C \in contexts : Q[P/r]C \equiv (QC)[P/r]$.

Let $P, Q \in singterms, r \in Idf$. Then

(∗3) $\{Q\} -a\twoheadrightarrow J \Rightarrow \{Q[P/r]\} -a\twoheadrightarrow \{R[P/r] \mid R \in J\}$,

(∗4) $P\ smd\_of\ Q \wedge \{P\} -a\twoheadrightarrow J \Rightarrow \{Q\} -a\twoheadrightarrow J$,

(∗5) $\tilde{Q} \equiv Q[P/r] \wedge \{\tilde{Q}\} -a\twoheadrightarrow \tilde{J}$
$\Rightarrow P\ smd\_of\ \tilde{Q} \wedge \{P\} -a\twoheadrightarrow \tilde{J}$
$\vee\ \exists J \subseteq grapes : \tilde{J} = \{R[P/r] \mid R \in J\} \wedge \{Q\} -a\twoheadrightarrow J$.

(∗1) and (∗2) are proved by induction on Q respectively C, for (∗2) use 3.17. To prove (∗3) we perform an induction on $Q \in singterms$. Let $\{Q\} -a\twoheadrightarrow J$. If $Q \equiv nil$ or $Q \equiv p \in Idf$, then $\neg(\{Q\} -a\twoheadrightarrow J)$.

<u>$Q \equiv aQ'$</u> for $a \in \{\tau\} \cup Vis$. Then the last rule applied must have been act$\rangle$, hence $J = dec(Q')$. $Q[P/r] \equiv a(Q'[P/r])$, by rule act$\rangle$ $Q[P/r] -a\twoheadrightarrow dec(Q'[P/r])$. By (∗1) $dec(Q'[P/r]) = \{R[P/r] \mid R \in J\}$.

<u>$Q \equiv Q_1 + Q_2$</u> for $Q_1, Q_2 \in singterms$. Then w.l.o.g. $\{Q_1\} -a\twoheadrightarrow J$. By ind. hyp. $\{Q_1[P/r]\} -a\twoheadrightarrow \{R[P/r] \mid R \in J\}$. $Q[P/r] \equiv Q_1[P/r] + Q_2[P/r]$. By sum$\rangle$ $Q[P/r] -a\twoheadrightarrow \{R[P/r] \mid R \in J\}$.

<u>$Q \equiv rec\, q.\tau Q'$</u> for $q \in Idf$. Due to Fact 1.9 we may assume $q \notin FI(P) \cup \{r\}$. Hence $Q[P/r] \equiv rec\, q.\tau(Q'[P/r])$. By rule rec$\rangle$ $\{Q[P/r]\} -\tau\twoheadrightarrow dec(Q'[P/r][Q[P/r]/q])$. By the substitution lemma (1.11) $Q'[P/r][Q[P/r]/q] \equiv Q'[Q/q][P/r]$. The last rule applied to prove $\{Q\} -a\twoheadrightarrow J$ must have been rec$\rangle$, hence $J = dec(Q'[Q/q])$ and $a = \tau$. Thus by (*1) $dec(Q'[Q/q][P/r]) = \{R[P/r] \mid R \in J\}$ which proves the claim.

□ (*3)

(*4) is easily checked by an induction on the length of the proof of $P\ smd\_of\ Q$. To prove (*5) let $\tilde{Q} \equiv Q[P/r] \ \wedge\ \{\tilde{Q}\} -a\twoheadrightarrow \tilde{J}$. We perform an induction on $Q \in singterms$.

<u>$Q \equiv nil$</u> Then $\tilde{Q} \equiv nil$ and $\neg(\{\tilde{Q}\} -a\twoheadrightarrow \tilde{J})$.

<u>$Q \equiv p$</u> for $p \in Idf$. If $p \neq r$, then $\tilde{Q} \equiv p$ and $\neg(\{\tilde{Q}\} -a\twoheadrightarrow \tilde{J})$. Else $p = r$, then $\tilde{Q} \equiv P$. Hence $P\ smd\_of\ \tilde{Q} \ \wedge\ \{P\} -a\twoheadrightarrow \tilde{J}$.

<u>$Q \equiv aQ'$</u> for $a \in \{\tau\} \cup Vis$. Then $\tilde{Q} \equiv a(Q'[P/r])$ and $\tilde{J} = dec(Q'[P/r])$. By act$\rangle$ $\{Q\} -a\twoheadrightarrow dec(Q')$, and by (*1) $\tilde{J} = \{R[P/r] \mid R \in dec(Q')\}$ which proves the claim.

<u>$Q \equiv Q_1 + Q_2$</u> for $Q_1, Q_2 \in singterms$. Then $\tilde{Q} \equiv Q_1[P/r] + Q_2[P/r]$. And w.l.o.g. $\{Q_1[P/r]\} -a\twoheadrightarrow \tilde{J}$. By ind. hyp. $P\ smd\_of\ Q_1[P/r] \ \vee \exists J :\ \tilde{J} = \{R[P/r] \mid R \in J\} \wedge \{Q_1\} -a\twoheadrightarrow J$. In the first case $P\ smd\_of\ \tilde{Q}$, in the second case by sum$\rangle$ $\{Q\} -a\twoheadrightarrow J$ follows.

<u>$Q \equiv rec\, q.\tau Q'$</u> for $q \in Idf$. Due to Fact 1.9 we may assume $q \notin FI(P) \cup \{r\}$. Hence $\tilde{Q} \equiv rec\, q.\tau(Q'[P/r])$. By rec$\rangle$ $a = \tau$ and $\tilde{J} = dec(Q'[P/r][Q[P/r]/q])$. By the substituition lemma (1.11) $Q'[P/r][Q[P/r]/q] \equiv Q'[Q/q][P/r]$. Hence by (*1) $\tilde{J} = \{R[P/r] \mid R \in dec(Q'[Q/q])\}$. And clearly by rec$\rangle$ $\{Q\} -\tau\twoheadrightarrow dec(Q'[Q/q])$. Hence the claim follows. □ (*5)

Proof of Proposition 6.19 continued.

<u>$P \equiv rec\, r.\tau\bar{R}$</u> for $r \in Idf$. Let $\mathcal{G}[\![\bar{R}]\!] = \langle S, D, Z\rangle$. Then $\mathcal{G}[\![P]\!] = \langle \bar{S}, \bar{D}, \{\langle P, \kappa\rangle\}\rangle$ where $\bar{S} = \{P\} \cup \{Q[P/r] \mid Q \in S\}$ and

$$\begin{aligned}\bar{D} = \quad & \Big\{\langle Q[P/r], a, \{\langle R[P/r], C\rangle \mid \langle R, C\rangle \in M\}\rangle \;\Big|\; \langle Q, a, M\rangle \in D\Big\} \\ \cup & \Big\{\langle Q, \tau, \{\langle R[P/r], C\rangle \mid \langle R, C\rangle \in Z\}\rangle \;\Big|\; Q \in \bar{S} \ \wedge\ P\ smd\_of\ Q\Big\}.\end{aligned}$$

1. $\gamma^{-1}(dec(P)) = \{\langle P, \kappa\rangle\}$ as $P \in singterms$.

2. Let $d \in \bar{D}$. We distinguish two cases.
Case 1. $d = \big\langle Q[P/r], a, \{\langle R[P/r], C\rangle \mid \langle R, C\rangle \in M\}\big\rangle$ for $\langle Q, a, M\rangle \in D$. By ind. hyp. $\{Q\} -a\twoheadrightarrow \gamma(M)$. By (*3) $\{Q[P/r]\} -a\twoheadrightarrow \{R[P/r] \mid R \in \gamma(M)\}$.
$\gamma\big(\{\langle R[P/r], C\rangle \mid \langle R, C\rangle \in M\}\big) = \{R[P/r]C \mid \langle R, C\rangle \in M\} \overset{(*2)}{=}$ $\{RC[P/r] \mid \langle R, C\rangle \in M\} = \{R[P/r] \mid R \in \gamma(M)\}$, this proves the claim.
Case 2. $d = \big\langle Q, \tau, \{\langle R[P/r], C\rangle \mid \langle R, C\rangle \in Z\}\big\rangle$ for $Q \in \bar{S} \wedge P\ smd\_of\ Q$. By rec⟩ $\{P\} -\tau\twoheadrightarrow dec(\bar{R}[P/r])$. By ind. hyp. 1. $Z = \gamma^{-1}(dec(\bar{R}))$, hence $\gamma(Z) = dec(\bar{R})$. And then $dec(\bar{R}[P/r]) \overset{(*1)}{=} \{R[P/r] \mid R \in dec(\bar{R})\} = \{R[P/r] \mid R \in \gamma(Z)\} =$ $\{RC[P/r] \mid \langle R, C\rangle \in Z\} \overset{(*2)}{=} \{R[P/r]C \mid \langle R, C\rangle \in Z\} =$ $\gamma\big(\{\langle R[P/r], C\rangle \mid \langle R, C\rangle \in Z\}\big)$. And then by (*4) the claim follows.

3. Let $\tilde{Q} \in \bar{S} \wedge \{\tilde{Q}\} -a\twoheadrightarrow \tilde{J}$. Then $\tilde{Q} \equiv Q[P/r]$ for $Q \in S \cup \{r\}$. In particular $Q \in singterms$. And then by (*5) there are two cases.
Case 1. $P\ smd\_of\ \tilde{Q} \wedge \{P\} -a\twoheadrightarrow \tilde{J}$. Then as the last rule applied to prove $\{P\} -a\twoheadrightarrow \tilde{J}$ must have been rec⟩, we know $a = \tau$ and $\tilde{J} = dec(\bar{R}[P/r])$. Clearly $\langle \tilde{Q}, \tau, X\rangle \in \bar{D}$, where $X = \{\langle R[P/r], C\rangle \mid \langle R, C\rangle \in Z\}$. In case 2 of 2. we have seen $\tilde{J} = \gamma(X)$, hence $\gamma^{-1}(\tilde{J}) = X$, which proves the claim.
Case 2. $\exists J \subseteq grapes : \tilde{J} = \{R[P/r] \mid R \in J\} \wedge \{Q\} -a\twoheadrightarrow J$. This implies $Q \not\equiv r$, thus $Q \in S$. Hence by ind. hyp. $\langle Q, a, \gamma^{-1}(J)\rangle \in D$. And then $\langle Q[P/r], a, X\rangle \in \bar{D}$, where $X = \{\langle R[P/r], C\rangle \mid \langle R, C\rangle \in \gamma^{-1}(J)\}$. Recall that $Q[P/r] \equiv \tilde{Q}$.
In case 1 of 2. we have seen that $\gamma(X) = \{R[P/r] \mid R \in \gamma\gamma^{-1}(J)\}$, and hence $\gamma(X) = \tilde{J}$. And thus $\gamma^{-1}(\tilde{J}) = X$, and the claim follows.

4. Clearly $P \in \bar{S}$. Proposition 6.19 □

The next lemma will be used in the proof of the consistency theorem to show that for the PrT-net construction it suffices to use synchronization transitions which stem from two singular transitions only. It is not necessary to consider synchronization transitions of higher order, i.e. synchronization transitions which stem from synchronization transitions. This is only possible due to the limitation to terms which satisfy *onesyn*.

Lemma 6.20 Let $I -a\twoheadrightarrow J$ and $onesyn(I)$. Then

$$\begin{array}{l} |I| = 1 \quad \vee \\ \exists Q_1, Q_2 \in grapes, C \in contexts, J_1, J_2 \subseteq grapes, a_1, a_2 \in Vis : \\ \quad I = \{Q_1 \llcorner C, Q_2 \lrcorner C\} \wedge J = J_1 \llcorner C \cup J_2 \lrcorner C \\ \quad \wedge\ \forall i \in \{1,2\} :\ \{Q_i\} -a_i\twoheadrightarrow J_i \wedge ([a_1, a_2])\mathcal{L}[\![C]\!] = a. \end{array}$$

Proof Let $I -a\twoheadrightarrow J$ and $onesyn(I)$. We perform an induction on the length of the proof of $I -a\twoheadrightarrow J$. If the last rule is ...

act⟩, sum⟩, or rec⟩ then obviously $|I| = 1$.

fun⟩ Then $I = I'f, J = J'f, bf = a$, and $I' -b\twoheadrightarrow J'$. As $onesyn(I)$ clearly $onesyn(I')$, hence by ind. hyp. there are two cases: If $|I'| = 1$, then $|I| = 1$. Otherwise $I' = \{Q_1 \llcorner C, Q_2 \lrcorner C\} \ \wedge \ J' = J_1 \llcorner C \cup J_2 \lrcorner C \ \wedge \ \forall i \in \{1,2\} : \{Q_i\} -a_i\twoheadrightarrow J_i \ \wedge \ [a_1, a_2]\mathcal{L}[\![C]\!] = b$. Hence for $\bar{C} :\equiv Cf$ the claim follows.

asyn⟩ Then $I = I'\llcorner \ \wedge \ J = J'\llcorner$ or $I = I'\lrcorner \ \wedge \ J = J'\lrcorner$. Analogous to the above case (with $\bar{C} :\equiv C\llcorner$ respectively $\bar{C} :\equiv C\lrcorner$) the claim follows.

syn⟩ Then $I = I_1\llcorner \cup I_2\lrcorner, J = J_1\llcorner \cup J_2\lrcorner, a = [a_1, a_2]$, and $\forall i \in \{1,2\} : I_i -a_i\twoheadrightarrow J_i \wedge a_i \in Vis$. As $onesyn(I)$ clearly $onesyn(I_1) \ \wedge \ onesyn(I_2)$. Now let $i \in \{1,2\}$ and assume $\exists Q_1, Q_2 \in grapes, C \in contexts, b_1, b_2 \in Vis : I_i = \{Q_1 \llcorner C, Q_2 \lrcorner C\} \ \wedge \ [b_1, b_2]\mathcal{L}[\![C]\!] = a_i$. As $onesyn(I)$ we know that $onesyn(C)$, and then $[b_1, b_2]\mathcal{L}[\![C]\!] \notin Vis$, contradicting $a_i \in Vis$. Hence by ind. hyp. $|I_1| = |I_2| = 1$. And then the second alternative of the claim follows for $C \equiv \kappa$. □

We are now ready to prove the consistency with respect to the distributed semantics. The proof is relatively easy due to the direct correspondence of the safe-net-semantics of the PrT-net construction and the distributed operational semantics. This direct correspondence in turn is due to our choice of **L** (Definition 6.1) and $\mathcal{R}$ (Definition 6.2).

Theorem 6.21 (distributed consistency)
Let $P \in qterms$ such that $\mathcal{G}[\![P]\!]$ is defined. Then

1. $\mathcal{G}[\![P]\!]$ is safe,
2. $Reach(Safenet(\mathcal{G}[\![P]\!])) \ = \ Reach(\mathcal{D}[\![P]\!])$,
3. $Transys(Safenet(\mathcal{G}[\![P]\!])) \ \sim \ \mathcal{T}[\![P]\!]$.

Proof 1. and 2. Let $\mathcal{G}[\![P]\!] = \langle S_P, D_P, Z_P\rangle$. Let

$$
\begin{aligned}
Z = \ & \gamma(Z_P), \ S = \{QC \mid Q \in S_P \ \wedge \ C \in contexts\}, \\
D = \ & \Big\{ \langle \{QC\}, b, \gamma(M)C\rangle \ \Big| \ \langle Q, a, M\rangle \in D_P \ \wedge C \in contexts \ \wedge \ a\mathcal{L}[\![C]\!] = b \neq \bot \Big\} \\
& \cup \Big\{ \langle \{Q_1C_1\llcorner C, Q_2C_2\lrcorner C\}, b\mathcal{L}[\![C]\!], \gamma(M_1)C_1\llcorner C \cup \gamma(M_2)C_2\lrcorner C\rangle \ \Big| \\
& \qquad \langle Q_1, a_1, M_1\rangle, \langle Q_2, a_2, M_2\rangle \in D_P \ \wedge \ C_1, C_2, C \in contexts \\
& \qquad \wedge \ \Big[a_1\mathcal{L}[\![C_1]\!], a_2\mathcal{L}[\![C_2]\!]\Big] = b \in EVis \ \wedge \ b\mathcal{L}[\![C]\!] \neq \bot \Big\}.
\end{aligned}
$$

We will prove $Reach(\langle S, D, Z\rangle) \ = \ Reach(\mathcal{D}[\![P]\!])$, (∗1)
which in turn with Theorem 6.14 2. and the analogue for safe nets of Lemma 4.11 1. implies 1. and 2.

$Reach(\langle S, D, Z\rangle) = \langle \hat{S}, \hat{D}, Z\rangle$, where $\hat{S} = \bigcup[Z\rangle_D$ and
$\hat{D} = \{d \in D \mid \exists M \in [Z\rangle_D : \bullet d \subseteq M\}$.
$Reach(\mathcal{D}[\![P]\!]) = \langle \tilde{S}, \tilde{D}, dec(P)\rangle$, where $\tilde{S} = \bigcup[dec(P)\rangle_{\mathbf{D}_{\gg}}$ and
$\tilde{D} = \{d \in \mathbf{D}_{\gg} \mid \exists M \in [dec(P)\rangle_{\mathbf{D}_{\gg}} : \bullet d \subseteq M\}$. We have

$$dec(P) \;=\; \gamma\gamma^{-1}(dec(P)) \;\overset{6.19\ 1.}{=}\; \gamma(Z_P) \;=\; Z. \qquad (*2)$$

Let us now prove $D \subseteq \mathbf{D}_{\gg}$. (*3)
Let $d \in D$, then there are two cases.
Case 1. $d = \langle\{QC\}, b, \gamma(M)C\rangle$ for $\langle Q, a, M\rangle \in D_P, C \in contexts$, and $a\mathcal{L}[\![C]\!] = b \neq \bot$. We perform an induction on the structure of C.

$\underline{C \equiv \kappa}$ Then $d = \langle\{Q\}, b, \gamma(M)\rangle$, and as $\mathcal{L}[\![\kappa]\!] = id$, $a = b$. By 6.19 2. $\{Q\} -a\twoheadrightarrow \gamma(M)$.

$\underline{C \equiv C'f}$ for $f \in Fun$. Then $d = \langle\{QC'f\}, b, \gamma(M)C'f\rangle$, for $\langle Q, a, M\rangle \in D_P, C' \in contexts$, and for $c \in Act$: $a\mathcal{L}[\![C']\!] = c$ and $cf = b$. Then also $d' := \langle\{QC'\}, c, \gamma(M)C'\rangle \in D$. By ind. hyp. $d' \in \mathbf{D}_{\gg}$. By fun$\rangle$ $d \in \mathbf{D}_{\gg}$.

$\underline{C \equiv C'\llcorner}$ ($C \equiv C'\lrcorner$ is analogous) Then $d = \langle\{QC'\llcorner\}, b, \gamma(M)C'\llcorner\rangle$ and $a\mathcal{L}[\![C']\!] = b$. Hence by ind. hyp. $\langle\{QC'\}, b, \gamma(M)C'\rangle \in \mathbf{D}_{\gg}$. By asyn$\rangle$ $d \in \mathbf{D}_{\gg}$.

Case 2. $d = \Big\langle \{Q_1C_1\llcorner C, Q_2C_2\lrcorner C\}, b\mathcal{L}[\![C]\!], \gamma(M_1)C_1\llcorner C \cup \gamma(M_2)C_2\lrcorner C\Big\rangle$ for $\langle Q_1, a_1, M_1\rangle, \langle Q_2, a_2, M_2\rangle \in D_P \;\wedge\; C_1, C_2, C \in contexts \;\wedge\; [a_1\mathcal{L}[\![C_1]\!], a_2\mathcal{L}[\![C_2]\!]] = b \in EVis \;\wedge\; b\mathcal{L}[\![C]\!] \neq \bot$. We perform an induction on the structure of C.

$\underline{C \equiv \kappa}$ Then $d = \Big\langle\{Q_1C_1\llcorner, Q_2C_2\lrcorner\}, b, \gamma(M_1)C_1\llcorner \cup \gamma(M_2)C_2\lrcorner\Big\rangle$. And as $a_1\mathcal{L}[\![C_1]\!]$, $a_2\mathcal{L}[\![C_2]\!] \in Vis$ we have $\forall i \in \{1,2\} : d_i := \Big\langle\{Q_iC_i\}, a_i\mathcal{L}[\![C_i]\!], \gamma(M_i)C_i\Big\rangle \in D$. By case 1 $\forall i \in \{1,2\} : d_i \in \mathbf{D}_{\gg}$. By syn$\rangle$ $d \in \mathbf{D}_{\gg}$.

$\underline{C \equiv C'f}$ for $f \in Fun$. Then
$d = \Big\langle\{Q_1C_1\llcorner C'f, Q_2C_2\lrcorner C'f\}, b\mathcal{L}[\![C'f]\!], \gamma(M_1)C_1\llcorner C'f \cup \gamma(M_2)C_2\lrcorner C'f\Big\rangle$, and as $b\mathcal{L}[\![C'f]\!] \neq \bot$ there exists $c \in Act : b\mathcal{L}[\![C']\!] = c$ and $cf = b\mathcal{L}[\![C'f]\!]$.
And then $d' := \Big\langle\{Q_1C_1\llcorner C', Q_2C_2\lrcorner C'\}, c, \gamma(M_1)C_1\llcorner C' \cup \gamma(M_2)C_2\lrcorner C'\Big\rangle \in D$. By ind. hyp. $d' \in \mathbf{D}_{\gg}$. By fun$\rangle$ then $d \in \mathbf{D}_{\gg}$.

$\underline{C \equiv C'\llcorner, \text{ and } C \equiv C'\lrcorner}$ are analogous using rule asyn$\rangle$. □ (*3)

Next to prove $M \in [Z\rangle_D \;\Rightarrow\; M \in [dec(P)\rangle_{\mathbf{D}_{\gg}}$ (*4)
we perform an induction on the length of $u \in D^*$ such that $Z[u\rangle M$.

$\underline{u = \varepsilon}$ Then $M = Z \overset{(*2)}{=} dec(P) \in [dec(P)\rangle_{\mathbf{D}_{\gg}}$.

$\underline{u = u'd}$ Then for some M' : $Z[u'\rangle M'$ and $M'[d\rangle M$. By ind. hyp. $M' \in [dec(P)\rangle_{\mathbf{D}_{\succ}}$. By (*3) $d \in \mathbf{D}_{\succ}$, hence $M \in [dec(P)\rangle_{\mathbf{D}_{\succ}}$. □ (*4)

Now by (*3) and (*4) clearly $\hat{S} \subseteq \tilde{S}$ and $\hat{D} \subseteq \tilde{D}$. (*5)

In order to prove the reverse inclusions, we proceed similarly. But note that the reverse of (*3) does not hold. Instead we will prove

$$d \in \mathbf{D}_{\succ} \ \wedge\ onesyn(\bullet d) \ \wedge\ \bullet d \subseteq S \quad \Rightarrow \quad d \in D \ \wedge\ onesyn(d\bullet). \qquad (*6)$$

Let $d = \langle I, a, J\rangle$ such that $I \ -a\twoheadrightarrow\ J \ \wedge\ I \subseteq S \ \wedge\ onesyn(I)$.
Case 1. $|I| = 1$. Then there exist $Q \in S_P \ \wedge\ C \in contexts$ such that $I = \{QC\}$. We perform an induction on the structure of C.

$\underline{C \equiv \kappa}$ Then $\{Q\} \ -a\twoheadrightarrow\ J$ for $Q \in S_P$. By 6.19 3. $\langle Q, a, \gamma^{-1}(J)\rangle \in D_P$. And then $\langle \{Q\}, a, \gamma\gamma^{-1}(J)\rangle \in D$. As $\gamma\gamma^{-1}(J) = J$ we conclude $d \in D$. By 6.17 we know that $onesyn(J)$.

$\underline{C \equiv C'f}$ Then $\{QC'f\} \ -a\twoheadrightarrow\ J$. The last rule applied to prove this must have been fun$\rangle$, hence $J = J'f$ and for $bf = a$: $\{QC'\} \ -b\twoheadrightarrow\ J'$.
Furthermore as $onesyn(QC'f)$ we know that $onesyn(QC')$ and $(EVis)f \cap Vis = \emptyset$. Hence by ind. hyp. $onesyn(J') \wedge \langle\{QC'\}, b, J'\rangle \in D$, i.e. $\langle Q, c, M\rangle \in D_P$ such that $J' = \gamma(M)C'$ and $c\mathcal{L}[\![C']\!] = b$. Hence also $\langle\{QC\}, a, J\rangle \in D$ and $onesyn(J)$.

$\underline{C \equiv C'\llcorner \text{ and } C \equiv C'\lrcorner}$ analogous using rule asyn$\rangle$.

Case 2. $|I| \neq 1$. Then by Lemma 6.20, for some $Q_1, Q_2 \in grapes, C \in contexts$, $J_1, J_2 \subseteq grapes, a_1, a_2 \in Vis : I = \{Q_1\llcorner C, Q_2\lrcorner C\} \ \wedge\ J = J_1\llcorner C \cup J_2\lrcorner C \ \wedge\ \forall i \in \{1,2\} : \{Q_i\} \ -a_i\twoheadrightarrow\ J_i \ \wedge\ [a_1, a_2]\mathcal{L}[\![C]\!] = a$.
As $I \subseteq S \ \wedge\ onesyn(I)$, clearly $\forall i \in \{1,2\} : Q_i \in S \ \wedge\ onesyn(Q_i)$, and $onesyn(C)$. Case 1 implies $\forall i \in \{1,2\} : \langle\{Q_i\}, a_i, J_i\rangle \in D \ \wedge\ onesyn(J_i)$. Hence for some $C_1, C_2 \in contexts$, there are for all $i \in \{1,2\}$ $\langle Q_i', b_i, M_i\rangle \in D_P$ such that $b_i\mathcal{L}[\![C_i]\!] = a_i$, $Q_i \equiv Q_i'C_i$, and $J_i = \gamma(M_i)C_i$. Hence also $\langle I, a, J\rangle \in D$, and clearly $onesyn(J)$. □ (*6)

To prove $M \in [dec(P)\rangle_{\mathbf{D}_{\succ}} \quad \Rightarrow \quad M \in [Z\rangle_D \ \wedge\ onesyn(M)$ (*7)
we perform an induction on the length of $u \in \mathbf{D}_{\succ}^*$ such that $dec(P)[u\rangle M$.

$\underline{u = \varepsilon}$ Then $M = dec(P) \overset{(*2)}{=} Z \in [Z\rangle_D$. And by 6.17 $onesyn(M)$.

$\underline{u = u'd}$ Then for some M' $dec(P)[u'\rangle M'$ and $M'[d\rangle M$. By ind. hyp. $M' \in [Z\rangle_D$ and $onesyn(M')$. Hence $\bullet d \subseteq M' \subseteq S$ and $onesyn(\bullet d)$. By (*6) $d \in D \ \wedge\ onesyn(d\bullet)$. Hence $M \in [Z\rangle_D$. Furthermore, as $M = M' - \bullet d + d\bullet$ we conclude $onesyn(M)$. □ (*7)

Now by (∗6) and (∗7) clearly $\tilde{S} \subseteq \hat{S}$ and $\tilde{D} \subseteq \hat{D}$. This and (∗5) and (∗2) imply (∗1). □ 2.

3. $\mathit{Transys}(\mathit{Safenet}(\mathcal{G}[\![P]\!]))$
= (by the analogue of Lemma 4.11 2. for safe nets) $\mathit{Transys}(\mathit{Reach}(\mathit{Safenet}(\mathcal{G}[\![P]\!])))$
= (by (2.)) $\mathit{Transys}(\mathit{Reach}(\mathcal{D}[\![P]\!]))$
= (again analogous to Lemma 4.11 2.) $\mathit{Transys}(\mathcal{D}[\![P]\!])$
$\sim$ (by Theorem 6.14 5.) $\mathcal{T}[\![P]\!]$. Theorem 6.21 □

Conclusion to Chapter 6

There is no comparable construction of PrT-nets for any abstract programming language in the literature known to the author. [Goltz, Reisig 85] construct predicate/transition nets for concrete CSP [Hoare 78], but the approach is completely different, there the individual tokens are used to model the data values of the programs while for the flow of control constructions of safe nets as in chapter 4 would have sufficed.

In conclusion to this chapter we want to discuss two points. The first one concerns the differences of the safe-net-semantics of the PrT-net of some term P and the safe Petri net construction $\mathcal{N}[\![P]\!]$ presented in chapter 4. The second point concerns the modelling of the $\|_A$-construct with finite PrT-nets.

With respect to the first point there are two differences. In the safe Petri net construction $\mathcal{N}[\![\cdot]\!]$ we have identified isomorphic extended safe Petri nets (Definition 4.8), while no comparable identification is made in our PrT-net construction (comparable would have been e.g. the identification of two PrT-nets if their safe-net-semantics produce isomorphic safe nets). As an example consider the term

$P \equiv a\,\mathit{nil}$, then $\mathcal{G}[\![P]\!]$ is 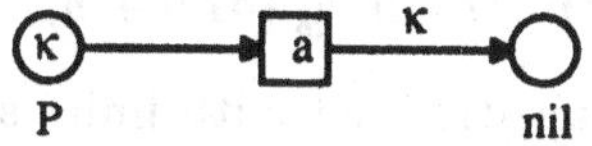

and $\mathit{Reach}(\mathit{Safenet}(\mathcal{G}[\![P]\!]))$ is 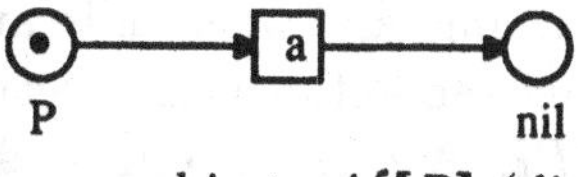

furthermore the latter net is isomorphic to $\mathcal{N}[\![P]\!]$ (disregarding the set of extensions, which is empty here). On the other hand $\mathcal{G}[\![P+P]\!]$ is

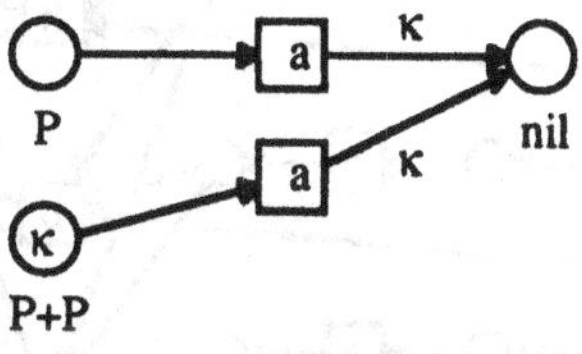

and $\mathit{Reach}(\mathit{Safenet}(\mathcal{G}[\![P+P]\!]))$ is 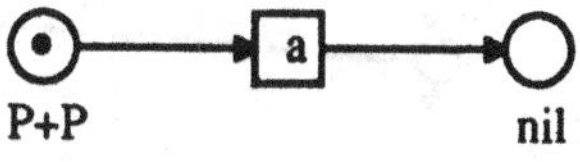

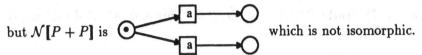

but $\mathcal{N}[\![P+P]\!]$ is 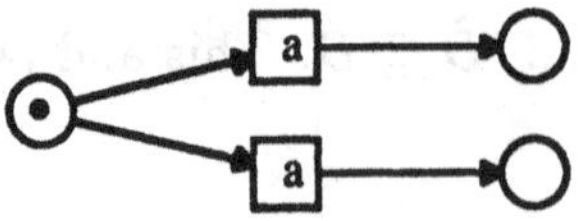 which is not isomorphic.

Note that due to the 'information' contained in the names (= dynamic predicates) of the PrT-nets, we do not need extensions as we did for $\mathcal{N}[\![\cdot]\!]$.

The second difference of the safe-net-semantics of the PrT-net of some term and the safe Petri net construction $\mathcal{N}[\![\cdot]\!]$ is that while the latter tries to keep the nets finite the former is rather wasteful with respect to infinity (although the PrT-nets are finite). Consider $P \equiv rec\, p.\tau a(pf)$, where $f = \{a \mapsto b\}$ (cf. the example on pp. 62 and 67). Then $\mathcal{G}[\![P]\!]$ is

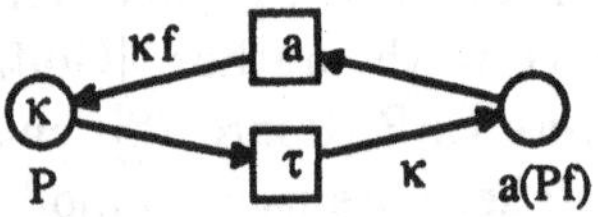

and the initial portion of $Reach(Safenet(\mathcal{G}[\![P]\!]))$ is

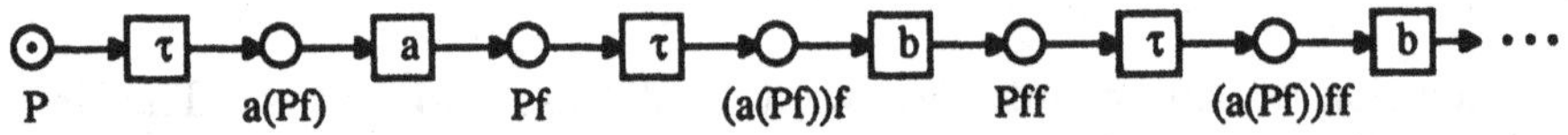

whereas $\mathcal{N}[\![P]\!]$ is 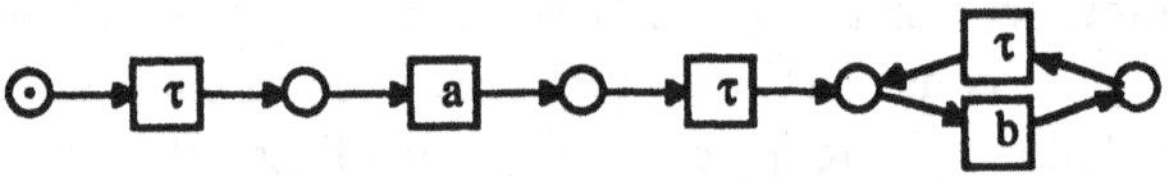 .

The last point to be discussed in this conclusion to chapter 6 concerns the $\|_A$-construct (Definition 1.12). It has been excluded in our PrT-net construction (see the discussion after Corollary 6.18). We now want to present the term

$$P \equiv rec\, p.\tau(ab\, nil \,\|_b\, (b\, nil + p))$$

to motivate that no predicate/transition net with finite sets of places and transitions, with a finite initial marking, and with finite annotations (even with different $\mathbf{L}$ and $\mathcal{R}$) can have a safe-net-semantics whose reachable subnet is isomorphic to the reachable subnet of $\mathcal{D}[\![P]\!]$. A related term is discussed in [Goltz 87, p. 115]. The initial portion of $Reach(\mathcal{D}[\![P]\!])$ may be sketched as

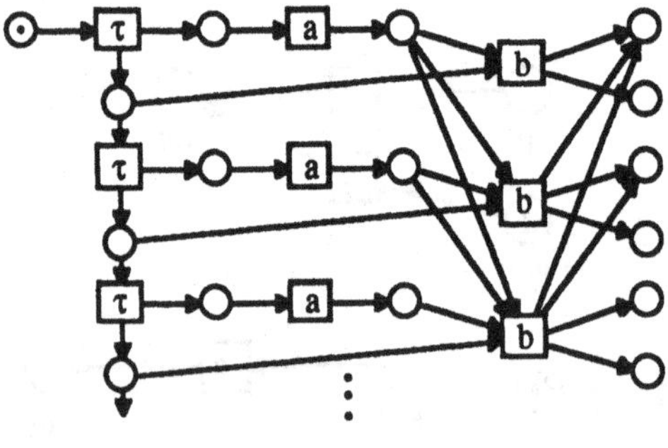

For any $n \geq 2$ there is a b-transition with n places in its presets, and all these b-transitions appear to be necessary. On the other hand if there would be a predicate/transition net with a finite number of transitions there would be one transition in it generating infinitely many transitions in the safe-net-semantics. And for every two of these transitions the presets have different cardinalities. But this is impossible as the initial marking and the annotations are finite.

The moral is that a term for which *onesyn* does not hold in general allows synchronizations to become arbitrarily complex dynamically (via recursion), and this cannot be modelled with finite predicate/transition nets. Hence the construction developed in this section also helps to emphasize an important difference of CCS and TCSP.

One could extend our construction to handle these arbitrarily complex synchronizations by taking not just pairs of singular transitions (of a shorthand PrT-net) to generate synchronization transitions. Instead one could define this generation inductively. But then, although the shorthand stays finite, the underlying longhand PrT-net would no longer be finite.

In summary we have given a completely new construction of PrT-nets for an abstract programming language which encloses finitary pure CCS (where every sum and recursion starts sequentially).

We have shown that this construction is consistent even with a distributed semantics. To this end we have transferred the distributed semantics of Degano et al. and Olderog to the set *qterms* which partially is a special case (w.r.t. sum and recursion) and partially is a generalization (w.r.t. parallel composition). For this set the semantics is technically simple. Furthermore a grape has a clear interpretation as a singular term occurring within some context, and hence also every token in the safe net $\mathcal{D}[\![P]\!]$ of a term P has a clear interpretation as a parallel subprocess of P which starts sequentially.

Conclusion

In conclusion we give an overview of the consistency results and on the interrelation of the three constructions for a term P, namely of

the (finite) transition system construction $\mathcal{F}[\![P]\!]$,
the (finite and) safe Petri net construction $\mathcal{N}[\![P]\!]$, and
the finite and strict predicate/transition net construction $\mathcal{G}[\![P]\!]$.

These constructions are not always defined, but if they are, we have the following picture.

extended transition systems		$\mathcal{E}[\![P]\!] \sim \mathcal{F}[\![P]\!] \cong Transys(\mathcal{N}[\![P]\!])$
		$\nearrow = \mathcal{E}[\![P]\!]_{1,2,4}$
tran-sition sys-tems	$\mathcal{T}[\![P]\!]$	
		$\searrow \sim Transys(\mathcal{D}[\![P]\!]) = Transys(Reach(\mathcal{D}[\![P]\!]))$
safe Petri nets	$\mathcal{D}[\![P]\!]$	$Reach(\mathcal{D}[\![P]\!]) = Reach(Safenet(\mathcal{G}[\![P]\!]))$

The starting point is the first stage of the (standard) interleaving operational semantics, namely the transition system $\mathcal{T}[\![P]\!]$. We have enhanced it with so-called extensions, which are derived by rules similar to the derivation of transitions (Definition 3.20), leading to the extended transition system $\mathcal{E}[\![P]\!]$. The projection to the first, second, and forth component of the latter equals $\mathcal{T}[\![P]\!]$. On the other hand the extended transition system is used for the proof of the strong bisimularity with $\mathcal{F}[\![P]\!]$ (Theorem 3.26).

The interrelation with the safe Petri net construction $\mathcal{N}[\![P]\!]$ is very strong, namely the extended transition system associated with $\mathcal{N}[\![P]\!]$ is isomorphic to $\mathcal{F}[\![P]\!]$ (Theorem 4.17), and hence also strongly bisimular to $\mathcal{E}[\![P]\!]$ (Corollary 4.18).

While going upwards in the above diagram adds the extension to $\mathcal{T}[\![P]\!]$, going downwards adds explicit parallelism to the semantics and leads to safe nets. Again the distributed semantics $\mathcal{D}[\![P]\!]$ agrees with the interleaving semantics, a result due to Degano, De Nicola, and Montanari which we recall in Theorem 6.14.

For our predicate/transition net construction we prove consistency with respect to the distributed semantics. In Theorem 6.21 one of the strongest conceivable consistency results is proved, i.e. the reachable part of the distributed semantics equals the reachable part of the safe-net-semantics of the constructed predicate/transition net.

This work helps solving the following problems: Abstract programming languages on the one hand and automata and Petri nets on the other hand are related. Sublanguages are indicated which are representable by the respective model. The sublanguage representable by finite automata is particularly interesting for automated theorem proving.

The implicit question raised in [Goltz 87] to what extent the construction of finite Petri nets given there can be extended is answered to the effect that no significant extension is possible.

The search for a good distributed semantics of abstract programming languages is enriched by an argument in favour of the semantics given by Degano et al., as the predicate/transition net construction of chapter 6 which has been developed independently is a closely related structure.

Every construction given in this work uses as target some kind of machine model, and hence supports the implementation of parallel processes. For a finite automaton the (unique) minimal automaton can effectively be constructed, hence with respect to strong bisimularity even an optimal implementation is possible. Petri nets can be seen as a parallel machine model. For an overview of their implementation see [Taubner 88].

We conclude by listing some directions for future research and some open problems.

In chapter 1 we have discussed the reachable subsystem, the quotient, and the existence of the minimal strongly bisimular transition system for some transition system. In order to avoid a distraction we did not transfer other notions and techniques from automata theory. Nevertheless the investigation of such a transference to transition systems and strong bisimularity (and other notions of equivalence) appears to be interesting.

We believe that it is undecidable whether for the transition system $\mathcal{T}[\![P]\!]$ of some term P a strongly bisimular transition system exists. However we were able to give a proof only for the weaker formulation given in Theorem 2.11. We conjecture that analogous to Rice's Theorem every non-trivial property of $\{\mathcal{T}[\![P]\!] \mid P \in terms\}$ is undecidable.

The apparently close relationship of $\mathcal{N}[\![P]\!]$ and $Safenet(\mathcal{G}[\![P]\!])$ should be established formally. In other words the safe net constructed for some term P should be interrelated with the safe-net-semantics of the predicate/transition net constructed for that term using some non-interleaving equivalence. In this work we have only established the strong bisimularity. A non-interleaving equivalence notion which is as convenient as bisimularity appears to be missing.

The invariant techniques for predicate/transition nets and coloured nets should be applied to the nets constructed in chapter 6. The comparatively simple structure of these nets should make it easier to use those techniques.

An investigation of the structure of the constructed predicate/transition nets paralleling that of section 4.4 for the safe net construction is also attractive. Furthermore it is interesting how the refinement techniques which have been developed for nets transfer to abstract programming languages. Conversely it is worthwhile to transfer logics and proof systems from abstract programming languages to nets.

For theoretical reasons it might be interesting to drop the limitations to *qterms* for the net constructions. For the PrT-net construction this should be possible using ideas from [Olderog 87], nevertheless some kind of well-guardedness would still be required as motivated at the end of section 1.7.

Practically more useful is an extension of the PrT-net construction for a language with value passing. When modelling the data values as in [Goltz, Reisig 85] we foresee no problems, even if the values are labels (= elements of *Vis*) as in [Engberg, Nielsen 86]. On the other hand allowing additionally also processes to be passed as values would be a very challenging extension.

Bibliography

[Agerwala 75] T.K.M. Agerwala: Towards a theory for the analysis and synthesis of systems exhibiting concurrency. Dissertation, The Johns Hopkins Univ., Baltimore, Maryland (1975)

[Arnold 82] A. Arnold: Synchronized behaviours of processes and rational relations. Acta Informatica 17 (1982) 21-29

[Austry, Boudol 84] D. Austry, G. Boudol: Algèbre de processus et synchronization. TCS 30 (1984) 91-131

[de Bakker 80] J. de Bakker: Mathematical theory of program correctness. Prentice-Hall 1980

[Barendregt 85] H.P. Barendregt: The lambda calculus - its syntax and semantics. North-Holland 1985

[Bergstra, Klop 84] J.A. Bergstra, J.W. Klop: The algebra of recursively defined processes and the algebra of regular processes. In: J. Paredaens(ed.): ICALP 84. Springer LNCS 172 (1984) 82-94

[Bergstra, Klop 85] J.A. Bergstra, J.W. Klop: Algebra of communicating processes with abstraction. TCS 37 (1985) 77-121

[Bergstra, Klop 86] J.A. Bergstra, J.W. Klop: Algebra of communicating processes. In: J.W. de Bakker et al.(eds.): Mathematics and computer science, Proc. of the CWI symposium Nov. 1983. North-Holland (1986) 89-138

[Bergstra, Klop 88] J.A. Bergstra, J.W. Klop: A complete inference system for regular processes with silent moves. In: F.R. Drake, J.K. Truss (eds.): Logic Colloquium '86. North-Holland (1988) 21-81

[Best 87] E. Best: COSY: Its relationship to nets and to CSP. In: W. Brauer et al.(eds.): Petri nets: Applications and relationships to other models of concurrency. Springer LNCS 255 (1987) 416-440

[Best, Devillers 87] E. Best, R. Devillers: Sequential and concurrent behaviour in Petri net theory. TCS 55 (1987) 87-136

[Best, Fernández 86] E. Best, C. Fernández: Notations and terminology on Petri net theory. Arbeitspapiere der GMD Nr. 195, Bonn (1986)

[Brauer 84] W. Brauer: Automatentheorie. Teubner 1984

[Brookes 83] S.D. Brookes: A model for communicating sequential processes. Carnegie-Mellon University, Report CMU-CS-83-149, 1983

[Brookes et al. 84] S.D. Brookes, C.A.R. Hoare, A.W. Roscoe: A theory of communicating sequential processes. Journal of the ACM 31 (1984) 560-599

[Brookes, Roscoe 85] S.D. Brookes, A.W. Roscoe: An improved failures model for communicating processes. In: S.D. Brookes et al.(eds.): Seminar on concurrency. Springer LNCS 197 (1985) 281-305

[Church 41] A. Church: The calculi of lambda conversion. Princeton University Press 1941

[Curry et al. 58] H.B. Curry, R. Feys, W. Craig: Combinatoric logic, Volume I. North-Holland 1958

[De Cindio et al. 82] F. De Cindio, G. De Michelis, L. Pomello, C. Simone: Superposed automata nets. In: C. Girault et al.(eds.): Application and theory of Petri nets. Springer IFB 52 (1982) 269-279

[De Cindio et al. 83] F. De Cindio, G. De Michelis, L. Pomello, C. Simone: Milner's communicating systems and Petri nets. In: A. Pagnoni, G. Rozenberg(eds.): Application and theory of Petri nets. Springer IFB 66 (1983) 40-59

[Degano et al. 85] P. Degano, R. De Nicola, U. Montanari: Partial ordering derivations for CCS. In: L. Budach(ed.): Fundamentals of computation theory. Springer LNCS 199 (1985) 520-533

[Degano et al. 87] P. Degano, R. De Nicola, U. Montanari: CCS is an (augmented) contact free C/E system. In: M.V. Zilli(ed.): Math. models for the semantics of parallelism. Springer LNCS 280 (1987) 144-165

[Degano et al. 88] P. Degano, R. De Nicola, U. Montanari: A distributed operational semantics for CCS based on condition/event systems. Acta Informatica 26 (1988) 59-91

[De Nicola, Hennessy 84] R. De Nicola, M.C.B. Hennessy: Testing equivalences for processes. TCS (1984) 83-133

[De Nicola, Hennessy 87] R. De Nicola, M.C.B. Hennessy: CCS without τ's. In: H. Ehrig et al.(eds.): TAPSOFT '87 Vol. 1. Springer LNCS 249 (1987) 138-152

[Dosch 87] W. Dosch: On a typed higher order functional calculus. Dissertation, Techn. Univ. München, 1987

[Engberg, Nielsen 86] U. Engberg, M. Nielsen: A calculus of communicating systems with label passing. Univ. Aarhus, Report DAIMI PB-208, 1986

[Geissler 85] J. Geissler: Zerlegung von diskreten Systemen mit Petri-Netzen. Dissertation, Univ. Kaiserslautern (1985) Report D 386

[Genrich 87] H.J. Genrich: Predicate/transition nets. In: W. Brauer et al.(eds.): Petri nets: Central models and their properties. Springer LNCS 254 (1987) 207-247

[van Glabbeck, Vaandrager 87] R. van Glabbeck, F. Vaandrager: Petri net models for algebraic theories of concurrency. In: J.W. de Bakker et al.(eds.): PARLE Vol. II. Springer LNCS 259 (1987) 224-242

[Goltz 87] U. Goltz: Über die Darstellung von CCS-Programmen durch Petrinetze. Dissertation, RWTH Aachen, 1987. Also available as GMD-Bericht Nr. 172, Oldenbourg Verlag 1988

[Goltz 88] U. Goltz: On representing CCS programs by finite Petri nets. In: M.P. Chytil et al.(eds.): MFCS. Springer LNCS 324 (1988) 339-350

[Goltz, Mycroft 84] U. Goltz, A. Mycroft: On the relationship of CCS and Petri nets. In: J. Paredaens(ed.): ICALP 84. Springer LNCS 172 (1984) 196-208

[Goltz, Reisig 83] U. Goltz, W. Reisig: The non-sequential behaviour of Petri nets. Information and Control 57 (1983) 125-147

[Goltz, Reisig 85] U. Goltz, W. Reisig: CSP-programs as nets with individual tokens. In: G. Rozenberg(ed.): Advances in Petri nets 1984. Springer LNCS 188 (1985) 169-196

[Greibach 78] S. Greibach: Remarks on blind and partially blind one-way multicounter machines. TCS 7 (1978) 310-324

[Hennessy 88] M. Hennessy: Algebraic theory of processes. MIT Press 1988

[Hoare 78] C.A.R. Hoare: Communicating sequential processes. Comm. ACM 21 (1978) 666-677

[Hoare 85] C.A.R. Hoare: Communicating sequential processes. Prentice-Hall 1985

[Hopcroft, Ullman 79] J.E. Hopcroft, J.D. Ullman: Introduction to automata theory, languages, and computation. Addison-Wesley 1979

[Jensen 87] K. Jensen: Coloured Petri nets. In: W. Brauer et al.(eds.): Petri nets: Central models and their properties. Springer LNCS 254 (1987) 248-299

[Kanellakis, Smolka 83] P.C. Kanellakis, S.A. Smolka: CCS expressions, finite state processes, and three problems of equivalence. In: Proc. 2nd Ann. ACM Symp. Principles of Distributed Computing, Montreal, Canada, Aug. 1983, 228-240

[Keller 76] R.M. Keller: Formal verification of parallel programs. Comm. ACM 19 (1976) 371-384

[Kiehn 88] A. Kiehn: On the interrelation between synchronized and non-synchronized behaviour of Petri nets. J. Inf. Process. Cybern. EIK 24 (1988) 3-18

[Kotov 78] V.E. Kotov: An algebra for parallelism based on Petri nets. In: J. Winkowski(ed.): MFCS. Springer LNCS 64 (1978) 39-55

[Lauer, Campbell 75] P.E. Lauer, R.H. Campbell: Formal semantics of a class of high-level primitives for coordinating concurrent processes. Acta Informatica 5 (1975) 297-332

[Loogen, Goltz 87] R. Loogen, U. Goltz: A non-interleaving semantic model for nondeterministic concurrent processes. RWTH Aachen, Report Informatik-Berichte Nr. 87-15, 1987

[Milne 85] G.J. Milne: CIRCAL and the representation of communication, concurrency, and time. ACM TOPLAS 7 (1985) 270-298

[Milner 80] R. Milner: A calculus of communicating systems. Springer LNCS 92 (1980)

[Milner 83] R. Milner: Calculi for synchrony and asynchrony. TCS 25 (1983) 267-310

[Milner 84] R. Milner: A complete inference system for a class of regular behaviours. JCSS 28 (1984) 439-466

[Milner 85] R. Milner: Lectures on a calculus of communicating systems. In: S.D. Brookes et al.(eds.): Seminar on concurrency. Springer LNCS 197 (1985) 197-220

[Milner 86] R. Milner: A complete axiomatisation for observational congruence of finite-state behaviours. Univ. Edinburgh, Report ECS-LFCS-86-8, 1986

[Minsky 67] M.L. Minsky: Computation - Finite and infinite machines. Prentice-Hall 1967

[Müller 85] K. Müller: Constructable Petri nets. Elektron. Inf.verarb. Kybern. EIK 21 (1985) 171-199

[Nielsen 87] M. Nielsen: CCS - and its relationship to net theory. In: W. Brauer et al.(eds.): Petri nets: Applications and relationships to other models of concurrency. Springer LNCS 255 (1987) 393-415

[Nivat 82] M. Nivat: Behaviours of processes and synchronized systems of processes. In: M. Broy, G. Schmidt(eds.): Theoretical Foundations of Programming Methodology. Reidel Publishing Co. (1982) 473-551

[Olderog 87] E.-R. Olderog: Operational Petri net semantics for CCSP. In: G. Rozenberg (ed.): Advances in Petri nets. Springer LNCS 266 (1987) 196-223

[Olderog, Hoare 86] E.-R. Olderog, C.A.R. Hoare: Specification-oriented semantics for communicating processes. Acta Informatica 23 (1986) 9-66

[Park 81] D. Park: Concurrency and automata on infinite sequences. In: P. Deussen (ed.): Proc. GI. Springer LNCS 104 (1981) 167-183

[Peterson 81] J.L. Peterson: Petri net theory and the modeling of systems. Prentice-Hall 1981

[Plotkin 81] G.D. Plotkin: A structural approach to operational semantics. Aarhus University, Report DAIMI FN-19, 1981

[Pomello 86] L. Pomello: Some equivalence notions for concurrent systems. In: G. Rozenberg(ed.): Advances in Petri nets 1985. Springer LNCS 222 (1986) 381-400

[Reisig 85] W. Reisig: Petri nets - An introduction. Springer 1985

[de Simone 85] R. de Simone: Higher-level synchronising devices in MEIJE-SCCS. TCS 37 (1985) 245-267

[Taubner 87] D. Taubner: Theoretical CSP and formal languages. Techn. Univ. München, Report TUM-I8706, 1987

[Taubner 88] D. Taubner: On the implementation of Petri nets. In: G. Rozenberg (ed.): Advances in Petri nets 1988. Springer LNCS 340 (1988) 418-439

[Thiagarajan 87] P.S. Thiagarajan: Elementary net systems. In: W. Brauer et al.(eds.): Petri nets: Central models and their properties. Springer LNCS 254 (1987) 26-59

[Valk 81] R. Valk: Generalizations of Petri nets. In: J. Gruska, M. Chytil: MFCS. Springer LNCS 118 (1981) 140-155

[Vogler 87] W. Vogler: Executions of Petri nets. In: Proc. of the 8th European workshop on application and theory of Petri nets, Zaragoza (1987) 551-564. Also available as Report TUM-I8806 Techn. Univ. München

[Winskel 87] G. Winskel: Event structures. In: W. Brauer et al.(eds.): Petri nets: Applications and relationships to other models of concurrency. Springer LNCS 255 (1987) 325-392

Mathematical notations

$\mathbb{N}$	$= \{0, 1, 2, \ldots\}$ natural numbers
$\mathbb{N}_1$	$= \{1, 2, \ldots\}$ positive natural numbers
$A - B$	set difference
B^A	the set of functions $f : A \to B$
id	identity (on the appropriate set)
$f\lceil_A$	restriction of the function f to the set A
pr_i	projection onto the i-th component
$\mathcal{P}(A)$	power set of the set A
$[a, b]$	the unordered pair of a and b

Abbreviations

w.r.t.	with respect to
ind. hyp.	induction hypothesis
i.h.	induction hypothesis
w.l.o.g.	without loss of generality
r.h.s.	right-hand side
l.h.s.	left-hand side

Summary of the sets of terms used

(page numbers refer to the definitions)

p. 14	*terms*	$\subset$	*conterms*	$= \{PC \mid P \in terms, C \in contexts\}$	p. 76
	$\cup$				
p. 16	$terms_\tau$				
	$\cup$		$\cup$		
p. 16	*qterms*				
	$\cup$				
p. 16	*singterms*	$\subset$	*grapes*	$= \{PC \mid P \in singterms, C \in contexts\}$	p. 140
			$\cup$		
			contexts		p. 76

Index

A 12
abbreviations 15, 18
abstract program 7, 14
abstract programming language 7
  semantics
    distributed operational 142
    interleaving operational 21
  syntax 8
abstraction *see* hiding
Act, $Act_{\perp}$ 13
action 13
action manipulation 13
Alph, $\overline{Alph}$ 13
α-congruence 10
arrows 22
  $P -a\rightarrow Q$ 23
  $P -a\rightarrow_{\tau} Q$ 39
  $I -a\twoheadrightarrow J$ 142
  $r -a\rightarrow_{D} s$ 22
  $r -a\rightarrow_{i} s$ 22
  $r =w\Rightarrow_{D} s$ 22
  $s -w\rightarrow_{D}$ 22
  $s =w\Rightarrow_{D}$ 22
  $s -w\not\rightarrow_{D}$ 22
  $s =w\not\Rightarrow_{D}$ 22
  $s \rightarrow_{D}$ 22
  $s \not\rightarrow_{D}$ 22
  $s \uparrow_{D}$ 22
  $P \rhd_{p} C$ 77
  $P \rhd_{p}$ 77
  $P \rhd$ 77
  $P \ntriangleright_{p}$ 77
  $P \ntriangleright$ 77
  $P \blacktriangleright p$ 78
  $P \not\blacktriangleright p$ 78
  $P \blacktriangleright$ 78
  $P \not\blacktriangleright$ 78
  $M_1[d\rangle M_2$ 98
  $M[I -a\twoheadrightarrow J\rangle M'$ 142
  $[Z\rangle_D$ 98
autobisimulation 25

Barendregt convention 11
bisimularity
  congruence 27
  strong 25, 63
  weak 27

change of bound identifier 10
cl 11
closed term 11
clterms *see cl*
consistent representation
  with Petri nets 99
  with transition systems 76
conterms 76
context relation ($\rhd$) 77
contexts 76
counter 49
  contained in a language 119

D 23
$\mathbf{D}_{\tau}$ 39
$\mathbf{D}_{\gg}$ 142
$\mathcal{D}[\![\cdot]\!]$ 142
dec 140
div 43
divergence free 27
divergences 27
divs 27

E 79
$\mathcal{E}[\![\cdot]\!]$ 79
equivalences 25
  $\doteq$ (abs. syntactic identity) 9
  $\equiv_\alpha$ (α-congruence) 10
  $\equiv$ (syntactic equality) 10
  $\cong$ (isomorphism)
    extended safe nets 100
    extended trans. systems 63
    transition systems 22
  $\sim$ (strong bisimularity)
    extended trans. systems 63
    transition systems 25
  $\overset{S,D}{\sim}$ 25
  $\sim_\$$ 25
  $\approx$ (weak bisimularity) 27
  $\approx_+$ (bisimulation congr.) 27
  $=_{\text{test}}$ (testing) 27
  $=_{\text{fail}}$ (failure) 27
  $=_{\text{div}}$ (divergence) 27
  $=_{\text{tr}}$ (trace) 27
EVis 13
extended safe net 99
extended transition system 62
  of an extended safe net 100
  of a term 79
extension
  safe net 99
  transition system 62
external choice 19

$\mathcal{F}[\![\cdot]\!]$ 64
failures 27
FI 9
fix 9
Fun 13
$Fun_\perp$ 62

$\mathcal{G}[\![\cdot]\!]$ 133
γ 131, 145
grape 140
  complete set of -s 140
grapes 140

hiding 13, 15
hot context relation ($\blacktriangleright$) 78
hot extension 63

identifier 8
  bound 9
  free 9
Idf 8
initials 27
internal non-determinism 15
invisible action 13

κ 76

L 126
$\mathcal{L}[\![\cdot]\!]$ 76

marking
  Petri net 98
  predicate/transition net 133
minimal transition system 31
μ-notation 9

$\mathcal{N}[\![\cdot]\!]$ 101
net 97
ni 82
nil 13
nil insertion 82
nilterms 82
ν 38

onesyn 146

$\mathcal{P}$ 165
parallel composition 14
  ACP 20
  CCS 15
  TCSP 15
  Winskel's 15
Petri net 97
  conventional notation 97
place invariant 115
plain term 8

predicate/transition net
  conventional notation 129
  shorthand notation 127
prefixing 13
proper termination 38
PrT-net *see* predicate/transition net

qterm 16
qterms 16
quotient of a transition system 30

$\mathcal{R}$ 127
Reach
  extended safe net 100
  extended transition system 63
  safe Petri net 99
  transition system 30
reachable markings 98
reachable subnet
  extended safe net 100
  safe Petri net 99
reachable subsystem
  extended transition system 63
  transition system 30
rec 8
Rec 11
regular term 57
renaming 13
  finite 70
representable 57
restriction 13, 15

Safenet 132
safe-net-semantics 132
safe Petri net 98
  of a qterm 142
safe predicate/transition net 132
sequential composition 18
$Sig_{\mathbf{A}}$ 13
σ 41
signature 8
singterms 16
singular term 16
singular transition 127
skip 18
smd_of 135
state machine decomposition 113
substitution lemma 12
subterm 11
sum 14
symbolic sum 129
symbolic transition rule 133
synchronization transition 127
syntactic substitution 10
Sysums 129

$\mathcal{T}[\![\cdot]\!]$ 23
$\mathcal{T}_\tau[\![\cdot]\!]$ 39
τ 13
Transys
  extended safe nets 100
  safe nets 99
term 10
terminating traces 47
terms 14
$terms_{\text{CCS}}$ 17
$terms_{\text{TCSP}}$ 19
$terms_\tau$ 16
$terms_\surd$ 18
$\surd$ (tick) 18
Ticks 18
traces
  Petri nets 119
  transition systems 27
$\surd$*traces* 47
transition system 21
  associated with a net 99
  of a term 23
Transys
  extended safe nets 100
  safe nets 99
Turing power 49

Vis 13